TERRAFORM CLI BOSS

NOVICE TO COMMAND LINE GURU

4 BOOKS IN 1

BOOK 1
TERRAFORM CLI BOSS: MASTERING THE BASICS

BOOK 2
TERRAFORM CLI BOSS: COMMAND LINE WIZARDRY

BOOK 3
TERRAFORM CLI BOSS: FROM NOVICE TO NINJA

BOOK 4
TERRAFORM CLI BOSS: EXPERT-LEVEL COMMANDS UNLEASHED

ROB BOTWRIGHT

Published by Rob Botwright
Library of Congress Cataloging-in-Publication Data
ISBN 978-1-83938-599-5
Cover design by Rizzo

Disclaimer

The contents of this book are based on extensive research and the best available historical sources. However, the author and publisher make no claims, promises, or guarantees about the accuracy, completeness, or adequacy of the information contained herein. The information in this book is provided on an "as is" basis, and the author and publisher disclaim any and all liability for any errors, omissions, or inaccuracies in the information or for any actions taken in reliance on such information.

The opinions and views expressed in this book are those of the author and do not necessarily reflect the official policy or position of any organization or individual mentioned in this book. Any reference to specific people, places, or events is intended only to provide historical context and is not intended to defame or malign any group, individual, or entity.

The information in this book is intended for educational and entertainment purposes only. It is not intended to be a substitute for professional advice or judgment. Readers are encouraged to conduct their own research and to seek professional advice where appropriate.

Every effort has been made to obtain necessary permissions and acknowledgments for all images and other copyrighted material used in this book. Any errors or omissions in this regard are unintentional, and the author and publisher will correct them in future editions.

BOOK 1 - TERRAFORM CLI BOSS: MASTERING THE BASICS

Introduction 5
Chapter 1: Introduction to Terraform and CLI 8
Chapter 2: Setting Up Your Terraform Environment 14
Chapter 3: Your First Terraform Commands 21
Chapter 4: Managing Terraform State 28
Chapter 5: Understanding Variables and Outputs 35
Chapter 6: Creating and Modifying Resources 42
Chapter 7: Terraform Modules and Workspaces 49
Chapter 8: Advanced CLI Techniques 56
Chapter 9: Handling Errors and Troubleshooting 64
Chapter 10: Best Practices for Terraform CLI Mastery 74

BOOK 2 - TERRAFORM CLI BOSS: COMMAND LINE WIZARDRY

Chapter 1: Mastering the Terraform CLI 83
Chapter 2: Advanced Configuration Management 86
Chapter 3: Harnessing the Power of HCL 93
Chapter 4: Dynamic Workflows with Variables 101
Chapter 5: Terraform Providers and Plugins 109
Chapter 6: Building Reusable Modules 118
Chapter 7: Remote State and Collaboration 126
Chapter 8: Infrastructure as Code Best Practices 133
Chapter 9: Extending Terraform Functionality 140
Chapter 10: Expert-Level Command Line Techniques 146

BOOK 3 - TERRAFORM CLI BOSS: FROM NOVICE TO NINJA

Chapter 1: Introduction to Terraform and CLI Basics 155
Chapter 2: Setting Up Your Terraform Environment 165
Chapter 3: Your First Steps with Terraform Commands 175
Chapter 4: Terraform Configuration Files Demystified 183
Chapter 5: Advanced Resource Management 188
Chapter 6: Terraform Modules and Reusability 194
Chapter 7: Collaboration and Version Control 200
Chapter 8: Extending Terraform Capabilities 206
Chapter 9: Debugging and Troubleshooting Techniques 213
Chapter 10: Becoming a Terraform CLI Ninja 220

BOOK 4 - TERRAFORM CLI BOSS: EXPERT-LEVEL COMMANDS UNLEASHED

Chapter 1: Mastering Advanced Terraform CLI Techniques 229
Chapter 2: Dynamic Configuration with Variables and Expressions 237
Chapter 3: Advanced Resource Management and Dependencies 244
Chapter 4: Harnessing Terraform Providers for Customization 251
Chapter 5: Advanced State Management Strategies 258
Chapter 6: Terraform Workspaces and Collaborative Workflows 265
Chapter 7: Extending Terraform with Custom Plugins 271
Chapter 8: Infrastructure Testing and Validation 278
Chapter 9: Advanced Debugging and Troubleshooting 285
Chapter 10: Achieving Infrastructure as Code Excellence 292
Conclusion 299

Introduction

Welcome to the ultimate journey through the world of Terraform and its powerful command-line interface with our comprehensive book bundle, "Terraform CLI Boss: Novice to Command Line Guru." In this carefully curated collection, we embark on a quest to transform you from a newcomer to the world of infrastructure as code into a seasoned command line guru, capable of harnessing Terraform's full potential.

In today's ever-evolving tech landscape, infrastructure as code (IaC) has emerged as a critical component of modern IT operations. Terraform, developed by HashiCorp, stands as one of the leading IaC tools, enabling you to define and provision infrastructure resources in a declarative and automated manner. The Terraform CLI, with its robust command set, serves as the gateway to this transformative world.

Our journey begins with "Book 1 - Terraform CLI Boss: Mastering the Basics." Here, we provide you with the fundamental knowledge and skills necessary to navigate the Terraform ecosystem. You'll learn how to set up your development environment, understand Terraform's core concepts, and master the essential commands for creating and managing infrastructure resources.

"Book 2 - Terraform CLI Boss: Command Line Wizardry" takes you to the next level, delving deep into advanced configuration management techniques. You'll become a wizard in using HashiCorp Configuration Language (HCL) to craft intricate infrastructure definitions. Dynamic workflows with variables, the customization of Terraform through providers and plugins, and the exploration of expert-level commands will be your new playground.

As we progress, "Book 3 - Terraform CLI Boss: From Novice to Ninja" continues the journey by introducing you to Terraform modules and workspaces. Here, you'll become a Terraform ninja, skilled in building reusable modules, optimizing collaborative workflows, and applying best practices to your projects. Your transformation into a Terraform virtuoso is well underway.

Finally, in "Book 4 - Terraform CLI Boss: Expert-Level Commands Unleashed," you'll ascend to the highest levels of Terraform mastery. This book will equip you with the knowledge and techniques needed to handle complex infrastructure scenarios with confidence. You'll explore advanced CLI techniques, infrastructure testing, and validation, ensuring that your Terraform projects are robust and resilient. With your expertise in debugging and troubleshooting, no challenge will be insurmountable.

Each book in this bundle is a stepping stone on your journey to becoming a Terraform CLI boss. Whether you're just starting or seeking to refine your skills, our goal is to provide you with a comprehensive and structured path to success. By the end of this adventure, you'll be a command-line guru, capable of crafting, managing, and optimizing infrastructure as code like a true Terraform expert.

So, without further ado, let's embark on this exhilarating voyage through the "Terraform CLI Boss" book bundle. Your mastery of Terraform's command-line interface awaits, and the possibilities are limitless. Let's unlock the full potential of Terraform together.

BOOK 1
TERRAFORM CLI BOSS
MASTERING THE BASICS

ROB BOTWRIGHT

Chapter 1: Introduction to Terraform and CLI

Terraform, a powerful open-source tool developed by HashiCorp, has revolutionized the way we manage and provision infrastructure in today's fast-paced, cloud-centric world. With its declarative syntax and robust ecosystem, Terraform enables organizations to define and manage their infrastructure as code (IaC), bringing efficiency, scalability, and consistency to the provisioning process. In this book, we will embark on a journey to master Terraform and its command-line interface (CLI), delving deep into its capabilities, best practices, and advanced techniques.

Our adventure begins with an introduction to Terraform and CLI basics, laying the foundation for what lies ahead. We'll explore the fundamentals, including understanding the concept of IaC and the core terminology associated with Terraform. As we dive into the CLI, you'll become familiar with essential commands and gain the confidence to navigate Terraform's command-line interface.

Once you've grasped the basics, we'll move on to setting up your Terraform environment. You'll learn how to install Terraform and configure your development environment to ensure a smooth and efficient workflow. Armed with this knowledge, you'll be ready to embark on your Terraform journey.

In Chapter 3, we take your first steps with Terraform commands, initiating a Terraform project and executing your first infrastructure provisioning commands. As you gain hands-on experience, you'll discover how Terraform simplifies infrastructure management, making it easier to build and maintain complex systems.

Chapter 4 demystifies Terraform configuration files, providing insights into HashiCorp Configuration Language (HCL) syntax.

You'll learn how to create and structure your configuration files effectively, setting the stage for more advanced configurations down the road.

Advanced resource management takes center stage in Chapter 5. Here, you'll dive into resource blocks and attributes, understanding how to define, manage, and interact with resources effectively. Resource dependencies will become second nature as you master Terraform's capabilities for managing complex infrastructure.

Chapter 6 introduces Terraform modules and the power of reusability. You'll discover how to modularize your infrastructure code, creating scalable, maintainable, and reusable components. With modules, you'll be able to streamline your workflow and enhance collaboration within your team.

Collaboration is key in modern infrastructure management, and Chapter 7 explores collaborative workflows with Terraform. We'll delve into remote state management and version control, ensuring you have the tools and strategies in place to work effectively with others on Terraform projects.

Extending Terraform's capabilities is the focus of Chapter 8. You'll learn about custom providers and plugins, allowing you to tailor Terraform to your specific needs. This chapter empowers you to take control of your infrastructure provisioning process, making it truly your own.

Chapter 9 takes a deep dive into debugging and troubleshooting techniques. As with any complex system, issues can arise, and you'll be well-prepared to diagnose and resolve them efficiently. We'll explore common error messages, best practices for debugging, and strategies for overcoming challenges.

Finally, Chapter 10 is dedicated to helping you become a Terraform CLI ninja. You'll uncover advanced command-line techniques and automation strategies, enabling you to optimize your workflow and tackle complex infrastructure projects with confidence.

As we journey through these chapters, you'll gain the skills and knowledge needed to become a Terraform expert. Whether you're a seasoned infrastructure professional or just starting your career in DevOps, this book will equip you with the tools to harness the full power of Terraform and its CLI.

By the end of this book, you'll be well-prepared to tackle real-world infrastructure challenges, develop best practices for IaC, and take your Terraform skills to the next level. So, let's embark on this exciting journey together and unlock the potential of Terraform: Infrastructure as Code. The command-line interface (CLI) is a powerful and versatile tool that lies at the heart of modern computing. It allows users to interact with computer systems and software through text-based commands. While the graphical user interface (GUI) is more visually intuitive, the CLI offers a level of control and automation that is unmatched. For many IT professionals, developers, and system administrators, the CLI is an essential part of their daily workflow. Next, we will delve into the essentials of the CLI, exploring its key concepts and capabilities. One of the fundamental concepts in the CLI is the notion of a command. A command is a specific instruction or action that you give to the computer by typing it in at the command prompt. Commands are typically composed of a command name followed by various options and arguments. Options are modifiers that you can add to a command to customize its behavior. Arguments are typically the targets or inputs that a command operates on. For example, if you wanted to list the files in a directory using the "ls" command, the directory name would be the argument. Commands can vary greatly in complexity, from simple ones that perform basic file operations to complex ones that configure system settings or execute complex scripts. The structure of a command is typically as follows: "command_name [options] [arguments]." The command name is the actual action you want to perform, such as "ls" for listing files or "mkdir" for creating a directory. Options are typically preceded by a hyphen or double hyphen and modify the behavior of the command. For example, the "-l" option with the "ls" command would display additional details about the files. Arguments are the specific items or targets that the command acts upon. In the case of the "ls" command, the argument would be the directory whose contents you want to list. Commands are case-sensitive, which means that "ls" and "LS" are treated as different commands. Most CLI systems provide a help system that you can access by using the "--help" or "-h" option with a command. This help system provides information about the command's usage, available options, and often includes examples. Learning to use the help system effectively is an essential skill for mastering the CLI. Another critical aspect of the CLI is the command prompt. The command prompt is the text that appears on the screen, indicating that the CLI is ready to accept your input. It typically includes information such as the current user, hostname, current directory, and a symbol (often a "$" or ">" character) to signify that it's waiting for your command. Understanding the information provided by the command prompt can help you navigate the file system and execute commands more effectively. The CLI operates within a command-line shell, which is a program that interprets your commands and interacts with the operating system. There are various command-line shells available, with Bash, PowerShell, and Command Prompt being some of the most common ones. Each shell has its own set of features and capabilities, making it important to choose the one that best suits your needs. The CLI allows for powerful automation through the use of scripts and batch files. Scripts are sequences of commands that can be saved and executed as a single unit. This capability enables you to automate repetitive tasks, manage system configurations, and perform complex operations. By creating and running scripts, you can save time and reduce the risk of human error. Additionally, the CLI provides a robust set of text-processing tools that allow you to manipulate and process data efficiently. Commands like "grep," "sed," and "awk" are essential for searching, filtering, and transforming text. They are particularly valuable for tasks such as log analysis, data extraction, and text manipulation. Navigating the file system is a core skill when using the CLI. Commands like "cd" (change directory), "pwd" (print working directory), "ls" (list files), and "mkdir" (make directory) are fundamental for file and directory management. Understanding how to move around the file system is essential for accessing files and directories and performing various tasks. The CLI also provides powerful networking capabilities, allowing you to perform tasks like network configuration, diagnostics, and testing. Commands like "ping," "netstat," and "ifconfig" provide insights into network connectivity and configuration. For administrators and network engineers, these tools are invaluable for troubleshooting and maintaining network infrastructure. In addition to its local capabilities, the CLI can be used to connect to remote systems via secure shell (SSH) or remote desktop protocols. This feature enables administrators to manage servers and devices remotely, providing access to resources and systems located elsewhere. By mastering remote access through the CLI, you can efficiently administer and troubleshoot remote systems without the need for physical access. Security is a paramount concern when using the CLI. Because the CLI provides direct access to the underlying system, it's crucial to practice secure CLI usage. This includes safeguarding your login credentials, limiting access to the CLI, and following security best practices. Furthermore, many CLI systems offer encryption and authentication mechanisms to protect sensitive data and ensure secure communication. As you progress in your CLI journey, you'll discover that many commands can be combined and piped together to create powerful command pipelines. This concept allows you to take the output of one command and use it as input for another, enabling complex operations and data transformations. For example, you can use the "grep" command to filter lines containing specific text and then pipe the results to the "sort" command to arrange them alphabetically. Command pipelines are a fundamental part of the CLI's versatility and efficiency. Mastering the CLI is an ongoing process that requires practice, exploration, and continuous learning. It's a valuable skill for IT professionals, developers, and anyone who wants to maximize their control over computer systems and automate tasks. Whether you're a novice user or an experienced sysadmin, the CLI offers a world of possibilities for managing and interacting with technology. In the chapters that follow, we will delve deeper into specific aspects of the CLI, exploring advanced techniques, scripting, and best practices. By the end of this book, you'll have the knowledge and confidence to navigate the CLI effectively and harness its power to simplify complex tasks and streamline your workflow.

Chapter 2: Setting Up Your Terraform Environment

Terraform is a versatile and powerful tool for managing infrastructure as code, but before you can start using it, you need to install it on your system. The installation process varies depending on your operating system, so let's explore the steps required for several common platforms. If you're running a Linux-based system, such as Ubuntu or CentOS, you can typically install Terraform using your package manager. For example, on Ubuntu, you can use the "apt" package manager, while on CentOS, "yum" or "dnf" is commonly used. To install Terraform on Ubuntu, you can open a terminal window and run the command "sudo apt-get install terraform." If you're using CentOS, you can use "sudo yum install terraform" or "sudo dnf install terraform," depending on your system. Once the installation is complete, you can verify it by running the command "terraform version" in the terminal, which should display the installed Terraform version. On macOS, you can use the popular package manager Homebrew to install Terraform. First, make sure you have Homebrew installed, and then run the command "brew install terraform" in your terminal. After the installation finishes, you can verify it by running "terraform version." For Windows users, Terraform offers a Windows installer package that simplifies the installation process. You can download the installer from the official Terraform website, double-click on it to run the installer, and follow the on-screen instructions. Once the installation is complete, open a Command Prompt or PowerShell window and run "terraform version" to confirm the installation. Terraform is also available as a standalone binary, which is convenient for users who prefer to manage their software manually or use package managers like Chocolatey on Windows. To install Terraform as a standalone binary, you can follow these general steps: First, visit the Terraform downloads page on the official website to get the latest release URL for your operating system. Next, download the Terraform binary by using a web browser or a command-line tool like "curl" or "wget." Once the download is complete, extract the binary from the archive (if applicable) and place it in a directory included in your system's PATH environment variable. You can check your system's PATH by running the command "echo $PATH" on Linux/macOS or "echo %PATH%" on Windows. After placing the Terraform binary in a PATH-accessible location, open a new terminal window and run "terraform version" to verify the installation. Keep in mind that the standalone binary installation method allows you to easily manage different Terraform versions on your system by downloading and placing the desired version in your PATH. For users who prefer containerization, Terraform is also available as a Docker container. You can pull the official Terraform Docker image from the Docker Hub using the "docker pull" command, like so: "docker pull hashicorp/terraform." Once the image is downloaded, you can use Docker to run Terraform commands within a container, providing isolation from your host system. Using Terraform as a Docker container is particularly useful for development and testing environments. It's worth noting that Terraform frequently releases new versions with bug fixes and feature updates, so it's a good practice to keep your installation up to date. You can check for the latest Terraform releases on the official website or use the "terraform version" command with the "-check-upgrade" flag to check for available updates. If a newer version is available, you can download and install it using the same installation method you used initially. Installing Terraform extensions, such as providers and modules, is an integral part of setting up your Terraform environment. Providers are responsible for managing resources in various infrastructure platforms like AWS, Azure, and Google Cloud. To use a specific provider, you need to install it and configure its credentials. Terraform providers are typically distributed as separate binary plugins or modules. To install a provider, download the provider binary from the official Terraform Registry or other trusted sources. Once you have the provider binary, place it in the ".terraform.d/plugins" directory within your Terraform configuration directory. You may need to create this directory if it doesn't already exist. After installing the provider, you can configure it in your Terraform configuration by specifying the provider block and providing the necessary configuration variables. For example, to configure the AWS provider, you would specify your AWS access key and secret key in the provider block. Modules, on the other hand, are reusable collections of Terraform configurations that encapsulate infrastructure resources and configurations. To use a module in your Terraform project, you need to install it and reference it in your main configuration files. Modules are typically stored in separate directories and can be sourced from various locations, such as a local file system, a Git repository, or the Terraform Registry. To install a module, create a directory within your Terraform project to store the module files. You can then copy or clone the module source code into this directory. Once the module is in place, you can reference it in your Terraform configuration using the "module" block and specifying the module source location. For instance, if you have a module named "web_server" in a subdirectory called "modules," you can reference it in your main configuration file like this: "module web_server { source = "./modules/web_server" }." This allows you to leverage the power of reusable infrastructure code by including and configuring modules within your Terraform projects. In addition to providers and modules, Terraform also supports plugins, which are extensions that add new features and functionality to Terraform. Plugins can enhance Terraform's capabilities by providing additional resources, data sources, and provisioners. Installing and managing plugins is straightforward, as Terraform handles the plugin installation process automatically. When you run a Terraform command that requires a particular plugin, such as "terraform init" or "terraform apply," Terraform checks if the necessary plugins are available and installs them if they are missing. These plugins are typically downloaded from the Terraform Registry, where they are hosted and maintained by the Terraform community. As part of the installation and configuration process, Terraform also requires authentication and access credentials to interact with cloud providers and APIs. These credentials are essential for Terraform to authenticate and authorize its actions, and they must be provided in a secure and controlled manner. The method for managing credentials varies depending on the provider and your specific use case. For many cloud providers, such as AWS, Azure, and Google Cloud, Terraform can use environment variables, configuration files, or IAM roles to access credentials securely. You can configure these credentials in your Terraform configuration files or use the provider-specific tools and methods recommended by the respective cloud providers. It's crucial to follow security best practices when managing credentials to ensure the protection of sensitive information. Overall, the installation and configuration of Terraform, providers, modules, and plugins are fundamental steps in preparing your Terraform environment. With Terraform properly installed and configured, you're ready to start defining your infrastructure as code, creating and managing resources, and automating your infrastructure provisioning and management tasks. In the subsequent chapters of this book, we'll explore how to write Terraform configurations, provision infrastructure, and leverage Terraform's powerful capabilities to build and manage your infrastructure efficiently. Configuring your development environment is a crucial step on your journey to becoming proficient with Terraform and its command-line interface (CLI). Your development environment is where you'll write, test, and manage your Terraform configurations, and it plays a pivotal role in your overall workflow. The process of setting up your environment involves preparing your local machine, configuring your Terraform settings, and ensuring that you have access to the necessary tools and resources. Next, we'll explore the key aspects of configuring your development environment for Terraform.

Before you begin configuring your development environment, you'll need to ensure that you have a few essential components in place. First and foremost, you'll need a computer or server that meets the minimum system requirements for running Terraform. Terraform is a lightweight tool, and it can run on a variety of operating systems, including Linux, macOS, and Windows. Make sure your system has sufficient disk space, memory, and CPU power to support your infrastructure provisioning tasks.

Next, you'll need to have a text editor or integrated development environment (IDE) installed on your machine. A good text editor or IDE can significantly enhance your productivity when working with Terraform configurations. Popular choices among Terraform users include Visual Studio Code, Sublime Text, and JetBrains IntelliJ IDEA, all of which offer Terraform extensions or plugins to streamline your workflow.

Another critical component of your development environment is version control. Version control systems like Git are essential for tracking changes to your Terraform code, collaborating with team members, and managing your project's history. If you're not already familiar with version control, it's worth investing time in learning the basics, as it's a fundamental skill for modern software development.

With the foundational components in place, it's time to focus on configuring your Terraform environment. One of the first steps is to install Terraform on your local machine, as discussed in the previous chapter. Ensure that you have the Terraform binary accessible in your system's PATH, so you can run Terraform commands from any directory in your terminal.

Once Terraform is installed, you should check the version to verify that the installation was successful. You can do this by running the "terraform version" command in your terminal. This command will display the currently installed Terraform version and any available upgrades.

Terraform configurations often require sensitive information, such as API keys, passwords, or access tokens. It's crucial to manage these secrets securely to protect your infrastructure and data. To handle sensitive data, Terraform provides several mechanisms, including environment variables, configuration files, and third-party secret management tools.

One common practice for managing sensitive information is to use environment variables. You can set environment variables with your secrets and then reference them in your Terraform configurations. This approach keeps sensitive data out of your configuration files and helps prevent accidental exposure. Make sure to follow security best practices when dealing with environment variables, and consider using a tool like HashiCorp Vault for more advanced secret management.

Another method for handling sensitive data is to use Terraform variables and input variables. You can define input variables in your Terraform configurations and prompt for their values interactively during Terraform execution. This approach allows you to enter sensitive information securely without exposing it in your configuration files. However, it's essential to be cautious when entering secrets interactively, especially if you're working in a shared or remote environment.

In addition to securing secrets, you should configure your Terraform settings to align with your specific use case. Terraform settings are typically defined in a configuration file named "terraform.tfvars" or "variables.tf." These settings can include values for variables, provider configurations, and backend configurations.

Provider configurations are particularly important, as they define the behavior and settings for the infrastructure providers you'll be using. For example, if you're working with AWS, you'll need to configure your AWS access and secret keys, as well as specify the AWS region you'll be operating in. These settings ensure that Terraform can authenticate and interact with your cloud provider's services effectively.

Backend configurations determine how Terraform manages state data. The state file contains information about your infrastructure, and it's critical to maintain its integrity and accessibility. Terraform supports various backends, such as local files, remote storage, and even database backends. You should choose a backend that suits your workflow and security requirements, and configure it accordingly.

In addition to the core Terraform settings, you may also need to configure authentication for remote services and APIs. For example, if your Terraform configurations interact with cloud provider APIs, you'll need to ensure that your credentials are set up correctly. This often involves creating service accounts, IAM roles, or access keys and configuring your environment to use them securely.

Terraform also offers the flexibility to configure remote state storage, which is particularly important in collaborative and team environments. By using remote state, you can centralize and share your Terraform state data, making it easier to collaborate on infrastructure projects. To configure remote state, you'll need to specify the backend settings in your Terraform configuration files and ensure that appropriate access controls are in place.

Once your Terraform environment is configured, it's a good practice to initialize your working directory using the "terraform init" command. This command prepares your configuration and downloads any necessary plugins or modules. Initialization is an essential step before you can apply or plan your Terraform configurations.

As you continue to work with Terraform, you may find that you need to install and configure additional tools and extensions to enhance your development environment. For example, you might use a tool like Terraform Format (terraform fmt) to automatically format your Terraform code according to best practices. Similarly, Terraform Lint (tflint) can help you catch errors and enforce coding standards in your configurations.

As your Terraform projects grow and become more complex, you may also want to consider using a continuous integration/continuous deployment (CI/CD) system. CI/CD pipelines can automate the testing, validation, and deployment of your Terraform configurations, streamlining your development and release processes.

In summary, configuring your development environment for Terraform is a critical step in your journey to mastering infrastructure as code. By setting up your local machine, managing secrets securely, configuring Terraform settings, and using the right tools, you'll be well-equipped to create, manage, and automate infrastructure deployments effectively. In the chapters that follow, we'll delve deeper into writing Terraform configurations, provisioning infrastructure, and exploring advanced techniques for managing infrastructure as code with Terraform.

Chapter 3: Your First Terraform Commands

Initializing a Terraform project is a foundational step in the process of using Terraform to manage your infrastructure as code. The initialization process ensures that your working directory is set up correctly, downloads any necessary plugins or modules, and prepares your Terraform configuration for use. Next, we'll explore the importance of initialization, the key steps involved, and how to effectively initialize a Terraform project.

When you first start working on a new Terraform project or configuration, it's crucial to initialize it before you can apply or plan any changes. Initialization sets up the necessary environment for Terraform to manage your infrastructure and resources effectively. One of the primary tasks during initialization is to download the provider plugins and modules specified in your configuration. These plugins and modules are essential for Terraform to communicate with infrastructure providers like AWS, Azure, Google Cloud, and others. By downloading and installing them, you ensure that Terraform has access to the necessary tools and resources to provision and manage your infrastructure.

To initialize a Terraform project, open a terminal window or command prompt and navigate to the directory containing your Terraform configuration files. Once you're in the correct directory, you can run the "terraform init" command. This command instructs Terraform to analyze your configuration files, identify the required plugins and modules, and download them from the Terraform Registry or other specified sources.

During initialization, Terraform generates a hidden directory called ".terraform" in your project directory. This directory contains the downloaded plugins, modules, and other metadata required for Terraform to function. It's worth noting that the ".terraform" directory is typically added to your project's version control system (e.g., Git) to ensure that all team members have access to the same dependencies when working on the project.

A critical aspect of initialization is the selection of a backend configuration. The backend configuration determines where Terraform stores its state data, which includes information about the infrastructure being managed. Terraform supports various backend types, such as local files, remote storage services (e.g., Amazon S3, Azure Blob Storage), and even database backends. The choice of a backend depends on your specific use case, workflow, and security requirements.

Configuring a backend is typically done by specifying the backend settings in your Terraform configuration files or by using command-line options. For example, to configure a backend that uses Amazon S3 for remote state storage, you would include the necessary configuration options in your Terraform configuration files. This might include specifying the AWS S3 bucket and key where the state file should be stored, as well as any AWS authentication credentials or roles required for access.

It's crucial to select an appropriate backend configuration that aligns with your project's needs. For collaborative projects with multiple contributors, a remote backend that allows for centralized state management is often preferred. This ensures that all team members are working with the same state data, reducing conflicts and enabling smoother collaboration.

Once the initialization process is complete, you can use Terraform commands like "terraform plan" and "terraform apply" to interact with your infrastructure. These commands leverage the information and resources set up during initialization to determine the changes required to bring your infrastructure to the desired state.

It's essential to note that initialization is not a one-time process; it should be performed whenever you start working on a new Terraform configuration or if you make changes to your existing configuration that affect the required plugins or modules. In a collaborative environment, all team members should run "terraform init" to ensure consistency and compatibility.

When you run "terraform init," Terraform checks for updates to the plugins and modules that your configuration depends on. If newer versions are available, Terraform downloads and installs them, keeping your project up to date. This automatic update feature helps ensure that your Terraform configurations continue to work seamlessly with the latest provider features and improvements.

Sometimes, you may encounter situations where Terraform initialization fails due to network issues, access restrictions, or other factors. In such cases, it's essential to diagnose and resolve the problem to ensure a successful initialization. Common issues may include firewall restrictions, proxy settings, or issues with network connectivity. By addressing these issues, you can ensure that Terraform can download the necessary dependencies and initialize your project correctly.

As your Terraform projects become more complex and involve multiple environments or stages (e.g., development, staging, production), you can use workspace management to streamline your workflow. Workspaces allow you to maintain separate state files for each environment while sharing the same configuration code. By using workspaces, you can switch between environments easily, apply changes independently, and maintain isolation between environments.

To create a new workspace, you can use the "terraform workspace new" command, specifying the name of the new workspace. For example, you can create workspaces named "dev," "staging," and "prod" to represent different environments. Each workspace has its own state file, which stores the infrastructure state for that specific environment.

To switch between workspaces, you can use the "terraform workspace select" command followed by the name of the workspace you want to switch to. This allows you to focus on a particular environment and apply changes or perform actions relevant to that environment.

Workspaces provide a structured approach to managing multiple environments within a single Terraform configuration. However, it's essential to follow best practices for managing state files in a team environment to avoid conflicts and ensure proper collaboration.

In summary, initializing a Terraform project is a crucial step in the infrastructure as code (IaC) process. It prepares your working directory by downloading necessary plugins and modules, setting up backend configurations, and ensuring that your Terraform environment is ready to provision and manage infrastructure. By understanding the initialization process and making informed choices about backends and workspaces, you can effectively manage your Terraform projects and maintain infrastructure consistency across different environments.

Creating your first resource with Terraform is an exciting step that allows you to put your infrastructure as code (IaC) skills into action. Resources are the building blocks of your infrastructure, representing the various components and services you want to provision and manage. Next, we'll explore the process of defining, configuring, and creating your first resource using Terraform.

Before you can create a resource, you need to define it in your Terraform configuration. A Terraform configuration is a set of declarative statements that describe the desired state of your infrastructure. Resource definitions are a fundamental part of your configuration, and they specify the type of resource you want to create, its properties, and any required settings.

Terraform configurations are typically stored in files with a ".tf" extension, and they can be organized into modules for reusability and maintainability. To create a resource, you'll need to define a resource block in your configuration file. A resource block begins with the resource type (e.g., "aws_instance" for an Amazon Web Services (AWS) EC2 instance) followed by a unique resource name and a set of configuration settings enclosed in curly braces.

For example, to define an AWS EC2 instance, you might create a resource block like this:

```arduino
Copy code
resource "aws_instance" "example" { ami = "ami-0c55b159cbfafe1f0" instance_type = "t2.micro" }
```

In this example, we've defined an AWS EC2 instance with the resource type "aws_instance" and the resource name "example." We've also specified two configuration settings: the Amazon Machine Image (AMI) ID and the instance type.

The AMI ID identifies the virtual machine image that the EC2 instance should be based on, while the instance type specifies the hardware characteristics of the instance, such as the number of CPU cores and the amount of memory.

Once you've defined your resource block, you can apply the Terraform configuration to create the resource. To do this, open a terminal window or command prompt, navigate to the directory containing your Terraform configuration, and run the "terraform apply" command.

Terraform will analyze your configuration, plan the changes required to reach the desired state (in this case, creating the resource), and then prompt you to confirm the changes. Review the proposed changes carefully, and if everything looks correct, type "yes" to proceed.

Terraform will then communicate with the target infrastructure provider (in this case, AWS) and instruct it to create the specified resource. You'll see progress updates and, once the resource is created, a confirmation message indicating that the operation was successful.

It's important to note that Terraform is designed to be idempotent, which means that you can apply the same configuration multiple times without causing unintended changes. If you run "terraform apply" again after creating a resource, Terraform will detect that the resource already exists and report that no changes are required.

To ensure that Terraform is aware of the resources it manages, it stores information about them in a state file. The state file is a JSON-formatted file that keeps track of the current state of your infrastructure. It records resource attributes, dependencies, and other essential information.

Terraform automatically manages the state file for you, and it's typically stored locally in a file named "terraform.tfstate." In a collaborative environment, it's common to use remote state storage, which stores the state file in a secure and shared location accessible to all team members.

By using remote state, you can avoid conflicts and ensure that everyone has access to the latest state information. Configuring remote state storage is done by specifying backend settings in your Terraform configuration files.

Now that you've successfully created your first resource, you can further customize and configure it to meet your specific requirements. Resource configuration options can vary depending on the resource type and provider, so it's essential to refer to the provider's documentation for details on available settings and attributes.

In addition to basic resource configuration, Terraform provides a wide range of features and capabilities for managing infrastructure. For example, you can use variables to parameterize your configurations, making them more flexible and reusable. Variables allow you to define dynamic values that can be provided at runtime or stored securely in variable files.

To illustrate, you might define a variable for the instance type in your AWS EC2 instance configuration like this:

arduinoCopy code

```
variable "instance_type" { description = "The type of AWS EC2
instance to create." default = "t2.micro" }
```

You can then reference this variable in your resource block:

csharpCopy code

```
resource "aws_instance" "example" { ami = "ami-
0c55b159cbfafe1f0" instance_type = var.instance_type }
```

By using variables, you can easily change the instance type for your EC2 instances without modifying the resource block directly.

Another powerful feature of Terraform is the use of data sources to query and retrieve information from your target infrastructure. Data sources allow you to access information like AMI IDs, IP addresses, and security group IDs dynamically. You can use this data to populate your resource configurations and ensure that your infrastructure remains up to date.

To demonstrate, let's say you want to retrieve the latest Amazon Linux 2 AMI ID for your EC2 instances. You can use a data source like this:

sqlCopy code

```
data "aws_ami" "latest" { most_recent = true owners =
["amazon"] filter { name = "name" values = ["amzn2-ami-hvm-
*"] } }
```
With this data source, you can obtain the latest Amazon Linux 2
AMI ID and use it in your resource block:
javaCopy code
```
resource "aws_instance" "example" { ami =
data.aws_ami.latest.id instance_type = "t2.micro" }
```
Terraform will automatically fetch the latest AMI ID when you
apply the configuration.

In addition to variables and data sources, Terraform provides a
wide array of functions, expressions, and operators for
manipulating values and performing computations within your
configurations. These features enable you to create dynamic and
flexible infrastructure definitions.

As you continue your journey with Terraform, you'll explore more
advanced topics such as resource dependencies, provisioners, and
remote backends. You'll also learn about strategies for organizing
and managing complex configurations and gain insights into best
practices for maintaining your infrastructure as code.

Creating your first resource with Terraform is an important
milestone, and it opens the door to efficiently managing and
automating your infrastructure. By understanding the basics of
resource definition, configuration, and management, you'll be
well-equipped to tackle more complex infrastructure challenges
and leverage the full potential of Terraform's capabilities.

Chapter 4: Managing Terraform State

Understanding state files is a fundamental aspect of using Terraform effectively to manage your infrastructure as code (IaC). State files play a crucial role in tracking the current state of your infrastructure, allowing Terraform to plan and apply changes accurately. Next, we'll explore the importance of state files, how they work, and best practices for managing them.

At its core, Terraform is a declarative tool that allows you to define the desired state of your infrastructure using configuration files. When you run Terraform commands like "terraform apply" or "terraform plan," Terraform compares the current state of your infrastructure with the desired state specified in your configuration.

To perform this comparison, Terraform relies on a state file, which is a JSON-formatted file that records information about the resources it manages. The state file contains details about the resources, their attributes, dependencies, and other metadata necessary for Terraform to understand and track the infrastructure.

One of the primary functions of the state file is to keep track of the resources Terraform manages. This includes resources like virtual machines, databases, storage buckets, and any other components defined in your Terraform configuration. Each resource is associated with a set of attributes and properties that describe its configuration and status.

For example, if you're managing an AWS EC2 instance, the state file would include information about the instance's ID, IP address, security groups, and other relevant details. Terraform uses this information to understand the current state of the resource and determine what changes, if any, need to be applied to reach the desired state defined in your configuration.

State files also store information about resource dependencies. In a complex infrastructure, resources often depend on each other, meaning that one resource relies on the existence or configuration of another. For example, a web server resource may depend on a database resource to store data. The state file captures these dependencies, ensuring that Terraform applies changes in the correct order to maintain consistency.

In addition to resource information, state files contain unique identifiers (known as resource addresses) for each resource. Resource addresses are a critical component of Terraform's tracking mechanism. They provide a way for Terraform to identify resources even if their names or other attributes change.

Resource addresses use a hierarchical format that reflects the structure of your configuration. For example, if you have a resource named "web_server" defined within a module named "app," its resource address might be "module.app.aws_instance.web_server." This structured approach allows Terraform to navigate and update resources accurately, even in complex configurations.

The state file also plays a role in managing resource lifecycle. When you initially create a resource with Terraform, it records the resource's configuration and status in the state file. As you make changes to your configuration and apply them, Terraform updates the state file to reflect the new state of your infrastructure.

Terraform is designed to be idempotent, which means you can run the same configuration repeatedly without causing unintended changes. When you apply your configuration, Terraform compares the desired state defined in your configuration with the current state stored in the state file. If there are differences, Terraform calculates the necessary actions to reach the desired state and applies them.

For example, if you change the instance type of an AWS EC2 instance from "t2.micro" to "t2.small" in your configuration,

Terraform will detect this change. It will update the state file with the new configuration and generate a plan to modify the existing EC2 instance to match the desired "t2.small" instance type.

It's important to note that the state file is typically stored locally by default. This means that the state file is located in the same directory as your Terraform configuration files, and it's often named "terraform.tfstate." However, in a collaborative or production environment, managing the state file locally can lead to issues, conflicts, and challenges with access control.

To address these concerns, Terraform provides support for remote state storage. Remote state storage involves storing the state file in a centralized, secure, and shared location that is accessible to all team members and automation processes. This centralization ensures that everyone is working with the same state data, reducing conflicts and enabling smoother collaboration.

There are several remote state storage options available, including cloud-based storage services like Amazon S3, Azure Blob Storage, and Google Cloud Storage. You can also use dedicated Terraform backends, such as HashiCorp Terraform Cloud or HashiCorp Consul, to manage your state.

To configure remote state storage, you specify the backend settings in your Terraform configuration files. These settings include the type of backend you want to use and any required authentication or access credentials.

For example, to configure remote state storage using Amazon S3 as the backend, you might include the following settings in your configuration:

vbnetCopy code

terraform { backend "s3" { bucket = "my-terraform-state-bucket" key = "my-project/terraform.tfstate" region = "us-east-1" encrypt = true acl = "private" } }

In this example, we've configured the S3 backend with the bucket name, key (object name), region, encryption, and access control list (ACL). This configuration tells Terraform to store the state file in the specified S3 bucket with the specified settings.

Once you've configured remote state storage, you can run "terraform init" and "terraform apply" as usual. Terraform will use the remote state backend to store and retrieve the state file, ensuring that it's centralized and accessible to all team members.

Managing state files is a critical aspect of Terraform's workflow, and it's important to follow best practices to ensure consistency and reliability. Here are some key best practices for managing Terraform state files:

Use remote state storage for collaboration: In team environments, always use remote state storage to centralize state data and avoid conflicts.

Encrypt sensitive state data: Enable encryption for state files, especially when storing them remotely, to protect sensitive information.

Implement access controls: Ensure that only authorized users and processes have access to state files and the remote state storage.

Use version control for configurations: Store your Terraform configurations in a version control system (e.g., Git) to track changes, collaborate, and maintain history.

Avoid sharing state files directly: Sharing state files outside of your team's controlled environment can lead to issues and conflicts. Use remote state storage instead.

Document state file locations: Clearly document the location and configuration of your state files to facilitate collaboration and troubleshooting.

In summary, state files are a critical component of Terraform's infrastructure management process. They track the current state of your infrastructure, resource dependencies, and configuration changes. By understanding how state files work and following best practices for managing them, you can ensure the reliability, security, and collaboration capabilities of your Terraform projects. State locking and management are essential aspects of using Terraform in collaborative environments to ensure data integrity and prevent conflicts. When multiple team members or automation processes work concurrently with Terraform, it's critical to implement state locking mechanisms to maintain consistency. Next, we'll explore the challenges posed by concurrent access to state files, the solutions provided by Terraform, and best practices for state locking and management.

As previously discussed, Terraform relies on state files to store information about the infrastructure it manages. These state files are JSON-formatted and contain data such as resource attributes, dependencies, and resource addresses. State files serve as the source of truth for Terraform, enabling it to understand the current state of the infrastructure.

When multiple individuals or automation systems collaborate on Terraform projects, they may perform concurrent operations, such as applying changes, destroying resources, or updating configurations. Concurrent access to state files can lead to race conditions, conflicts, and data inconsistencies if not managed properly. To address these challenges, Terraform offers state locking mechanisms that ensure only one entity can modify the state at any given time. State locking is particularly crucial in situations where multiple users or automation processes interact with a shared state file.

Terraform supports various backend types for storing state, and the state locking mechanism may vary depending on the chosen backend. Common state backends include local files, Amazon S3, Azure Blob Storage, Google Cloud Storage, and dedicated Terraform backends like HashiCorp Terraform Cloud or HashiCorp Consul. Local file state backends, which are often used for individual or development environments, provide simple locking mechanisms. When Terraform initializes and configures a local file backend, it creates a lock file alongside the state file. This lock file is used to coordinate access to the state file. For example, if one user runs "terraform apply" to update the infrastructure, Terraform will attempt to acquire a lock on the state file. If the lock is already held by another process (e.g., a different user or automation system), Terraform will wait until the lock is released before proceeding. Once the lock is acquired, Terraform performs the planned operation, updates the state, and releases the lock.

This locking mechanism ensures that only one user or process can modify the state at any given time, preventing conflicts and data corruption. However, it also means that other users or processes must wait for the lock to be released, which can introduce delays in a collaborative environment.

For remote state backends like Amazon S3, Azure Blob Storage, or Google Cloud Storage, state locking is implemented differently. These remote backends typically leverage the built-in locking capabilities of the underlying storage service to coordinate access.

For example, Amazon S3 provides support for object locking, which can be used to prevent concurrent access to state files. When Terraform initializes a remote S3 backend, it configures object locking settings to ensure that only one entity can modify the state file at a time. This eliminates the need for explicit lock files and allows multiple users and automation processes to interact with the state concurrently.

Similarly, other remote state backends employ their respective locking mechanisms to coordinate access and maintain data integrity. These mechanisms are designed to handle concurrent operations gracefully and prevent conflicts.

Dedicated Terraform backends like HashiCorp Terraform Cloud offer advanced state management capabilities, including fine-grained access control and audit logging. Terraform Cloud provides centralized state storage, locking, and collaboration features, making it an excellent choice for teams working on infrastructure projects.

When using Terraform Cloud or other dedicated backends, you can configure access control policies to define who can read, write, and modify the state. This granular control allows you to restrict access to sensitive infrastructure data and ensure that only authorized users can make changes.

In addition to locking mechanisms provided by Terraform backends, it's essential to follow best practices for state management in collaborative environments:

Use Remote State Storage: Always use remote state storage, especially in collaborative environments, to centralize state data and enable concurrent access.

Leverage Backend Locking: Choose a remote state backend that supports built-in locking mechanisms, such as Amazon S3, Azure Blob Storage, or dedicated Terraform backends.

Configure Access Control: Implement access control policies to define who can access and modify the state in dedicated Terraform backends or remote storage services.

Follow Naming Conventions: Establish naming conventions for state files to ensure clarity and consistency, especially when managing multiple environments or projects.

Implement Change Workflow: Define a workflow for making changes to infrastructure configurations, including planning, applying changes, and reviewing state modifications.

Monitor Locking: Regularly monitor state locking and access to detect and resolve any issues or conflicts promptly.

Backup State Files: Maintain backups of state files to recover from unexpected issues or data corruption.

In summary, state locking and management are vital components of Terraform's collaborative workflow. By using the appropriate state backend, implementing access control, and following best practices, you can ensure data integrity, prevent conflicts, and enable efficient collaboration when working with Terraform in team environments.

Chapter 5: Understanding Variables and Outputs

Declaring variables is a fundamental concept in Terraform that allows you to parameterize your configurations and make them more flexible and reusable. Variables serve as placeholders for values that can be provided at runtime, enabling you to customize your infrastructure definitions without modifying the configuration itself. Next, we'll explore the importance of declaring variables, how to define and use them, and best practices for managing variables in Terraform.

Variables in Terraform provide a way to abstract and generalize your configuration by separating values from the configuration logic. Instead of hardcoding specific values like IP addresses, instance types, or resource names directly into your configuration files, you can define variables to represent these values.

To declare a variable in Terraform, you use the "variable" block within your configuration. A variable block specifies the variable's name, optional description, and default value.

For example, to declare a variable named "instance_type" that represents the type of an AWS EC2 instance, you can define it as follows:

arduinoCopy code

variable "instance_type" { description = "The type of AWS EC2 instance to create." default = "t2.micro" }

In this example, we've declared a variable named "instance_type" with a description and a default value of "t2.micro." The description provides additional context for the variable's purpose, helping users understand its intended use.

Once you've declared a variable, you can reference it throughout your configuration by using its name. Variables are interpolated into your configuration, replacing their placeholders with their values.

For instance, if you want to use the "instance_type" variable within a resource block to specify the instance type for an AWS EC2 instance, you can do so like this:

csharpCopy code

```
resource "aws_instance" "example" { ami = "ami-0c55b159cbfafe1f0" instance_type = var.instance_type }
```

In this code snippet, we've used the "var.instance_type" syntax to reference the value of the "instance_type" variable.

By declaring variables and referencing them in your configuration, you make your infrastructure definitions more dynamic and adaptable. Variables enable you to:

Promote Reusability: Variables allow you to create configurations that can be reused across different environments or projects with varying settings.

Enhance Maintainability: Separating values into variables makes your configuration files cleaner and easier to maintain, as changes can be made in one place.

Customize Deployments: You can use different values for variables when applying the same configuration to different environments, such as development, staging, and production.

Facilitate Collaboration: Variables provide a standard way for team members to customize configurations without requiring in-depth knowledge of the underlying Terraform code.

Variables can have various data types, including strings, numbers, lists, maps, and bools. Terraform automatically infers the data type from the default value you provide. However, you can explicitly specify the data type using the "type" attribute in the variable block if needed.

For example, to declare a variable as a list of strings, you can use the following syntax:

goCopy code

```
variable "availability_zones" { description = "A list of availability zones for resources." type = list(string) default = ["us-east-1a", "us-east-1b", "us-east-1c"] }
```

In this case, we've explicitly specified the data type as "list(string)" to indicate that the "availability_zones" variable should contain a list of string values.

Variables can also be provided with values at runtime in several ways. The most common methods for supplying variable values are through variable files, environment variables, or interactive prompts during Terraform commands.

Variable files are JSON or HCL files that specify values for variables. You can create a variable file and pass it to Terraform using the "-var-file" option when running commands like "terraform apply" or "terraform plan."

For instance, if you have a variable file named "variables.tfvars" with the following content:

hclCopy code

instance_type = "t2.small" availability_zones = ["us-west-2a", "us-west-2b"]

You can apply it to your configuration using:

csharpCopy code

```
terraform apply -var -file=variables.tfvars
```

Alternatively, you can set variable values using environment variables. Variables in Terraform can be assigned values by specifying environment variables with the naming convention "TF_VAR_variable_name."

For example, to set the "instance_type" variable using an environment variable, you can do the following:

bashCopy code

```
export TF_VAR_instance_type= "t2.small"
```

Now, when you run Terraform commands, it will use the value from the environment variable for the "instance_type" variable.

Terraform also supports interactive prompts for variables. If a variable doesn't have a value specified through any other method, Terraform will prompt you for it during command execution. This interactive approach can be useful when working with sensitive data or variables that may vary between runs.

To leverage interactive prompts, simply omit the default value for a variable in its declaration.

In addition to declaring and using variables, Terraform allows you to set variable values directly within a configuration file using variable assignment. This can be helpful for small-scale configurations or for providing default values within a module.

For example, you can set the value of a variable directly within a configuration file like this:

hclCopy code

```
variable "instance_type" { description = "The type of AWS EC2 instance to create." default = "t2.micro" } variable "availability_zones" { description = "A list of availability zones for resources." default = ["us-east-1a", "us-east-1b", "us-east-1c"] } # Override the default value of the "instance_type" variable. variable "instance_type" { default = "t2.small" }
```

In this example, we've overridden the default value of the "instance_type" variable within the same configuration file.

While variable assignment within configuration files can be convenient, it's essential to maintain consistency and avoid conflicts when working on larger projects with multiple contributors.

To manage variables effectively in Terraform projects, consider the following best practices:

Use Descriptive Names: Choose meaningful names for variables to enhance clarity and understanding of their purpose.

Provide Descriptions: Include descriptions for variables to document their intended use and any specific requirements.

Organize Variables: Group related variables together in your configuration files to improve organization and readability.

Centralize Variable Definitions: Consider defining variables in a separate module or variable file that can be reused across multiple configurations.

Avoid Overly Specific Default Values: Default values should be general enough to accommodate various use cases. Reserve specific values for variable assignments.

Document Variable Sources: Clearly document where variable values can be sourced, whether from variable files, environment variables, or interactive prompts.

Test Variable Assignments: Verify that variable assignments and values are correctly set and applied in your Terraform configurations.

By following these best practices and understanding how to declare, define, and use variables in Terraform, you can harness the power of parameterization to create more flexible, maintainable, and reusable infrastructure as code.

Retrieving outputs is a crucial step in Terraform's workflow that allows you to obtain information about the resources and infrastructure you've provisioned. Outputs in Terraform provide a way to expose specific attributes or values from your infrastructure to be used by other Terraform configurations, scripts, or external systems. Next, we'll explore the significance of outputs, how to declare and use them, and best practices for retrieving and managing outputs in Terraform.

Outputs serve as a means of communication between different parts of your Terraform infrastructure. While variables allow you to parameterize and customize configurations, outputs enable you to extract and share specific information about your infrastructure's current state.

To declare an output in Terraform, you use the "output" block within your configuration. An output block specifies the output's name, description (optional), and the value or reference you want to expose.

For example, if you want to retrieve the public IP address of an AWS EC2 instance, you can declare an output like this:

hclCopy code

output "public_ip" { description = "The public IP address of the EC2 instance." value = aws_instance.example.public_ip }

In this declaration, we've created an output named "public_ip" with a description and a value referencing the public IP address of the "aws_instance" resource named "example."

Once you've declared an output, you can reference it from other parts of your Terraform configuration or from external scripts and tools. Outputs are valuable for various purposes, including providing information to users, sharing data between Terraform configurations, and integrating with external systems.

To access an output value in another Terraform configuration, you can use the "module" syntax to reference the output from the module where it's defined. For example, if you have a module named "web_server" that declares an output named "public_ip," you can access it like this:

hclCopy code

```
module "web_server" { source = "./modules/web_server" # other module configuration settings # Access the output from the "web_server" module. web_server_public_ip = module.web_server.public_ip }
```

In this example, we've used the "module.web_server.public_ip" syntax to access the "public_ip" output from the "web_server" module.

Terraform allows you to retrieve outputs from both the root module (the main configuration) and child modules, making it possible to share information across different parts of your infrastructure.

Outputs can be especially useful when you want to obtain dynamically generated values from your infrastructure. For instance, you might retrieve the DNS name of a load balancer, the ID of a database instance, or the endpoint URL of an API gateway.

In addition to retrieving outputs within Terraform configurations, you can use the "terraform output" command to display the values of declared outputs. Running "terraform output" in the command line will list all the defined outputs and their current values for the active workspace.

For example, if you have defined the "public_ip" output as shown earlier, you can use the "terraform output" command to view its value:

bashCopy code

```
terraform output public_ip
```

Terraform will display the value of the "public_ip" output, making it accessible for scripting or automation purposes.

When working with outputs, it's essential to consider best practices for managing and utilizing them effectively:

Use Descriptive Names: Assign meaningful names to outputs to provide clear and understandable information to users and consumers.

Document Outputs: Include descriptions for outputs to document their purpose, usage, and any specific considerations.

Select Relevant Information: Outputs should expose information that is useful and necessary for consumers, avoiding excessive or unnecessary data exposure.

Update Outputs Carefully: When modifying outputs, be cautious about backward compatibility and ensure that existing consumers can still access the data they expect.

Test Outputs: Verify that outputs provide accurate and up-to-date information about your infrastructure, especially when dealing with dynamically changing values.

Secure Sensitive Information: Avoid exposing sensitive or confidential data through outputs. If necessary, use encryption or access controls to protect sensitive information.

Version Outputs: When outputs are consumed by external systems or scripts, consider versioning to ensure compatibility as your infrastructure evolves.

Outputs play a pivotal role in making infrastructure information accessible, shareable, and usable in Terraform. Whether you're retrieving IP addresses, DNS names, or other resource attributes, outputs enable you to integrate your infrastructure with external systems and automate tasks effectively.

When designing Terraform configurations, consider how outputs can provide valuable insights into your infrastructure's state and enable seamless interactions with downstream processes, monitoring tools, or deployment pipelines.

By following best practices and understanding how to declare, reference, and manage outputs, you can enhance the transparency and usability of your Terraform configurations, facilitating collaboration and automation in your infrastructure projects.

Chapter 6: Creating and Modifying Resources

Resource blocks and attributes are fundamental components of Terraform configurations that enable you to define and manage infrastructure resources. In Terraform, a resource block represents a specific resource or service in your cloud or on-premises environment, while attributes provide access to the properties and details of those resources. Next, we'll delve into the significance of resource blocks and attributes, explore how to declare and configure them, and understand their role in defining infrastructure as code.

Resource blocks are the building blocks of your Terraform configurations. They define the resources or services you want to provision and manage, such as virtual machines, databases, load balancers, or cloud storage buckets. Resource blocks specify the resource type, name, and configuration parameters. To declare a resource block in Terraform, you use the following syntax:

hclCopy code

resource "resource_type" "resource_name" { # Configuration settings for the resource }

"resource_type" specifies the type of resource you're creating, such as "aws_instance" for an Amazon Web Services (AWS) EC2 instance.

"resource_name" is a user-defined name for the resource block, which is used to reference the resource in other parts of your configuration.

For example, to create an AWS EC2 instance resource named "example," you can use the following resource block:

hclCopy code

resource "aws_instance" "example" { ami = "ami-0c55b159cbfafe1f0" instance_type = "t2.micro" }

In this code snippet, we've declared a resource block of type "aws_instance" with the name "example." The block contains configuration settings for the EC2 instance, such as the Amazon Machine Image (AMI) ID and the instance type.

Resource attributes, on the other hand, provide access to specific properties and details of the resources defined in resource blocks. Attributes allow you to retrieve information about a resource, such as its IP address, DNS name, or unique identifier.

To access an attribute of a resource, you use the following syntax:

hclCopy code

resource_type.resource_name.attribute_name

"resource_type" is the type of the resource you're accessing.

"resource_name" is the name of the resource block.

"attribute_name" is the name of the attribute you want to retrieve.

For example, to access the public IP address of the "example" EC2 instance resource declared earlier, you can use the following attribute reference:

hclCopy code

aws_instance.example.public_ip

Attributes in Terraform can be used in various ways within your configurations. You can assign them to variables, use them as inputs for other resources, or include them in outputs to make resource information accessible to other parts of your infrastructure.

Resource blocks and attributes play a pivotal role in defining infrastructure as code (IaC) in Terraform. They allow you to express your infrastructure requirements in a declarative manner, specifying what resources should exist and how they should be configured without worrying about the underlying implementation details.

Terraform providers, which are responsible for interacting with specific cloud or infrastructure platforms, define the available resource types and their attributes. Different providers offer a wide range of resources, enabling you to manage diverse aspects of your infrastructure across various platforms.

When working with resource blocks and attributes, it's essential to understand some key concepts and best practices:

Resource Lifecycle: Terraform manages the lifecycle of resources, including creation, modification, and deletion. It ensures that your infrastructure matches the desired state defined in your configurations.

Resource Dependencies: Resources often have dependencies on other resources, which are automatically managed by Terraform. Terraform determines the order in which resources are created or modified to satisfy dependencies.

Resource Names: Resource names should be unique within a configuration and follow naming conventions that make them easily identifiable and maintainable.

Resource Reusability: Resource blocks can be reused within the same configuration or across different configurations and modules, promoting code reusability.

Resource Inputs: Resource configuration settings, such as the AMI ID or instance type in the example above, are inputs that can be parameterized using variables for flexibility.

Resource Outputs: Resources often produce attributes that can be captured as outputs, allowing you to expose resource information to other parts of your infrastructure.

Resource State: Terraform maintains the state of managed resources in a state file, which is used to track the current state of your infrastructure.

Resource Updates: Terraform calculates and applies updates to resources by comparing the desired state with the current state, minimizing unnecessary changes.

Resource Deletion: Deleting a resource in Terraform requires careful consideration, as it can result in the loss of data and potential service disruptions.

In summary, resource blocks and attributes form the core of Terraform configurations, enabling you to define, configure, and manage infrastructure resources with precision. By understanding their role and following best practices, you can harness the power of Terraform to create, modify, and maintain infrastructure as code efficiently and reliably.

Managing resource changes is a crucial aspect of using Terraform effectively to maintain and evolve your infrastructure as code. In Terraform, changes to infrastructure are inevitable as your requirements evolve, and it's essential to understand how Terraform handles these changes and how you can control and manage them. Next, we'll explore the process of managing resource changes, the different types of changes, and strategies for handling updates while ensuring infrastructure stability.

Terraform's approach to managing resource changes is centered around the concept of the desired state. When you declare your infrastructure in Terraform configurations, you specify the desired state—the state you want your infrastructure to be in. Terraform's job is to make the actual state of your infrastructure match this desired state.

Resource changes occur when there is a discrepancy between the desired state and the actual state of a resource. These discrepancies can be due to configuration updates, external factors, or changes in the infrastructure platform itself.

Terraform is designed to handle three primary types of resource changes: create, update, and delete. Understanding these types of changes is essential for effective infrastructure management.

Create: A create change occurs when Terraform detects that a resource specified in your configuration does not exist in the current infrastructure state. In response, Terraform will create the resource to align with the desired state. This typically happens when you add a new resource block to your configuration.

Update: An update change occurs when there is a discrepancy between the desired state and the current state of a resource. Terraform will modify the resource to bring it in line with the desired state. Updates can include changes to configuration settings, such as modifying instance types, security groups, or other resource attributes.

Delete: A delete change occurs when a resource exists in the current infrastructure state but is not specified in the desired state. Terraform will delete the resource to align with the desired state. Delete changes often result from removing resource blocks from your configuration. Terraform's change management process is driven by its planning and execution phases. When you run a Terraform command like "terraform apply," Terraform performs a planning step to determine what changes are needed to reconcile the desired state with the current state. This planning phase generates a detailed execution plan that outlines the actions Terraform will take. The execution plan includes information about which resources will be created, updated, or deleted. Terraform also identifies any potential risks or conflicts that may arise during the execution of the plan. During the planning phase, Terraform evaluates dependencies between resources to determine the order in which changes should be applied. This dependency analysis ensures that resources are created or modified in a way that satisfies their interdependencies.

After generating the execution plan, Terraform prompts you to review and approve it before proceeding with the changes. This manual review step allows you to verify the proposed changes and prevent unintended modifications to your infrastructure.

Once you approve the plan, Terraform executes the changes in the specified order. Terraform applies the changes to the infrastructure while tracking the progress of each resource operation. If any part of the execution encounters errors or issues, Terraform will attempt to roll back changes to ensure that the infrastructure remains in a consistent state.

Resource changes are a common occurrence in Terraform, especially as you iterate on your infrastructure configurations and adapt to evolving requirements. To manage resource changes effectively, consider the following strategies and best practices:

Plan and Review Changes: Always run "terraform plan" before applying changes to understand the scope and impact of modifications. Review the plan carefully to ensure that it aligns with your expectations.

Use Variables for Flexibility: Parameterize your configurations using variables to make it easier to adapt to changes. Variables allow you to customize resource settings without modifying the configuration directly.

Resource Dependencies: Define dependencies explicitly between resources to ensure that changes are applied in the correct order. Terraform will automatically manage resource dependencies based on your configuration.

Monitor for External Changes: Keep an eye on changes made directly to the infrastructure outside of Terraform. External changes may require corresponding updates in your Terraform configuration.

Version Control: Use version control systems like Git to track changes to your Terraform configurations. This helps maintain a history of configuration changes and facilitates collaboration.

Backups and Snapshots: Consider creating backups or snapshots of critical resources before applying changes, especially for resources with potential data loss.

Infrastructure Testing: Implement testing and validation procedures to catch errors or issues early in the development process. Automated testing can help identify problems before they impact production.

Infrastructure as Code (IaC) Practices: Adhere to IaC best practices, such as modularization, documentation, and code reviews, to ensure the maintainability and reliability of your configurations.

Rollback Plans: Be prepared with rollback plans in case a change encounters unforeseen issues. Terraform's state management allows you to roll back to a previous state if needed.

Use State Locking: Implement state locking mechanisms, especially in collaborative environments, to prevent concurrent changes that may lead to conflicts.

In summary, managing resource changes is a fundamental aspect of Terraform's workflow. By understanding the types of changes, leveraging Terraform's planning and execution phases, and following best practices, you can confidently evolve your infrastructure as code while ensuring stability and reliability in your environments.

Chapter 7: Terraform Modules and Workspaces

Modularizing your infrastructure is a key practice in Terraform that promotes maintainability, reusability, and collaboration in your infrastructure as code (IaC) projects. Terraform's modular design allows you to break down complex configurations into smaller, manageable components called modules. Next, we'll explore the importance of modularization, how to create and use Terraform modules, and best practices for structuring your infrastructure codebase.

Infrastructure projects often grow in complexity as the number of resources, configurations, and environments increases. Without proper organization, managing large and intricate Terraform configurations can become challenging and error-prone. This is where modularization comes into play.

Modularization involves dividing your Terraform configurations into reusable and logically separated modules. Each module encapsulates a specific set of resources, configurations, or functionality. Think of modules as building blocks that you can assemble to construct your infrastructure.

The benefits of modularization in Terraform are manifold. First and foremost, it enhances maintainability. By breaking down configurations into smaller modules, you create manageable pieces of code that are easier to develop, test, and maintain.

Secondly, modularization encourages code reuse. You can create modules for common infrastructure patterns or components, such as web servers, databases, or networking configurations. These modules can be shared and reused across different projects, saving time and effort.

Moreover, modularization promotes collaboration. Multiple team members can work on different modules simultaneously, as long as they adhere to the module's interface and contract.

This parallel development enables faster progress and better collaboration in larger teams.

To create a Terraform module, you organize related resource blocks, variables, and outputs into a directory with a specific structure. A typical module directory structure includes a main.tf file for resource definitions, variables.tf for variable declarations, outputs.tf for output definitions, and optionally other files for additional configuration.

For instance, let's say you want to create a Terraform module for an AWS Virtual Private Cloud (VPC). You could structure your module directory like this:

cssCopy code

my_vpc_module/ | ├── main.tf   ├── variables.tf   └── outputs.tf

In the main.tf file, you would define the AWS VPC resource, subnets, security groups, and other related resources and configurations specific to the VPC module.

Variables.tf would contain declarations for variables that allow users of the module to customize the VPC's settings, such as the CIDR block, subnet configurations, or tags.

Outputs.tf would define any information you want to expose to users of the module, such as the VPC ID, subnet IDs, or other relevant attributes.

To use a Terraform module in your main configuration, you can reference it using the module block. For example:

hclCopy code

```
module "my_vpc" { source = "./path/to/my_vpc_module" cidr_block = "10.0.0.0/16" subnet_count = 3 }
```

In this code snippet, we're using the "my_vpc_module" module to create a VPC with a specified CIDR block and subnet count. The "source" attribute points to the module's directory.

Modules can also accept inputs in the form of variables and produce outputs, allowing you to customize and retrieve information from modules. This abstraction makes modules highly flexible and reusable.

Here are some best practices for modularizing your infrastructure codebase effectively:

Single Responsibility: Aim for modules with a single responsibility or focus. Each module should encapsulate a specific piece of functionality or resource type.

Abstraction Levels: Consider different levels of abstraction. You can create high-level modules that use lower-level modules. High-level modules provide a simpler interface for common use cases, while low-level modules offer more fine-grained control.

Consistent Interfaces: Define clear and consistent interfaces for your modules. Use variable names, input values, and output attributes that are intuitive and self-explanatory.

Reusability: Design modules with reusability in mind. Make sure modules are generic enough to be used across different projects or environments.

Version Control: Use version control systems like Git to manage and version your modules. This helps track changes, collaborate with others, and maintain a history of module updates.

Documentation: Include documentation within your modules to explain their purpose, inputs, outputs, and usage. Clear documentation makes modules more accessible to users.

Testing: Implement testing and validation procedures for your modules to ensure they work as expected. Automated testing can catch issues early in development.

Immutable Infrastructure: Embrace the concept of immutable infrastructure, where changes to infrastructure are achieved by creating new resources or modules rather than modifying existing ones. This approach simplifies changes and rollbacks.

Separation of Concerns: Separate modules for different layers of your architecture, such as networking, compute, databases, and security. This separation improves clarity and reduces complexity.

Standardized Naming: Establish standardized naming conventions for your modules and their resources. Consistent naming makes it easier to identify and manage resources.

Use Community Modules: Leverage community-contributed Terraform modules from the Terraform Registry or other sources. Community modules can save time and provide tested solutions for common infrastructure needs.

In summary, modularizing your infrastructure in Terraform is a powerful practice that promotes maintainability, reusability, and collaboration. By breaking down complex configurations into smaller, self-contained modules and following best practices, you can efficiently manage and scale your infrastructure projects while ensuring consistency and reliability.

Workspace strategies are a fundamental aspect of Terraform's workflow that enable you to manage and isolate different states of your infrastructure. In Terraform, a workspace is a separate environment for managing infrastructure configurations and state. Workspaces are particularly valuable when you need to work with multiple environments, such as development, staging, and production, or when collaborating with a team of developers on the same project. Next, we'll delve into workspace strategies, their use cases, and best practices for leveraging workspaces effectively in your Terraform projects.

Workspaces in Terraform are akin to different sandboxes where you can develop, test, and maintain your infrastructure configurations independently. Each workspace has its own state, variables, and configurations, allowing you to work on different aspects of your infrastructure in parallel without interfering with one another.

One of the primary use cases for workspaces is managing multiple environments. For example, you might have a development workspace where you iterate quickly on configurations, a staging workspace for pre-production testing, and a production workspace for your live infrastructure. By creating separate workspaces for each environment, you can isolate changes and state while maintaining consistency across your infrastructure.

To create a new workspace, you can use the "terraform workspace new" command and provide a name for the workspace. For instance:

bashCopy code

```
terraform workspace new development
```

This command creates a new workspace named "development." You can switch between workspaces using the "terraform workspace select" command. For example:

bashCopy code

```
terraform workspace select staging
```

Terraform also provides a default workspace named "default," which is automatically created when you initialize a new project. By default, Terraform commands operate in the "default" workspace if another workspace is not explicitly selected.

Each workspace maintains its own state file, which tracks the current state of the infrastructure for that workspace. This separation ensures that changes made in one workspace do not impact the state or resources of other workspaces.

Workspaces are valuable not only for managing different environments but also for handling feature branches, pull requests, and collaborative development. In a team setting, developers can create their own workspaces for feature development or bug fixes. This allows each developer to work independently on their changes without affecting the shared infrastructure.

For example, a developer working on a feature branch can create a workspace specific to that branch. They can make changes, test them, and collaborate with other team members in a controlled environment. Once the changes are ready, they can merge the branch and apply the changes to the appropriate workspace, such as the development or staging environment.

Here are some best practices and strategies for effectively using workspaces in your Terraform projects:

Naming Conventions: Establish clear naming conventions for your workspaces to ensure consistency and readability. Use names that reflect the purpose or environment of each workspace, such as "dev," "stage," or "prod."

Workspace State: Be aware that each workspace has its own state file. Ensure that you select the correct workspace before running Terraform commands to avoid unintended changes.

Isolation: Leverage workspaces to isolate changes and state between environments. Avoid sharing workspaces for different environments to prevent accidental changes in production.

Branch-Based Workspaces: Consider creating workspaces for feature branches or pull requests to enable parallel development and testing of new features.

Workspace Initialization: When creating a new workspace, initialize it with the necessary backend configuration and variables specific to that environment. Customize workspace settings as needed.

State Locking: Implement state locking mechanisms, especially in collaborative environments, to prevent concurrent changes that may lead to conflicts. Terraform's state locking feature helps ensure safe access to shared state files.

Remote State: Store workspace state in a centralized and version-controlled location, such as an object store or a remote state backend. This ensures that state is accessible to all team members and is not stored locally.

Pipeline Integration: Integrate workspace management into your CI/CD pipelines. Use Terraform commands to create, select, and destroy workspaces as part of your deployment process.

Cleanup and Deletion: Develop a process for cleaning up and deleting unused workspaces to prevent clutter and resource consumption.

Workspace Variables: Define workspace-specific variables or use variable files to customize configurations for each workspace. This allows you to adapt configurations for different environments while maintaining a single codebase.

Documentation: Document workspace purposes, conventions, and procedures to guide team members on workspace usage and best practices.

In summary, workspace strategies are a powerful tool for managing and isolating different states of your Terraform infrastructure. By using workspaces effectively, you can work on multiple environments, collaborate with team members, and develop features or fixes in parallel while maintaining a high degree of control and consistency in your infrastructure projects.

Chapter 8: Advanced CLI Techniques

Terraform CLI offers a wide array of features and functionalities for managing infrastructure as code (IaC) projects, and mastering some tips and tricks can greatly enhance your Terraform workflow. Next, we'll explore various Terraform CLI tips and techniques that can help you work more efficiently, troubleshoot issues, and streamline your infrastructure management processes.

Aliases for Commands: You can create custom aliases for Terraform commands to save time and reduce typing. For example, you can set up an alias like "t" for "terraform" to shorten your commands.

Environment Variables: Utilize environment variables to set common configuration values like your AWS access and secret keys. This prevents the need to hardcode sensitive information in your configurations.

Terraform Cloud: Consider using Terraform Cloud for collaborative and automated workflows. Terraform Cloud provides features like remote state management, version control integration, and run triggers for automation.

Remote State: Store your Terraform state files remotely in a secure and versioned location, such as an S3 bucket with versioning enabled. This ensures that your state is backed up, accessible to your team, and protected from data loss.

Workspaces for Environments: Leverage Terraform workspaces to manage different environments (e.g., dev, stage, prod) with the same configuration. Workspaces help you avoid duplicating code and maintain separate state files.

Resource Graph Visualization: Use the "terraform graph" command to generate a visual representation of your resource graph. This can be helpful for understanding dependencies and relationships between resources.

Terraform fmt: Keep your configuration files consistently formatted by running "terraform fmt." This command automatically reformats your code according to Terraform's style guide.

Terraform validate: Validate your configuration files with "terraform validate" to catch syntax errors and detect potential issues before applying changes.

Terraform import: If you have existing infrastructure, you can import it into Terraform using the "terraform import" command. This allows you to manage existing resources with Terraform.

State Commands: Familiarize yourself with state management commands like "terraform state list," "terraform state show," and "terraform state rm" for troubleshooting and managing state files.

Terraform Taint and Untaint: Use "terraform taint" to mark a resource for recreation during the next "terraform apply" and "terraform untaint" to clear the taint status. This is helpful when you need to recreate specific resources intentionally.

Conditional Resource Creation: Employ conditional resource creation with the "count" and "for_each" arguments to control when and how resources are provisioned based on variables or conditions.

Provider Configuration Blocks: In multi-cloud or multi-region setups, utilize provider configuration blocks to define different providers with distinct settings, such as access keys and regions.

Locking State: Implement state locking mechanisms to prevent concurrent access to your state files. Many remote state backends offer built-in locking capabilities.

Terraform Variables: Leverage Terraform variables and variable files to parameterize your configurations and make them more adaptable to different environments.

Terraform Outputs: Use Terraform outputs to expose specific information about your infrastructure that can be used by external scripts, tools, or other Terraform configurations.

Conditional Resource Updates: Control when resources get updated by using "depends_on" to establish dependencies between resources. This can help prevent unexpected resource changes.

Resource Data Sources: Data sources allow you to query existing resources and retrieve information to use in your configurations. This is valuable for referencing external resources.

Terraform Backends: Choose an appropriate backend for your state management, such as Amazon S3, Azure Blob Storage, or Terraform Cloud. Different backends offer various features and performance characteristics.

Terraform Destroy: Test your "terraform destroy" commands in non-production environments before running them in production. This helps avoid accidental deletions.

Dynamic Blocks: Utilize dynamic blocks to create resource configurations programmatically based on variables or data. This can simplify the management of multiple similar resources.

External Data Sources: If Terraform lacks a specific data source, consider using an external data source that interacts with an API or external tool to retrieve information.

Terraform Init Options: Customize the behavior of "terraform init" using options like "-upgrade" to update provider plugins or "-backend-config" to set backend configuration variables.

Terraform Plan Output: Save the output of "terraform plan" to a file with "terraform plan -out=plan.tfout" and apply it later using "terraform apply plan.tfout."

Provider Documentation: Refer to provider documentation for additional provider-specific options and features. Providers often have unique settings and capabilities beyond the core Terraform functionality.

Remote Execution: Consider using remote execution environments like Docker or cloud-based CI/CD platforms for Terraform operations to ensure consistency and reproducibility.

Dry Run with -detailed-exitcode: Use "terraform apply - detailed-exitcode" to perform a dry run and receive detailed exit codes. This can be useful for incorporating Terraform into automation scripts.

Work with Modules: Leverage modules to modularize and reuse your Terraform configurations. Well-structured modules can make your infrastructure code more maintainable and adaptable.

Use Terraform Functions: Explore Terraform's built-in functions to manipulate and transform data within your configurations. Functions like "element," "lookup," and "format" can simplify complex configuration logic.

Monitor Changes: Implement change management processes to review and approve proposed infrastructure changes before applying them in production environments.

Terraform Profiler: Consider using third-party tools like "tfsec" and "Terraform Profiler" to analyze your Terraform code for security vulnerabilities and performance optimizations.

Incremental Changes: When modifying existing resources, aim for incremental changes rather than replacing entire resources. This can minimize disruptions and reduce the risk of downtime.

Terraform Cloud Workspaces: Utilize Terraform Cloud workspaces for centralized management of state, variables, and runs in a collaborative and controlled environment.

Review Execution Plans: Carefully review the execution plans generated by "terraform plan" to understand the scope and impact of changes before applying them.

Alias for Remote State Data: Use resource aliases when referencing remote state data to avoid conflicts when multiple resources share the same name.

In summary, mastering the Terraform CLI and its associated tips and tricks can significantly enhance your infrastructure management capabilities. By incorporating these techniques into your workflow, you can work more efficiently, reduce errors, and maintain a higher level of control over your infrastructure as code projects.

Leveraging CLI plugins and extensions is a valuable approach to enhance your Terraform experience by extending its capabilities and integrating it with external tools. Terraform's ecosystem includes a variety of community-developed plugins and extensions that can streamline workflows, provide additional functionalities, and facilitate integration with different cloud providers, services, and systems. Next, we'll explore the benefits of CLI plugins and extensions, how to discover and install them, and some popular options to consider incorporating into your Terraform workflow.

Terraform's extensibility is one of its strengths, as it allows you to tailor the tool to your specific infrastructure and workflow needs. CLI plugins and extensions serve as powerful tools that expand Terraform's functionality beyond its core features. They can automate common tasks, integrate with third-party services, enhance the user interface, and provide valuable insights into your infrastructure.

The Terraform ecosystem offers several types of plugins and extensions:

Providers: Providers are plugins that enable Terraform to interact with specific cloud platforms or services. They define the resources, data sources, and authentication mechanisms required to manage infrastructure on a particular platform.

Provisioners: Provisioners are plugins that allow you to run scripts or commands on instances after they've been created. They are useful for tasks like configuring software, installing packages, or running tests.

Modules: Modules are reusable configurations that can be shared and incorporated into different Terraform projects. While not technically plugins, they are a form of extension that can simplify the creation of complex infrastructure.

Custom Functions: Terraform supports custom functions that can be defined in Go and compiled into plugins. These functions can be used in your configurations to perform specific operations or calculations.

Discovering and installing CLI plugins and extensions is straightforward. You can find a wide range of community-contributed plugins and extensions on the Terraform Registry, which serves as a central repository for Terraform modules and providers.

To install a provider, you typically add it to your Terraform configuration by specifying its version and source URL. For example:

```hcl
hclCopy code
provider "aws" { region = "us-west-2" }
```

In this configuration snippet, the "aws" provider is specified, and the desired region is set.

To use a provisioner, you include it in a resource block like this:

```hcl
hclCopy code
resource "aws_instance" "example" { # ... provisioner "local-exec" { command = "echo 'Hello, Terraform'" } }
```

In this example, a "local-exec" provisioner is defined to run the "echo" command on the created AWS instance.

Modules are incorporated into your configurations by specifying their source URL:

```hcl
hclCopy code
module "vpc" { source = "terraform-aws-modules/vpc/aws" # ... }
```

Here, a module named "vpc" is sourced from the "terraform-aws-modules/vpc/aws" GitHub repository.

Custom functions are created by writing Go code and compiling it into a plugin. These functions can be used in Terraform configurations by referencing them.

Here are some popular CLI plugins and extensions to consider integrating into your Terraform workflow:

Terraform Cloud: Terraform Cloud offers a cloud-based collaboration and automation platform for Terraform projects. It provides remote state management, version control integration, and a user-friendly interface for running Terraform commands.

tfenv: tfenv is a version manager for Terraform that allows you to easily switch between different Terraform versions on your local machine. This is helpful for managing projects with varying Terraform requirements.

Terragrunt: Terragrunt is a wrapper for Terraform that simplifies the management of remote state, configuration inheritance, and organization of infrastructure code. It's particularly useful for managing complex infrastructures with multiple environments.

tfsec: tfsec is a security scanner for your Terraform code that identifies potential security vulnerabilities and provides recommendations for improving your configurations.

Terraform Landscape: Terraform Landscape is a code formatting and styling tool for Terraform configurations that enforces best practices and improves code readability.

pre-commit Hooks: Use pre-commit hooks to enforce code quality and style standards in your Terraform projects before committing changes. Tools like "pre-commit" and "terraform-docs" can be integrated into your Git workflow.

Vault: HashiCorp Vault can be integrated with Terraform to securely manage secrets, credentials, and sensitive data used in your infrastructure configurations.

Terraform AWS Workspace: Terraform AWS Workspace is a Terraform Cloud workspace configured with AWS-specific settings and pre-installed AWS CLI tools, streamlining AWS infrastructure management.

Snyk Infrastructure as Code (IaC) Scanner: Snyk's IaC Scanner can scan your Terraform configurations for security vulnerabilities and misconfigurations, providing remediation advice.

Terraformer: Terraformer is a tool that generates Terraform configurations from existing cloud resources, enabling you to import and manage your infrastructure as code.

Terrahelp: Terrahelp is a Terraform documentation generator that automatically generates documentation for your Terraform configurations, making it easier for your team to understand and use your code.

Terratest: Terratest is a testing framework for Terraform that allows you to write automated tests for your infrastructure code to ensure its correctness and reliability.

Copper: Copper is a tool that helps manage Terraform modules and makes it easier to publish, version, and share them within your organization.

Landscape: Landscape is a Terraform code formatting tool that enforces best practices and keeps your codebase clean and consistent.

Driftctl: Driftctl is a drift detection tool for Terraform that helps you identify and track changes in your cloud infrastructure, ensuring it remains compliant with your desired state.

In summary, leveraging CLI plugins and extensions in your Terraform workflow can significantly enhance your infrastructure management capabilities. These plugins and extensions provide valuable features, automate tasks, and integrate Terraform with other tools and services, ultimately simplifying and improving your infrastructure as code practices.

Chapter 9: Handling Errors and Troubleshooting

Common error messages can be encountered when working with Terraform, and understanding them is essential for troubleshooting and debugging your infrastructure code. Next, we will explore some of the most frequently encountered Terraform error messages, their potential causes, and how to address them effectively.

"Error: Provider configuration not present": This error occurs when Terraform cannot find a provider configuration for a specific resource. Ensure that you have defined the required provider configuration for the resource, including the provider alias and its settings.

"Error: Missing required argument": Terraform expects certain arguments for a resource or module, and this error indicates that a required argument is not provided. Review the resource/module documentation and add the missing argument to your configuration.

"Error: Resource not found": This error may occur when Terraform attempts to destroy a resource that no longer exists. Verify that the resource still exists and that there are no typos in the resource name.

"Error: Value for undeclared variable": Terraform reports this error when a variable is referenced without being declared in the configuration. Declare the variable using a "variable" block in your configuration.

"Error: Variable not found": Similar to the previous error, this message indicates that Terraform cannot find a declared variable. Ensure that the variable name is spelled correctly and defined within your configuration.

"Error: Invalid function argument": Terraform functions require valid arguments, and this error is raised when an invalid argument is provided. Review the function documentation and verify that the arguments match the expected types.

"Error: Reference to undeclared resource": When you reference a resource that is not defined in your configuration, Terraform will raise this error. Ensure that the resource is defined or that there are no typos in the resource reference.

"Error: Invalid index": This error occurs when you attempt to access an element in a list or map using an invalid index. Verify that the index is within the bounds of the list or map.

"Error: Invalid character": Terraform may report this error when your configuration contains invalid characters or syntax. Review the code and correct any syntax errors or special characters.

"Error: Provider not found": When Terraform cannot find the required provider, this error is raised. Verify that you have configured the provider correctly and that it is available in your environment.

"Error: Invalid block type": Terraform enforces a specific structure for configuration blocks, and this error indicates that you've used an invalid block type. Check the resource or module documentation to ensure you are using the correct block types.

"Error: Invalid attribute name": Resource attributes must match the attribute names specified in the provider's documentation. Double-check that you are referencing valid attributes for the resource.

"Error: Conflicting resource instance key": This error may occur when you define multiple resources with the same "for_each" key, causing conflicts. Ensure that each resource instance has a unique key or adjust the key definition.

"Error: Unauthorized": If you receive an "unauthorized" error, it means that your credentials or access permissions are insufficient to perform the requested action. Check your credentials, IAM roles, or access policies to ensure they grant the necessary permissions.

"Error: Quota exceeded": Some cloud providers have quotas or limits on resource creation. This error indicates that you've reached a quota limit, and you may need to request a quota increase.

"Error: Resource already exists": Terraform attempts to create a resource that already exists in your environment. Ensure that the resource is not already provisioned and that Terraform's state is consistent.

"Error: Variable cannot be assigned": Terraform variables are immutable, and this error occurs when you attempt to assign a new value to a variable. Instead, define variables with different values in separate configurations.

"Error: Failed to load root module": This error typically occurs when Terraform cannot locate or access the root module configuration file. Ensure that you are running Terraform from the correct directory and that the configuration file exists.

"Error: Invalid or unknown key": This error indicates that you have specified an invalid or unknown key in a resource or module block. Double-check the documentation for the correct key names.

"Error: Module not found": Terraform may report this error if it cannot locate a referenced module. Verify that the module source URL is correct and that the module is accessible.

"Error: Incompatible block type": Terraform requires specific block types for certain resource configurations, and this error arises when using an incompatible block type. Consult the resource documentation to ensure you are using the correct block.

"Error: Invalid provider alias": Terraform provider aliases must be valid identifiers, and this error occurs when an invalid alias is used. Verify that the alias conforms to Terraform's naming conventions.

"Error: Invalid input variable value": When a variable's value does not match its declared type or constraints, Terraform will raise this error. Ensure that variable values adhere to the specified type and constraints.

"Error: Resource in use": Some resources cannot be deleted because they are in use. Check if the resource is referenced by other resources or dependencies.

"Error: Invalid output name": Output names must adhere to naming conventions, and this error occurs when using an invalid output name. Review your output definitions and ensure they comply with naming requirements.

"Error: Unexpected token": Syntax errors, such as misplaced or missing tokens, can trigger this error. Carefully review your code for syntax issues and correct them.

"Error: Failed to create or update the state file": This error can occur when Terraform encounters issues writing to or locking the state file. Verify that the state file location is accessible and that there are no conflicting processes.

"Error: Invalid count argument": Terraform's "count" argument must evaluate to a number, and this error arises when an invalid expression is used. Ensure that your "count" expressions are correctly formatted and result in numerical values.

"Error: Variable not set": If you attempt to use a variable that is not set, Terraform will raise this error. Make sure you've provided a value for all required variables.

"Error: Resource dependencies are not supported": Some resources or modules may not support dependencies, and this error occurs when you try to define dependencies for such resources. Review the resource/module documentation for dependency limitations.

"Error: No matching resource found": Terraform may report this error when it cannot find a resource with the specified attributes. Verify that the resource exists and that the attribute values are accurate.

"Error: Data source not found": Data sources must be correctly defined, and this error is raised when Terraform cannot locate a specified data source. Check your data source definitions and ensure that the source is accessible.

"Error: Invalid provider version constraint": This error occurs when you specify an invalid or incompatible provider version constraint in your configuration. Ensure that the provider version constraint is accurate and matches the available versions.

"Error: Duplicate resource instance": Terraform requires resource instances to have unique names, and this error occurs when you define multiple resources with the same name. Provide unique names for your resources or adjust the resource definitions.

"Error: Provider initialization required": This error can occur when Terraform encounters issues initializing a provider. Check that your provider configuration is accurate, and verify that the required credentials and access are available.

To effectively address Terraform error messages:

Consult Documentation: Refer to the Terraform documentation, resource/provider documentation, and module documentation for guidance on resolving specific errors.

Double-Check Configuration: Review your Terraform configurations for typos, missing arguments, and incorrect references.

Validate Variables: Ensure that variable values match their declared types and constraints.

Inspect State: Examine the Terraform state file to understand the current state of your infrastructure and identify any inconsistencies.

Check Provider Versions: Verify that you are using compatible provider versions and that the providers are correctly configured.

Use Terraform Commands: Leverage Terraform commands like "terraform plan" and "terraform apply" to detect and rectify errors in your configurations.

Isolate Issues: Isolate problematic resources or modules to narrow down the source of the error and simplify debugging.

Testing: Implement testing strategies using tools like Terratest to validate your infrastructure code and configurations.

In summary, understanding and addressing common Terraform error messages is crucial for effectively managing your infrastructure as code projects. By familiarizing yourself with these errors and following best practices for troubleshooting and debugging, you can minimize downtime, maintain reliable infrastructure, and streamline your Terraform workflow.

Debugging and troubleshooting are essential skills for anyone working with Terraform, as they enable you to identify and resolve issues in your infrastructure code effectively. Next, we will explore various debugging and troubleshooting techniques that can help you diagnose and fix problems in your Terraform configurations and deployments.

Understand the Error: When encountering an error or unexpected behavior, start by carefully reading the error message. The error message often provides valuable information about what went wrong, where the issue occurred, and what Terraform was trying to do.

Review the Configuration: Inspect your Terraform configuration files to ensure that the resource definitions, variables, and settings are correct. Typos, missing arguments, or misconfigured blocks can lead to errors.

Check Variable Values: If variables are involved in the error, verify that their values match the expected data types and constraints. Use the "terraform validate" command to check variable values before applying changes.

Examine Dependencies: Analyze the resource dependencies in your configuration. Ensure that resources are created in the correct order, and dependencies are properly defined using "depends_on" or other relevant mechanisms.

Inspect Terraform State: Use the "terraform show" and "terraform state list" commands to examine the Terraform state file. This can help you understand the current state of your infrastructure and identify any discrepancies.

Enable Debug Logging: Enable debug logging with the "TF_LOG" environment variable to get detailed information about Terraform's internal operations. Set "TF_LOG=DEBUG" before running Terraform commands.

Check Provider Versions: Verify that you are using compatible provider versions for your Terraform configurations. Provider version constraints should be accurate and up-to-date.

Review Resource Attributes: Double-check that you are referencing valid attributes for the resources you are managing. Resource attribute names should match the provider's documentation.

Inspect Terraform Plan: Run "terraform plan" to generate an execution plan. Review the plan to understand what Terraform intends to do before applying changes. The plan can help you identify issues in your configuration logic.

Dry Run Commands: Use "terraform apply" with the "-detailed-exitcode" flag to perform a dry run. This will check the proposed changes without actually applying them and provide detailed exit codes for further analysis.

Terraform Graph Visualization: Generate a visual representation of your resource graph using "terraform graph." This can help you visualize dependencies and relationships between resources.

Module Testing: If you are using modules, test them in isolation to ensure they work correctly before integrating them into your main configuration. Isolating modules can simplify troubleshooting.

Check for Quotas: Some cloud providers impose resource quotas or limits. Ensure that you have not exceeded these limits, as it can lead to errors.

Use Terraform Taint: The "terraform taint" command allows you to mark a resource for recreation during the next "terraform apply." This can be useful when a resource needs to be rebuilt due to issues.

Review Logs: Examine logs and error messages from the underlying cloud providers, as they may provide additional insights into issues related to infrastructure resources.

Validate Variables: Implement input validation for variables in your configurations to catch invalid values early. You can use validation expressions and conditionals to ensure variable values meet your requirements.

Check Permissions and Credentials: Verify that the credentials and access permissions used by Terraform are correct. Insufficient permissions can result in authentication or authorization errors.

Test Locally: Test your Terraform configurations in a local development environment or sandbox before applying changes in a production environment. This allows you to catch issues early.

Incremental Changes: When modifying existing resources, aim for incremental changes rather than replacing entire resources. This minimizes disruptions and reduces the risk of errors.

Version Control: Use version control systems like Git to track changes to your Terraform configurations. This allows you to revert to previous versions in case of issues.

Interactive Debugging: For complex issues, consider using the "terraform console" command to interactively evaluate expressions and inspect variable values within your Terraform configuration.

Break Down Configurations: If you encounter issues in large configurations, try breaking them down into smaller, more manageable modules and configurations. Isolating the problematic area can simplify debugging.

Check Data Sources: Verify that data sources used in your configuration provide accurate and up-to-date information. Changes in data sources can impact your infrastructure.

Custom Functions: If you have custom functions in your configurations, review the function code to ensure it behaves as expected and handles edge cases.

Inspect State Locks: Terraform uses state locks to prevent concurrent access to state files. Ensure that state locks are functioning correctly and are not causing conflicts.

Collaboration and Communication: Collaborate with team members to share insights and collectively troubleshoot issues. Effective communication can lead to faster problem resolution.

Monitor Resources: Implement resource monitoring and alerts to detect issues in your infrastructure. Monitoring tools can provide early warnings of problems.

Consult Community and Forums: Utilize online forums, communities, and Terraform-specific resources to seek help from the community. Many issues have been encountered and resolved by others.

Practice Rollbacks: Have a rollback plan in place for your infrastructure changes. Being prepared to revert to a stable state can mitigate the impact of critical issues.

Documentation: Maintain comprehensive documentation for your Terraform configurations, including information on variables, dependencies, and resource settings. Well-documented code is easier to troubleshoot.

Infrastructure as Code Validation Tools: Use third-party validation tools like "tfsec" and "Terraform fmt" to enforce code quality and security standards in your configurations.

Learn from Errors: Treat errors as opportunities to learn and improve your Terraform skills. Document the root causes and solutions to prevent similar issues in the future.

Redeploy Resources: In some cases, redeploying affected resources or modules can resolve issues. Use "terraform taint" or "terraform destroy" followed by "terraform apply" to recreate resources.

Resource-Specific Troubleshooting: For resource-specific issues, consult the provider's documentation and community forums for guidance. Provider-specific issues may have unique solutions.

Backup State: Regularly back up your Terraform state files to prevent data loss in case of accidental corruption or deletion.

In summary, debugging and troubleshooting are integral aspects of working with Terraform, and they require a systematic approach to identify and address issues effectively. By following these techniques, collaborating with peers, and continuously learning from errors, you can maintain a robust and reliable infrastructure as code practice and confidently manage your infrastructure with Terraform.

Chapter 10: Best Practices for Terraform CLI Mastery

Coding standards and style guidelines are crucial for maintaining consistency and readability in your Terraform configurations. Establishing and adhering to these standards not only makes your code more accessible to collaborators but also enhances its maintainability and reduces the likelihood of errors.

Consistency Matters: Consistency in code formatting and structure is vital for a seamless collaboration experience within a team. When all team members follow the same standards, it becomes easier to understand and work with the code.

Terraform Format (Terraform Fmt): Use the "terraform fmt" command to automatically format your Terraform configurations. This command enforces the official Terraform style guide and ensures consistent indentation, spacing, and line breaks.

Indentation: Stick to a consistent indentation style throughout your codebase. Common choices are two spaces, four spaces, or tabs, but the key is to remain consistent across all files.

Spacing: Maintain consistent spacing around operators, arguments, and blocks. This includes spacing around equal signs, colons, and parentheses.

Line Length: Limit the length of lines to enhance readability. Aim to keep lines below 80-120 characters to prevent horizontal scrolling.

Comments: Use comments generously to explain the purpose of your code, especially for complex or non-obvious sections. Clearly document what each resource or module does.

Inline Comments: Include inline comments to clarify specific lines or expressions. These comments can help readers understand your thought process and intentions.

Header Comments: Begin each Terraform file with a header comment that provides an overview of the file's purpose, author, and modification history.

Module Documentation: If you create custom modules, document their usage, inputs, and outputs. This documentation helps users understand how to use the module effectively.

Naming Conventions: Follow consistent naming conventions for variables, resources, and modules. Use descriptive names that convey the purpose of the item. For example, use "my_instance" instead of vague names like "instance1" or "server."

Resource Names: Consider using a standardized naming scheme for resources. Incorporate resource type and role into the name. For example, "aws_instance" followed by a descriptive name like "web_server."

Variable Names: Use meaningful variable names that indicate their purpose. Avoid single-letter or overly abbreviated variable names. For instance, use "region" instead of "r" for specifying a region.

Constants: Define constants as variables in your configuration for values that might change in the future, such as default tags, AMI IDs, or common values used across resources.

Resource Blocks: Format resource blocks consistently. Place resource attributes in alphabetical order to make it easier to locate specific attributes.

Data Blocks: Apply the same formatting guidelines to data blocks as resource blocks. Consistency improves the visual structure of your code.

Input and Output Blocks: When defining input and output variables for modules, use consistent formatting and provide descriptions for each variable. This enhances the module's usability and documentation.

Provider Blocks: Group provider configurations together at the top of your configuration files. Use a consistent naming convention for provider aliases and include any required authentication details.

Conditional Expressions: Format conditional expressions (e.g., "count" and "for_each") with clear line breaks and indentation. Avoid complex, unreadable conditions within resource blocks.

Quoting String Values: Enclose string values in double quotes for consistency and readability. While Terraform accepts both single and double quotes, using double quotes is a common practice.

Heredoc Syntax: When using heredoc syntax for multiline strings, maintain consistent indentation and consider using the <<- delimiter to remove leading whitespace.

Provider Blocks: Group provider configurations together at the top of your configuration files. Use a consistent naming convention for provider aliases and include any required authentication details.

Conditional Expressions: Format conditional expressions (e.g., "count" and "for_each") with clear line breaks and indentation. Avoid complex, unreadable conditions within resource blocks.

Quoting String Values: Enclose string values in double quotes for consistency and readability. While Terraform accepts both single and double quotes, using double quotes is a common practice.

Heredoc Syntax: When using heredoc syntax for multiline strings, maintain consistent indentation and consider using the <<- delimiter to remove leading whitespace.

Sensitive Data: Avoid hardcoding sensitive data like passwords or API keys in your configurations. Instead, use Terraform variables or external secret management tools.

Module Reusability: Design your modules to be reusable and configurable. Ensure that modules can be customized for different use cases by providing input variables for important parameters.

Documentation Generators: Consider using documentation generators like "terraform-docs" to automatically generate documentation from your code. This can save time and ensure that your documentation stays up-to-date.

Testing and Validation: Implement validation tools such as "tfsec" and automated tests using "Terratest" to enforce coding standards and catch issues early.

Version Control: Use version control systems like Git to track changes to your Terraform configurations. Create meaningful commit messages to describe the purpose of each change.

Peer Reviews: Encourage peer reviews of code changes within your team. Reviewers can provide valuable feedback and help ensure that coding standards are followed.

Linting: Utilize linters and static analysis tools to automatically identify code style violations and inconsistencies. Tools like "terraform-ls" and "tflint" can assist in this regard.

Refactoring: Periodically review and refactor your code to improve its clarity and maintainability. As your infrastructure evolves, update your code accordingly.

Educate Team Members: Train team members on coding standards and style guidelines to ensure everyone follows the same conventions.

Enforce Standards: If possible, use CI/CD pipelines to enforce coding standards and style guidelines automatically. This can prevent code that doesn't adhere to standards from being deployed.

Documentation Consistency: Ensure consistency in documentation format and style across your codebase. A standardized approach to documentation makes it easier to locate information.

In summary, coding standards and style guidelines are essential for writing clean, maintainable, and collaborative Terraform configurations. By adhering to these guidelines, you can enhance the quality of your infrastructure as code, streamline development workflows, and promote consistency within your team or organization.

Continuous Integration and Continuous Deployment (CI/CD) have become integral components of modern software development and infrastructure as code practices. Next, we will delve into the best practices for integrating Terraform into your CI/CD pipeline and optimizing your workflow for efficient and reliable infrastructure deployments.

Version Control Integration: Start by integrating your Terraform codebase with a version control system like Git. Version control allows you to track changes, collaborate with team members, and maintain a history of your infrastructure code.

Repository Organization: Organize your Terraform codebase within a structured repository. Use directories and subdirectories to categorize configurations, modules, and environment-specific code.

Infrastructure as Code Repositories: Consider creating separate repositories for different environments or stages, such as development, staging, and production. This isolation helps manage configurations and deployments for each environment independently.

Branching Strategy: Implement a branching strategy in your version control system to separate feature development, bug fixes, and releases. Common strategies include "feature branches" and "git flow."

Code Review Workflow: Introduce a code review process for Terraform changes. Code reviews help ensure that infrastructure code is of high quality, follows coding standards, and adheres to best practices.

Automated Testing: Implement automated testing as part of your CI/CD pipeline. Use tools like "Terratest" to validate your Terraform code and infrastructure changes, including unit tests and integration tests.

Infrastructure Validation: Before applying changes, validate your Terraform configurations using the "terraform validate" command. This step checks for syntactic errors and validates that resource configurations are well-formed.

Terraform Linting: Incorporate a Terraform linter like "tflint" or "terraform fmt" into your CI/CD pipeline to enforce code formatting and style guidelines.

Security Scanning: Integrate security scanning tools to identify vulnerabilities and security issues in your Terraform code. Tools like "tfsec" can help you identify security misconfigurations.

Environment Variables: Store sensitive information such as API keys, secrets, and credentials as environment variables in your CI/CD environment. Avoid hardcoding these values directly in your Terraform code.

Secret Management: Implement a secret management solution to securely store and retrieve sensitive data required by your

Terraform configurations. Services like HashiCorp Vault or AWS Secrets Manager can be valuable for this purpose.

Immutable Infrastructure: Strive for immutable infrastructure by recreating resources and environments rather than modifying them in-place. This approach enhances predictability and reduces configuration drift.

Parallelism: Leverage parallel execution in your CI/CD pipeline to speed up infrastructure provisioning. Execute Terraform plans and applies concurrently for different environments or modules when possible.

Automated Apply and Destroy: Automate the "terraform apply" and "terraform destroy" processes within your CI/CD pipeline. Use conditional checks and manual approvals to control when changes are applied.

Rollback Strategy: Establish a rollback strategy to revert to a known good state in case of failures during deployment. This can involve using Git branches or automated rollback scripts.

Infrastructure State Management: Store Terraform state files in a centralized location, such as an object storage bucket or a state management service like Terraform Cloud or AWS S3. Ensure proper access controls and versioning for state files.

State Locking: Implement state locking to prevent concurrent Terraform operations that can lead to state corruption. State locking is especially critical in collaborative environments.

Backup State Files: Regularly back up your Terraform state files to prevent data loss in case of accidental corruption or deletion.

Workspace Strategies: Utilize Terraform workspaces to manage multiple environments and configurations within a single codebase. Workspaces enable you to maintain separate states for different environments.

Remote Backends: Consider using remote backends like Terraform Cloud, AWS S3, or Azure Blob Storage for storing Terraform states. Remote backends provide additional features like collaboration, locking, and versioning.

Deployment Notifications: Implement notifications and alerts for CI/CD pipeline events, including successful deployments, failures, and rollbacks. Monitoring and notifications help maintain visibility into your infrastructure changes.

Infrastructure as Code Promotion: Promote Terraform configurations and modules through different environments (e.g., from staging to production) using a defined promotion process. Ensure that configurations are thoroughly tested before promotion.

Infrastructure Documentation: Maintain comprehensive documentation for your infrastructure code and deployments. Document the purpose of each configuration, variables, and input/output values.

Infrastructure Diagrams: Create visual diagrams of your infrastructure to provide a clear overview of the relationships between resources. Tools like "terraform-graph" can assist in generating infrastructure diagrams.

Rolling Updates: When updating infrastructure, implement rolling updates or blue-green deployments to minimize downtime and ensure smooth transitions.

Monitoring and Logging: Integrate monitoring and logging solutions to track the health and performance of your infrastructure. Tools like Prometheus, Grafana, and centralized logging platforms can be valuable.

Change Management: Establish change management processes and approval workflows for infrastructure changes. Ensure that changes are reviewed, approved, and tracked.

Testing Environments: Create replica testing environments that closely mimic production to validate changes before deployment. Realistic testing environments help catch issues early.

Backup and Restore: Implement backup and restore procedures for critical infrastructure components and data stores. Test backup and restore processes periodically.

Incremental Changes: Apply changes incrementally to minimize the blast radius of potential issues. Avoid making large, complex changes in a single deployment.

Deployment Rollback: Be prepared to execute rollback procedures quickly in case of deployment failures or critical issues. Test rollback procedures regularly.

Security and Compliance Scanning: Use security and compliance scanning tools to assess your infrastructure for vulnerabilities and ensure adherence to industry regulations.

Infrastructure Self-Healing: Implement self-healing mechanisms that automatically recover from common infrastructure failures. Automation can reduce manual intervention and downtime.

Feedback Loop: Establish a feedback loop within your team to gather input and insights on the CI/CD process. Continuously improve your workflows based on feedback.

Continuous Learning: Stay updated with Terraform best practices, new features, and community contributions. Attend webinars, conferences, and participate in Terraform-related forums and communities. In summary, integrating Terraform into your CI/CD pipeline and following these best practices can significantly enhance the reliability, security, and efficiency of your infrastructure deployments. By adopting a systematic approach to managing infrastructure as code, you can streamline your workflows, minimize errors, and deliver stable and scalable infrastructure.

BOOK 2
TERRAFORM CLI BOSS
COMMAND LINE WIZARDRY

ROB BOTWRIGHT

Chapter 1: Mastering the Terraform CLI

The Terraform CLI (Command Line Interface) workflow is a fundamental aspect of working with Terraform, enabling you to manage infrastructure as code efficiently and effectively. Next, we will explore the Terraform CLI workflow, step by step, to understand how to create, modify, and maintain infrastructure using Terraform.

To begin, the Terraform CLI workflow starts with the creation of Terraform configuration files. These files, often with a **.tf** extension, define the desired state of your infrastructure. Within these configuration files, you specify the resources, variables, and settings that Terraform will use to provision and manage your infrastructure.

Once you have defined your Terraform configuration files, the next step in the workflow is to initialize your Terraform environment. Initialization is performed using the **terraform init** command. This command downloads and installs the necessary providers and modules as specified in your configuration, ensuring that Terraform has all the required dependencies.

After initialization, you are ready to create an execution plan. The execution plan is a detailed outline of the changes that Terraform will make to your infrastructure to reach the desired state. To generate an execution plan, you use the **terraform plan** command. This command analyzes your configuration files, compares the current state of your infrastructure with the desired state, and produces a plan with a list of actions to achieve the desired state.

Once you have reviewed the execution plan and are satisfied with the proposed changes, the next step is to apply the changes to your infrastructure. You use the **terraform apply** command for this purpose. Terraform will execute the plan and make the necessary changes to your infrastructure resources, creating, updating, or deleting resources as needed.

During the apply process, Terraform may prompt you to confirm the changes before proceeding. This confirmation step helps prevent unintended changes to your infrastructure. You can use the -**auto-approve** flag with **terraform apply** to automate the approval process if desired.

As the apply process progresses, Terraform provides real-time feedback on the status of each resource being created or modified. You can monitor the progress in your terminal, and Terraform will report any errors or warnings encountered during the operation.

Once the apply process is complete, your infrastructure should be in the desired state as defined in your configuration files. Terraform will generate a summary of the changes made, including any resources created, modified, or destroyed. This summary is displayed in the terminal for your review.

With your infrastructure provisioned and configured, you can now start using it for your applications or services. Terraform has successfully translated your infrastructure as code into a live environment that matches your specifications.

When you need to make changes to your infrastructure, whether it's adding new resources, modifying existing ones, or making other adjustments, you can return to your Terraform configuration files. Edit the relevant configuration files to reflect the desired changes.

After making changes to your configuration files, it's essential to re-run the **terraform plan** command. This step generates a new execution plan that captures the modifications you've made. Review the plan to ensure it accurately reflects your intentions and doesn't introduce unexpected changes.

If the execution plan aligns with your expectations, proceed to apply the changes using the **terraform apply** command. Terraform will once again execute the plan and apply the necessary updates to your infrastructure.

Throughout the Terraform CLI workflow, you can use various Terraform commands to manage and inspect your infrastructure. For example, the **terraform show** command allows you to view the current state of your resources. You can use the **terraform**

state command to perform various state-related operations, such as moving resources between Terraform workspaces.

Terraform also provides commands like **terraform destroy** to tear down and destroy resources created by Terraform. This can be useful when you no longer need a specific set of resources or want to clean up your infrastructure.

When working with larger-scale infrastructure deployments or collaborative environments, it's crucial to consider state management carefully. Terraform uses a state file to keep track of the current state of your infrastructure. This state file contains important information about the resources Terraform manages, such as their IDs, attributes, and dependencies.

To ensure safe and consistent state management, it's recommended to use remote backends for storing your Terraform state. Remote backends, such as Terraform Cloud or cloud-based object storage services like AWS S3 or Azure Blob Storage, provide features like state locking and versioning. They also enable collaboration among team members working on the same infrastructure.

The Terraform CLI workflow is designed to be flexible and adaptable to various use cases and project requirements. As your infrastructure evolves, you can continue to iterate through the workflow, making changes to your Terraform configuration files, generating and reviewing execution plans, and applying updates to your infrastructure.

By following best practices, maintaining version control, implementing testing and validation processes, and embracing automation, you can establish a robust Terraform CLI workflow that simplifies infrastructure management and ensures the reliability and scalability of your systems.

In summary, the Terraform CLI workflow empowers you to manage infrastructure as code with precision and efficiency. It offers a structured approach to defining, provisioning, and maintaining infrastructure, enabling you to embrace infrastructure as code practices and deliver infrastructure changes with confidence.

Chapter 2: Advanced Configuration Management

Advanced configuration techniques in Terraform allow you to take full control of your infrastructure as code, enabling you to tackle complex scenarios and achieve greater flexibility in managing your resources. Next, we will explore advanced techniques that go beyond the basics, providing you with the tools and strategies to address unique requirements in your infrastructure.

One advanced configuration technique is the use of Terraform modules. Modules allow you to encapsulate and reuse blocks of infrastructure code, promoting modularity and maintainability. By creating custom modules, you can abstract complex configurations into reusable components that can be shared across different projects or teams.

Parameterizing modules is another powerful technique. It allows you to make modules more versatile by defining input variables that customize module behavior. These variables can be used to adjust settings, such as resource names, sizes, or counts, when using the module. By making your modules parameterized, you can create a single module that adapts to various use cases.

Conditional resource creation using the **count** argument is an advanced technique that lets you dynamically create or destroy resources based on specific conditions. By setting the **count** argument to 0 or 1 within a resource block, you can control whether that resource is created or not, depending on the value of a variable or condition.

The Terraform **for_each** argument extends the capabilities of conditional resource creation. It allows you to create multiple instances of a resource with different configurations based on a map or set of strings. This technique is particularly useful when managing resources that share similar settings but need slight variations.

Dynamic blocks offer a way to generate resource configurations dynamically. You can use dynamic blocks to create resource blocks based on the elements of a list or map. This is helpful when working with dynamic data, such as a list of IP addresses or a collection of data sources.

In some cases, you may need to modify or extend existing resources from providers. The **terraform-provider-exists** is a third-party Terraform provider that enables you to manage resources that already exist outside of Terraform. This provider allows you to import external resources and manipulate them within your Terraform configuration.

Terraform's ability to handle remote backends like Terraform Cloud, AWS S3, or Azure Blob Storage is essential for advanced workflows. Remote backends provide features such as state locking, versioning, and collaboration, making them suitable for large-scale, team-oriented projects.

Variable validation is a powerful technique to ensure that the values provided for variables meet specific criteria. You can define custom validation rules using the **validation** block within variable declarations. This helps prevent misconfigurations and ensures that your infrastructure adheres to predefined constraints.

In complex deployments, managing input variables can become challenging. Terragrunt is a tool that helps manage Terraform configurations at scale by providing additional features like configuration inheritance, remote state management, and a simpler way to organize Terraform code.

To avoid hardcoding sensitive data like passwords and API keys in your Terraform configurations, leverage secret management solutions. HashiCorp Vault and AWS Secrets Manager are examples of services that can securely store and provide access to sensitive data when needed.

Advanced configuration techniques also include using data sources effectively. Data sources allow you to retrieve information from external systems or services and use it within your Terraform configurations. You can use data sources to fetch data such as AWS AMI IDs, security group IDs, or the latest available version of an artifact from a repository.

Dynamic expressions with functions like **element**, **lookup**, and **slice** enable you to manipulate and extract data dynamically. These functions are valuable when working with lists, maps, and complex data structures within your configurations.

In cases where you need to orchestrate complex workflows, external provisioners like Ansible or Chef can be integrated into your Terraform configurations. This allows you to perform custom actions or configurations on instances after they are created by Terraform.

Remote execution of Terraform configurations can be achieved by leveraging remote state and remote backends. This is especially useful when working in distributed or team environments, as it enables collaboration on the same infrastructure codebase while maintaining a centralized state.

For managing multiple environments (e.g., development, staging, and production) with similar configurations, Terraform workspaces are a convenient technique. Workspaces allow you to maintain separate states for each environment within the same codebase, reducing duplication and ensuring consistency.

Testing your infrastructure code is crucial for advanced configuration management. Terratest is a tool designed for writing and running automated tests against your Terraform configurations. By testing your code, you can identify issues early in the development process and ensure that your infrastructure behaves as expected.

Terraform providers are essential for interacting with various cloud and infrastructure platforms. Sometimes, custom providers are required to extend Terraform's capabilities. You can develop custom providers using the Terraform Plugin SDK to interact with APIs or services that Terraform does not natively support.

Implementing remote execution and orchestration with tools like Jenkins, CircleCI, or GitLab CI/CD enables you to automate Terraform workflows further. These CI/CD systems allow you to trigger Terraform actions, manage secrets, and integrate testing and validation into your pipeline.

When dealing with Terraform codebases of considerable size, it's beneficial to establish coding standards and style guidelines. Consistency in code formatting and documentation helps maintain code quality and readability, making it easier for teams to collaborate effectively.

In summary, advanced configuration techniques in Terraform open the door to a wide range of possibilities for managing infrastructure as code. By mastering these techniques, you can address complex use cases, create reusable and dynamic configurations, and integrate Terraform seamlessly into your development and operations workflows. Managing configuration changes is a critical aspect of working with Terraform, as it ensures the reliability and stability of your infrastructure over time. Next, we will explore strategies and best practices for handling configuration changes, whether they involve updating resource settings, modifying infrastructure layouts, or scaling your environment.

One fundamental concept in managing configuration changes is understanding the impact of changes to your infrastructure. Terraform provides the **terraform plan** command, which generates an execution plan that outlines the proposed changes to your infrastructure. Reviewing this plan is a crucial step to assess the potential impact before applying any modifications.

Before making changes, it's essential to follow version control best practices. By using version control systems like Git, you can track changes to your Terraform configurations, collaborate with team members, and maintain a history of modifications. This provides a clear audit trail and facilitates collaboration among developers and operations teams.

When planning configuration changes, consider the use of Terraform workspaces. Workspaces allow you to manage multiple environments, such as development, staging, and production, within the same codebase. Each workspace maintains its own state, enabling you to make changes independently and avoid conflicts.

Another aspect of managing configuration changes is handling variables effectively. Terraform allows you to define input variables that parameterize your configurations. By organizing your variables and providing default values, you can make your configurations more flexible and adaptable to different scenarios. When modifying infrastructure, you may encounter scenarios where you need to add, update, or remove resources. For resource modifications, Terraform offers several techniques, such as updating resource attributes, scaling resources horizontally or vertically, and replacing resources when necessary.

The **terraform apply** command is used to apply changes to your infrastructure. This command can be used to add new resources, update existing ones, or delete resources that are no longer needed. It's important to review the execution plan generated by **terraform plan** before applying changes to ensure that they align with your intentions.

Terraform also provides conditional resource creation and destruction using the **count** argument within resource blocks. By setting the **count** argument to 0, you can prevent the creation of specific resources, and by setting it to 1 or more, you can create resources based on specific conditions or variables.

To facilitate the management of resource attributes, consider using data sources. Data sources allow you to query information from external systems or services and use it within your Terraform configurations. This is useful for dynamically populating attributes or using data from other resources.

Resource replacement is a technique used when you need to change a resource's configuration in a way that cannot be updated in place. In such cases, Terraform replaces the existing resource with a new one that matches the desired configuration. Careful planning and validation are necessary to ensure that resource replacement is performed correctly and safely. Modifying infrastructure layouts involves making structural changes to your Terraform code. This may include restructuring your modules, reorganizing resources, or adjusting the hierarchy of your configurations. Terraform's modularity and configuration organization best practices can help you manage these changes effectively. When making structural changes, it's important to consider the dependencies between resources and modules. Changes in one part of your configuration can affect other resources or modules. You can use Terraform's dependency management to control the order in which resources are created or modified. When scaling your environment, whether by adding more instances or expanding your infrastructure to new regions or cloud providers, Terraform provides flexibility. You can use input variables and conditional logic to parameterize your configurations, making it easier to scale resources dynamically. Scaling horizontally involves adding more instances or resources to handle increased workload or traffic. You can use Terraform's **count** argument or **for_each** argument to dynamically create multiple instances based on a variable or condition. This approach enables you to scale resources up or down as needed.

Scaling vertically involves modifying the attributes or settings of existing resources to handle increased demand. You can update resource attributes, such as instance sizes, by modifying your Terraform configurations. Ensure that you review the execution plan and test changes in a controlled environment to avoid disruptions.

Terraform modules are instrumental in scaling your infrastructure. By creating reusable and parameterized modules, you can easily replicate resource configurations across different environments and regions. This helps maintain consistency and simplifies the process of scaling your infrastructure.

Monitoring and testing are essential aspects of managing configuration changes. Implementing automated tests using tools like Terratest or test-driven development (TDD) practices can help catch issues early and ensure that your infrastructure behaves as expected after changes are made.

When managing changes collaboratively in a team, it's crucial to establish a workflow and communication process. Use version control systems, create branches for feature development, and conduct code reviews to ensure that changes are reviewed and validated by team members.

To handle configuration changes in a multi-environment setup, adopt infrastructure as code (IaC) promotion practices. Promote changes from development to staging to production, following a well-defined process that includes testing and validation at each stage.

Rollback strategies are essential in case changes introduce unexpected issues or disruptions to your infrastructure. Having a rollback plan in place allows you to revert to a known good state quickly. Testing rollback procedures is equally important to ensure that they work as intended.

Continuous integration and continuous deployment (CI/CD) pipelines can automate the testing and deployment of configuration changes. Integrate Terraform into your CI/CD workflows to enforce testing, validation, and version control before applying changes to production environments.

Secret management solutions like HashiCorp Vault or AWS Secrets Manager can help protect sensitive data in your configurations. Avoid hardcoding secrets directly in your code and instead retrieve them securely from these services.

Chapter 3: Harnessing the Power of HCL

Next, we will take a deep dive into HashiCorp Configuration Language (HCL), the language used to define Terraform configurations. HCL is a powerful and expressive language that enables you to describe your infrastructure as code in a clear and concise manner.

At its core, HCL is designed to be human-readable and easy to understand. This readability is a significant advantage, as it allows both developers and operations teams to collaborate effectively on infrastructure code.

HCL uses a declarative syntax, meaning you specify what you want your infrastructure to look like rather than describing how to achieve that state. This declarative approach is intuitive and aligns with the concept of desired state, a fundamental principle of Terraform.

HCL configurations are written in files with a .tf extension, making it easy to identify Terraform configuration files within your project.

HCL supports comments, which can be useful for providing explanations, context, or documentation within your configuration files. Comments in HCL are preceded by the # symbol for single-line comments or enclosed in /* */ for multi-line comments.

HCL configuration files consist of blocks, which are containers for resource definitions, data source lookups, and various settings. Each block begins with an opening curly brace { and ends with a closing curly brace }.

Inside blocks, you define arguments and their values. Arguments are key-value pairs that configure the behavior of the block. The key is the argument name, and the value can be a string, number, boolean, or more complex data structures.

HCL uses a simple assignment syntax to set argument values. For example, to set the **name** argument of a resource block, you can write **name = "my-instance"**.

HCL supports interpolation, a powerful feature that allows you to embed expressions within your configurations. Interpolation is denoted by **${}** and allows you to reference variables, functions, and resource attributes.

Variables in HCL enable you to parameterize your configurations. You can declare variables at the top of your configuration files using the **variable** block and assign default values if needed.

HCL also supports input variables, which are external values passed into your configurations. Input variables allow you to customize your configurations without modifying the code directly.

In addition to variables, HCL provides functions that you can use to manipulate and transform data within your configurations. Functions are invoked using the **function()** syntax and are valuable for tasks like string manipulation or conditional logic.

Resource blocks are a fundamental aspect of HCL configurations. Resource blocks define the infrastructure resources you want to create or manage. Each resource block includes a resource type, a name for the resource instance, and a set of arguments that configure the resource.

Resource types are specific to each Terraform provider and correspond to the types of resources that provider can manage. For example, the AWS provider includes resource types like **aws_instance** for EC2 instances and **aws_s3_bucket** for S3 buckets.

Resource names must be unique within a configuration file and provide a way to reference and manage specific instances of a resource.

Resource arguments define the desired state of the resource. These arguments vary depending on the resource type and include settings such as instance size, region, or access control. To reference attributes of a resource, you can use interpolation. Resource attributes are properties of the resource instance that you want to access or use in other parts of your configuration.

Data sources in HCL allow you to query and retrieve information from external systems or services. Data sources provide a way to interact with data that is not managed by Terraform but is essential for configuring your infrastructure.

To use a data source, you define a data block, specify the data source type, and provide any required arguments. Once defined, you can reference the data source attributes in your configuration.

HCL also supports expressions, which are used for more complex computations and transformations. Expressions can include mathematical operations, string concatenation, and conditionals.

Conditionals in HCL allow you to create dynamic configurations that adapt to different scenarios. You can use the **if** and **else** statements to create conditional logic within your configurations.

HCL has a built-in **for** expression that enables you to iterate over lists or maps and perform operations on each element. This is particularly useful when working with dynamic data or generating resource configurations programmatically.

To maintain clean and organized configurations, HCL allows you to split your configuration into multiple files and use the **module** block to encapsulate reusable configurations. Modules enable you to abstract complex configurations and promote code reuse.

HCL also supports functions for working with collections, such as lists and maps. Functions like **length()**, **element()**, and **for** loops make it easier to manipulate and process data structures within your configurations.

To ensure that your configurations adhere to a consistent style and format, you can use Terraform's built-in formatting tool, **terraform fmt**. This tool automatically formats your HCL code according to Terraform's style guidelines, making your code more readable and maintainable.

HCL configurations should be well-documented to provide clarity and context to other team members. Using comments and clear variable and resource names can significantly improve the comprehensibility of your code.

When working with HCL, it's essential to validate your configurations using **terraform validate** to catch syntax errors and detect potential issues before applying changes to your infrastructure.

HCL is designed to be provider-agnostic, meaning you can use it with various cloud and infrastructure providers. Each provider has its set of resource types and data sources, which are defined using HCL in provider-specific modules.

HCL's modular and extensible nature makes it a versatile language for managing infrastructure across different cloud providers and services.

In summary, HCL is a powerful and expressive language that forms the foundation of Terraform configurations. By mastering HCL's syntax, blocks, variables, and functions, you can create clear, adaptable, and maintainable infrastructure as code that defines your infrastructure's desired state and automates its management.

Next, we will explore best practices for writing HashiCorp Configuration Language (HCL) code effectively in Terraform configurations. Following these best practices will help you create maintainable, efficient, and error-free infrastructure as code.

One of the fundamental principles of HCL best practices is readability. Your HCL code should be easy to read and understand by both yourself and your team members. Use meaningful names for variables, resources, and modules, and avoid overly cryptic or abbreviated identifiers.

Consistency in your HCL code is essential. Adhere to a consistent style and formatting throughout your configurations. Terraform provides a built-in formatting tool, **terraform fmt**, to automatically enforce consistent formatting and style.

To enhance the readability of your HCL code, use comments effectively. Comments provide context and explanations for specific code blocks, variables, or resource configurations. While HCL supports both single-line (#) and multi-line (/* */) comments, prefer single-line comments for conciseness.

Well-documented HCL code is not only easier to understand but also facilitates collaboration among team members. Provide clear and concise explanations for variables, resource configurations, and complex logic. Documentation should answer questions about why certain decisions were made and what specific configurations achieve.

Use descriptive names for variables, resources, and modules. Avoid generic names like "var1" or "resource2" and instead choose meaningful names that reflect their purpose and usage. For example, use **instance_type** instead of **type** for an EC2 instance's instance type.

When defining variables, include a description that explains their purpose and usage. This documentation helps users of your code understand the intended role of each variable and how to provide values when using your module or configuration.

Organize your HCL code logically within your configuration files. Group related resources and variables together to create a clear structure. This makes it easier to locate specific sections of your code and understand the relationships between resources.

To enhance modularity and code reuse, consider encapsulating related resource configurations and variables into reusable modules. Modules should have a clear and well-documented interface, specifying the input variables they expect and the output values they provide.

Avoid hardcoding values directly into your resource configurations. Instead, use variables to parameterize your configurations. This allows you to customize your infrastructure easily for different environments and use cases.

Follow a naming convention for your variables and stick to it consistently. Common naming conventions include snake_case or camelCase for variable names. Choose a convention that aligns with your team's preferences and maintain it throughout your codebase.

Leverage Terraform's built-in variable validation to enforce constraints on input variables. Use the **validation** block within variable declarations to specify allowed values, ranges, or patterns. This helps prevent misconfigurations and ensures that your infrastructure adheres to predefined constraints.

When working with sensitive data like passwords, API keys, or access tokens, avoid hardcoding them directly into your configurations. Instead, use secret management solutions like HashiCorp Vault or AWS Secrets Manager to securely store and retrieve sensitive information.

Use Terraform's built-in functions to simplify complex operations or transformations within your HCL code. Functions like **join()**, **map()**, and **element()** can help you manipulate data structures and perform calculations.

Minimize code duplication by creating reusable functions or modules for common tasks or patterns. For example, if you frequently configure security groups with specific rules, create a reusable module for defining security groups.

When dealing with conditional logic in your HCL code, keep it concise and easy to follow. Use conditional expressions and functions like **if** and **coalesce()** to handle different scenarios effectively.

Avoid resource sprawl by carefully managing the creation and deletion of resources. Use conditional resource creation and destruction techniques like the **count** argument to control when resources are created or destroyed based on specific conditions.

To facilitate code testing and validation, structure your configurations to be testable. Separate your resource configurations from your business logic, making it easier to write unit tests for your infrastructure code.

Embrace the "infrastructure as code" (IaC) philosophy by treating your HCL code like software. Apply software development best practices such as version control, code reviews, and continuous integration to your infrastructure codebase.

Regularly review and refactor your HCL code to improve its quality and maintainability. Identify opportunities to simplify configurations, remove redundancy, and enhance documentation.

Use Terraform's dependency management features to specify relationships between resources. This ensures that resources are created or modified in the correct order, preventing issues related to resource dependencies.

Implement testing and validation processes for your HCL code to catch errors and ensure that your infrastructure behaves as expected. Tools like Terratest can help you write automated tests for your Terraform configurations.

Consider implementing a code review process within your team to ensure that code adheres to best practices and quality standards. Code reviews provide an opportunity to share knowledge, catch issues early, and promote consistency.

When working with multiple environments (e.g., development, staging, production), maintain separate state files for each environment. This reduces the risk of accidentally modifying or destroying resources in the wrong environment.

Integrate your HCL code into a continuous integration and continuous deployment (CI/CD) pipeline to automate the testing and deployment of infrastructure changes. CI/CD pipelines help enforce testing, validation, and version control before applying changes to production environments.

Implement rollback strategies in case configuration changes introduce unexpected issues. Having a plan for reverting to a known good state can minimize downtime and disruptions.

Finally, keep up to date with Terraform and HCL best practices and recommendations by regularly checking official documentation, community resources, and release notes. Staying informed ensures that you can leverage new features and improvements in your infrastructure as code workflows.

In summary, HCL best practices encompass readability, consistency, documentation, organization, modularity, and automation. By following these best practices, you can create maintainable, efficient, and error-free Terraform configurations that effectively define and manage your infrastructure as code.

Chapter 4: Dynamic Workflows with Variables

In Terraform, variables play a crucial role in parameterizing and customizing your infrastructure configurations, and understanding variable types and their usage is essential for effective infrastructure as code (IaC) development.

Variables in Terraform are placeholders for values that can be provided when you run **terraform apply**, allowing you to customize your infrastructure configurations without modifying the underlying code.

There are several variable types in Terraform, each serving specific purposes and use cases, and it's important to choose the appropriate type for your needs.

The most common variable type is the input variable, which allows you to accept values from external sources when running Terraform, such as from the command line, environment variables, or variable definition files.

Input variables are defined in your Terraform configurations using the **variable** block and can specify a name, type, and an optional default value.

For example, you can define an input variable named **region** with a default value of **"us-west-2"** like this:

hclCopy code

variable "region" { type = string default = "us-west-2" }

The **type** attribute in the **variable** block defines the expected data type of the variable, ensuring that Terraform validates and enforces type constraints during configuration loading.

Terraform supports various data types for input variables, including **string, number, bool, list, map**, and more, allowing you to work with a wide range of values and structures.

For example, you can define an input variable of type **list** to accept a list of strings like this:

hclCopy code

variable "instance_types" { type = list(string) default = ["t2.micro", "m4.large", "c5.xlarge"] }

Input variables provide flexibility for customizing your configurations, enabling you to create generic modules and configurations that can be reused across different projects and environments.

To use input variables in your configurations, you can reference them using interpolation syntax **${var.variable_name}**, where **variable_name** is the name of the input variable.

For example, if you want to use the **region** variable defined earlier in a resource block, you can do so like this:

hclCopy code

resource "aws_instance" "example" { ami = "ami-12345678" instance_type = "t2.micro" region = var.region }

Terraform also supports local values, which are computed values derived from input variables or other expressions within your configurations.

Local values are defined using the **locals** block and allow you to create intermediate values, perform calculations, or concatenate strings to simplify your configurations.

Here's an example of defining a local value to generate an S3 bucket name based on the **project_name** input variable:

hclCopy code

locals { s3_bucket_name = "${var.project_name}-data" }

With this local value, you can reference **local.s3_bucket_name** in resource configurations, making your code more readable and reducing redundancy.

Output variables in Terraform enable you to expose values from your configurations, such as resource attributes or computed values, for external use or reference in other Terraform modules.

Output variables are defined using the **output** block and can specify a name and value to expose.

For instance, you can define an output variable to expose the public IP address of an EC2 instance like this:

hclCopy code

```
output        "instance_public_ip"        {        value        =
aws_instance.example.public_ip }
```

Once defined, output variables can be retrieved using **terraform output** or referenced in other configurations that depend on the outputs.

Variable definition files, often named with a **.tfvars** extension, are used to specify values for input variables when running **terraform apply** or **terraform plan**.

These files provide a convenient way to separate variable values from your configuration code, making it easier to manage different environments or configurations without modifying the main codebase.

To use a variable definition file, you can create a file with your desired variable values in HCL syntax. For example, a **variables.tfvars** file might contain:

hclCopy code

```
region = "us-east-1" project_name = "my-project"
```

You can then apply your configurations using these variable values like this:

bashCopy code

```
terraform apply -var-file=variables.tfvars
```

Terraform also supports environment variables for providing variable values, allowing you to pass values as environment variables prefixed with **TF_VAR_**.

For example, to set the **region** variable using an environment variable, you can do:

bashCopy code

```
export TF_VAR_region="us-west-2"
```

Terraform will automatically recognize and use these environment variables as variable values.

Input variables can also have descriptions provided in their **variable** block, which serve as documentation for the variable's purpose and usage. This documentation is useful for maintaining and sharing configurations within a team.

When defining input variables, consider providing default values when appropriate. Default values help simplify the usage of your modules or configurations, making it easier for users who don't need to specify values explicitly.

To provide default values for input variables, you can simply include a **default** attribute in the **variable** block.

For instance, if you have an input variable named **instance_type**, you can set a default value like this:

hclCopy code

```
variable "instance_type" { type = string default = "t2.micro" }
```

This allows users to override the default value if necessary but provides a sensible default for most cases.

Terraform also allows you to define variable validation rules within the **variable** block. Validation rules help ensure that input variable values meet specific criteria, such as being within a certain range or matching a particular pattern.

For example, you can define a validation rule to ensure that the **port** variable is an integer within the range of 1 to 65535:

hclCopy code

```
variable "port" { type = number validation { condition = var.port >= 1 && var.port <= 65535 error_message = "Port must be between 1 and 65535." } }
```

With this validation rule, Terraform will check that the **port** variable meets the specified conditions and provide an error message if the validation fails.

In addition to input variables, local values, and output variables, Terraform also provides sensitive variables, which are designed to handle secret or sensitive data, such as passwords, API keys, or access tokens, with care.

Sensitive variables are a special type of input variable that can be marked as sensitive using the **sensitive** argument within the **variable** block.

For example, to define a sensitive variable for an API key, you can do:

hclCopy code

variable "api_key" { type = string sensitive = true }

When a variable is marked as sensitive, its values are treated with extra care by Terraform. They are not shown in logs or displayed in the console output, helping to protect sensitive information.

To use a sensitive variable in your configurations, you can reference it like any other input variable, and Terraform will handle the sensitivity automatically.

In summary, Terraform supports various types of variables, including input variables, local values, output variables, and sensitive variables, each serving specific purposes in customizing, documenting, and sharing your infrastructure configurations.

Understanding how to define, use, and provide values for these variables is essential for creating flexible, maintainable, and secure infrastructure as code.

Dynamic variable configurations are a powerful aspect of Terraform that enable you to adapt and customize your infrastructure configurations based on various conditions and inputs.

One common scenario for using dynamic variable configurations is when you need to manage multiple environments, such as development, staging, and production, with slight variations in configuration values.

To handle such scenarios, Terraform allows you to define different variable values for each environment by leveraging variable definition files or environment variables.

For example, you can create separate variable definition files like **dev.tfvars**, **staging.tfvars**, and **production.tfvars**, each containing environment-specific variable values.

By using the **-var-file** flag with **terraform apply**, you can specify which variable definition file to use for a particular environment, allowing you to easily switch between configurations.

Another approach is to use environment variables, setting the values for input variables prefixed with **TF_VAR_** for each environment. This method provides flexibility and allows you to manage configurations without changing variable definition files.

Dynamic variable configurations are particularly valuable when you need to manage resources across multiple regions or cloud providers.

For example, if you want to create AWS EC2 instances in different regions, you can define a region-specific variable that determines the AWS region for each set of instances.

With dynamic variable configurations, you can easily scale and adapt your infrastructure to meet changing requirements or deploy resources across different regions or environments.

Another way to achieve dynamic configurations is by using conditional logic within your Terraform code, allowing you to make decisions based on the values of input variables or other factors.

Terraform supports conditional expressions, which you can use to create conditional logic within your configurations.

For instance, you can use the **count** argument within resource blocks to conditionally create or destroy resources based on the value of an input variable.

Consider the example of creating an AWS EC2 instance only if a variable named **create_instance** is set to **true**:

hclCopy code

```
resource "aws_instance" "example" { ami = "ami-12345678" instance_type = "t2.micro" count = var.create_instance ? 1 : 0 }
```

In this example, the **count** argument evaluates the value of **var.create_instance** and creates the EC2 instance if the condition is **true**, or skips it if the condition is **false**.

Conditional logic allows you to make decisions about resource creation, modification, or deletion based on the values of input variables or other dynamic factors.

Terraform also provides conditional functions like **coalesce()** and **if()**, which enable you to perform more complex conditional operations within your configurations.

For example, you can use the **coalesce()** function to choose between two values based on a condition:

```
hclCopy code
variable "use_default_ami" { type = bool default = false }
resource "aws_instance" "example" { ami = coalesce(var.use_default_ami ? "ami-default" : var.custom_ami, "ami-fallback") instance_type = "t2.micro" }
```

In this example, the **ami** argument selects either the **var.custom_ami** value if **var.use_default_ami** is **true**, or falls back to **"ami-fallback"** if no custom AMI is provided.

Conditional functions like **coalesce()** and **if()** expand your ability to create dynamic configurations that adapt to different scenarios and conditions.

Dynamic variable configurations are also useful when working with variable lists or maps to define resource configurations or values based on specific conditions.

For instance, you can define a map variable that maps environment names to AWS region names:

```
hclCopy code
variable "environment_to_region" { type = map(string) default = { "dev" = "us-west-2" "stg" = "us-east-1" "prod" = "us-west-1" } }
```

Then, you can use this map to dynamically select the AWS region based on the environment:

```
hclCopy code
```

```
resource "aws_instance" "example" { ami = "ami-12345678"
instance_type = "t2.micro" region =
var.environment_to_region[var.environment] }
```

In this example, the **var.environment** input variable determines which environment-specific AWS region to use, allowing you to customize resource configurations based on the environment.

Dynamic variable configurations extend the capabilities of Terraform, enabling you to create flexible, adaptive, and reusable infrastructure code that can handle varying conditions, environments, and requirements.

Using dynamic configurations effectively requires a clear understanding of variable definitions, conditional logic, and the specific use cases you want to address.

By mastering dynamic variable configurations, you can streamline your infrastructure management, reduce redundancy, and create configurations that automatically adapt to different scenarios and needs.

Chapter 5: Terraform Providers and Plugins

Understanding Terraform providers is fundamental to mastering infrastructure as code (IaC) with Terraform.

Providers are plugins that enable Terraform to interact with various cloud, infrastructure, and service platforms, allowing you to manage resources across different environments from a single configuration.

Each provider in Terraform is responsible for communicating with a specific API, managing resource lifecycle, and handling authentication.

Providers are essential components of Terraform, and they play a central role in defining and managing infrastructure resources.

To use a specific provider in your Terraform configurations, you must declare it within your configuration using the **provider** block.

The **provider** block specifies the provider's name and any required configuration details, such as authentication credentials, endpoint URLs, or region settings.

For example, when working with AWS, you can define an AWS provider block as follows:

hclCopy code

provider "aws" { region = "us-east-1" access_key = "your-access-key" secret_key = "your-secret-key" }

In this example, the **provider** block configures the AWS provider with the specified region and access credentials.

Terraform supports a wide range of providers for various cloud providers, infrastructure platforms, and services.

Some of the most commonly used providers include AWS, Azure, Google Cloud, VMware, and Kubernetes, but there are many more providers available to cover a diverse set of environments.

Providers are responsible for defining and managing resources, which represent the infrastructure components you want to create and manage.

Each provider offers a set of resource types specific to the platform or service it interacts with.

Resource types in Terraform represent various components like virtual machines, databases, networks, and more, depending on the provider.

For instance, when working with AWS, you can create an EC2 instance resource using the **aws_instance** resource type:

hclCopy code

resource "aws_instance" "example" { ami = "ami-12345678" instance_type = "t2.micro" }

In this example, **aws_instance** is the resource type provided by the AWS provider, and it allows you to define and manage EC2 instances.

Resource configurations include attributes that specify the desired state of the resource, such as its AMI ID, instance type, and other properties.

Terraform providers are responsible for translating resource configurations into API requests to create, update, or delete resources as needed.

Providers also handle the management of resource state, tracking the current state of resources in a state file, which allows Terraform to understand the differences between the desired and actual infrastructure states.

Providers can also manage dependencies between resources, ensuring that resources are created or modified in the correct order to maintain consistency and avoid errors.

Providers are versioned separately from Terraform itself, which means that provider updates and releases can occur independently of Terraform releases.

This allows providers to evolve and adapt to changes in the platforms or services they interact with, providing users with access to new features and improvements.

To use a specific provider version in your Terraform configuration, you can specify the provider version constraint within the **provider** block.

For example, to use version 3.0.0 or later of the AWS provider, you can define it as follows:

hclCopy code

provider "aws" { region = "us-east-1" version = "~> 3.0" access_key = "your-access-key" secret_key = "your-secret-key" }

By specifying a version constraint like **~> 3.0**, you allow Terraform to use any version equal to or later than 3.0 but less than 4.0 of the AWS provider.

Terraform providers are available through the official Terraform Registry, which serves as a central repository for provider plugins and their documentation.

The Terraform Registry makes it easy to discover and install providers, ensuring that you're using the latest and recommended versions for your configurations.

To install a provider, you can use the **terraform init** command, which downloads the necessary provider plugins and initializes your Terraform workspace.

For example, running **terraform init** in a configuration that uses the AWS provider will automatically download and install the AWS provider plugin.

Providers can also be developed and maintained by the community, which means that you can find providers for a wide range of services and platforms beyond those officially supported by HashiCorp.

Community-maintained providers are typically hosted on version control systems like GitHub, and you can reference them in your configurations by specifying their source URL.

For example, you can reference a community-maintained provider hosted on GitHub like this:

hclCopy code

provider "my_custom_provider" { source = "github.com/username/my_custom_provider" version = "1.0.0" }

By specifying the source and version, you can use community providers just like official ones in your Terraform configurations.

Terraform also supports data sources, which allow you to query and retrieve information from external resources or services that are managed by providers.

Data sources enable you to access information like existing resources, network configurations, or authentication details.

To use a data source in your Terraform configuration, you can define it using the **data** block and specify its source and configuration details.

For example, you can use a data source to retrieve information about an AWS VPC:

hclCopy code

```
data "aws_vpc" "example" { tags = { Name = "my-vpc" } }
```

In this example, the **aws_vpc** data source retrieves details about the AWS VPC with the specified tags.

Data sources are read-only and provide information that you can use within your configurations, such as attributes that can be interpolated into resource configurations.

Terraform providers are extensible, which means that you can create custom providers to interact with your own internal systems, APIs, or services.

Custom providers allow you to integrate Terraform with platforms or resources that are unique to your organization.

To develop a custom provider, you can use the Terraform SDK, a set of tools and libraries provided by HashiCorp to simplify provider development.

Custom providers are written in Go and can be distributed as standalone plugins, allowing you to share them with others in your organization or the wider Terraform community.

By creating custom providers, you can leverage Terraform's infrastructure as code capabilities to manage your entire technology stack, from infrastructure and applications to custom services and configurations.

Terraform providers are a fundamental part of infrastructure as code with Terraform, enabling you to define, manage, and automate infrastructure resources across various platforms and services.

By understanding how to declare and configure providers, manage resource lifecycles, and use data sources, you can harness the power of Terraform to create, modify, and maintain infrastructure in a consistent and repeatable manner.

Providers also allow you to adapt to changes in the infrastructure landscape and integrate Terraform with a wide range of environments, both cloud-based and on-premises, making it a versatile tool for modern infrastructure management.

Custom providers and plugins extend the capabilities of Terraform, allowing you to manage resources and configurations in your infrastructure that are not covered by official or community-maintained providers.
By developing custom providers and plugins, you gain the flexibility to integrate Terraform with your organization's specific services, APIs, or platforms, creating a unified infrastructure management solution.
Custom providers are a type of plugin that interact with external systems or services, enabling Terraform to communicate with resources unique to your environment.
These providers are written in Go using the Terraform SDK and can be distributed as standalone binary plugins.
Developing a custom provider involves defining resource types, data sources, and handling CRUD operations for managing resources in your target system.
To create a custom provider, you'll need to write Go code that interfaces with the target API or service and implement the necessary Terraform functions and methods to enable resource management.
Custom providers should adhere to Terraform's conventions and standards, ensuring a consistent and user-friendly experience for Terraform users.
One of the essential components of a custom provider is the schema definition, which describes the attributes, arguments, and settings for resource types and data sources.
The schema defines how resources and data sources are configured and provides validation rules and documentation to guide users.
Creating a custom provider schema involves defining resource blocks with attributes, data sources with query parameters, and specifying their types, constraints, and descriptions.
The schema definition ensures that Terraform users can configure and use your custom provider effectively.

Resource types in custom providers represent the infrastructure components you want to manage, such as virtual machines, databases, or custom services.

To define a resource type, you'll need to create a Go struct that represents the resource's configuration, state, and attributes.

This struct should implement the necessary CRUD methods for creating, reading, updating, and deleting resources, ensuring that Terraform can manage them appropriately.

When developing a custom provider, you should consider resource dependencies and how they interact within your infrastructure.

Terraform manages resource dependencies automatically, but it's crucial to define them accurately in your custom provider to ensure that resources are created, modified, or deleted in the correct order.

Custom providers can also implement data sources, which allow you to query external systems or services to retrieve information that can be used within your Terraform configurations.

Data sources provide read-only access to external data and allow Terraform to access information like existing resources, network configurations, or authentication details.

To create a data source in your custom provider, you'll need to define a Go struct that represents the data source configuration and implement the data source's query logic.

Data sources are queried during Terraform's plan and apply phases, providing information that can be interpolated into resource configurations.

Custom providers and plugins can be distributed and installed in Terraform workspaces using the same mechanisms as official providers.

Terraform automatically detects and loads custom providers and plugins when you run **terraform init**, ensuring that they are available for use in your configurations.

Custom providers should be versioned and released following Semantic Versioning (SemVer) practices to maintain compatibility with Terraform and ensure smooth updates.

By developing custom providers and plugins, you can integrate Terraform with your organization's unique infrastructure, services, and workflows, creating a centralized and automated infrastructure management solution.

Custom providers allow you to define resource types and data sources that are specific to your environment, providing a consistent and standardized way to manage infrastructure components.

To develop custom providers, you'll need to become familiar with the Terraform SDK and the Go programming language, as well as the specific APIs or services you intend to interact with.

The Terraform SDK provides libraries and tools for building custom providers, including code generation tools that simplify the creation of provider schemas and resource implementations.

When developing custom providers, it's essential to follow best practices and conventions to ensure a seamless experience for Terraform users.

Consider providing comprehensive documentation for your custom provider, including examples, usage guidelines, and troubleshooting information to assist users in adopting and troubleshooting your provider.

Custom providers can be shared with the Terraform community by publishing them on platforms like GitHub or the Terraform Registry, making them accessible to a broader audience and contributing to the Terraform ecosystem.

Plugins extend the functionality of Terraform by adding new features or capabilities beyond what is available in the core Terraform tool.

Plugins can be written in various programming languages, including Go, Python, Ruby, and more, depending on the Terraform provider or extension you are creating.

To create a custom plugin, you'll need to understand the Terraform Plugin Protocol, which defines how Terraform interacts with plugins to perform actions like resource management, state storage, and variable interpolation.

Custom plugins can enhance Terraform in various ways, such as adding support for custom functions, external data sources, or custom provisioners.

When developing custom plugins, you'll need to adhere to the Plugin Protocol specifications to ensure compatibility with Terraform.

Plugins are responsible for handling various aspects of Terraform's functionality, including variable interpolation, state management, and resource provisioning.

For example, a custom plugin can extend Terraform's capabilities by introducing a new function that performs complex calculations or by providing an external data source that retrieves data from an external system.

Developing custom plugins involves implementing the necessary functions and interfaces defined by the Plugin Protocol, as well as handling any required configuration or state management.

Once a custom plugin is developed, it can be distributed and installed in Terraform workspaces alongside official and custom providers.

Terraform automatically loads and manages plugins during the **terraform init** process, making them available for use in your configurations.

Custom plugins should also be versioned and released following best practices to ensure compatibility and a smooth user experience.

By creating custom plugins, you can extend Terraform's capabilities and tailor it to your specific requirements, allowing you to automate and manage your infrastructure more effectively.

Custom plugins provide a way to integrate custom logic, external data sources, or third-party services into your Terraform workflows, enhancing your infrastructure as code practices.

To develop custom plugins, you'll need to understand the Plugin Protocol and the specific functionality you want to add to Terraform.

Custom plugins can be distributed and shared within your organization or with the broader Terraform community, contributing to the ecosystem of Terraform extensions and integrations.

In summary, custom providers and plugins are powerful tools that enable you to extend and enhance Terraform's capabilities, making it a versatile and adaptable infrastructure as code solution. Custom providers allow you to manage resources and configurations specific to your environment, while custom plugins can add new features and functionality to Terraform.

By mastering the development of custom providers and plugins, you can tailor Terraform to your organization's unique infrastructure needs and automate complex workflows, ultimately improving your infrastructure management practices.

Chapter 6: Building Reusable Modules

Creating modular infrastructure is a fundamental practice in infrastructure as code (IaC) that enables you to build, manage, and scale your infrastructure more effectively.

Modular infrastructure refers to the practice of breaking down your infrastructure code into smaller, reusable components or modules.

Each module focuses on a specific piece of infrastructure, such as a virtual machine, database, or network, and is designed to be self-contained and independent.

Modular infrastructure allows you to abstract and encapsulate infrastructure components, making it easier to manage and maintain your infrastructure codebase.

One of the primary benefits of modular infrastructure is reusability. You can create modules for common infrastructure patterns and reuse them across different projects or environments.

For example, you can create a module for deploying a web application that includes all the necessary resources, configurations, and dependencies.

By reusing this module in multiple projects, you ensure consistency and reduce duplication of code, making it easier to maintain and update your infrastructure.

Modular infrastructure also promotes collaboration within your team or organization. Team members can work on different modules simultaneously, knowing that each module has well-defined inputs, outputs, and responsibilities.

This parallel development approach increases productivity and accelerates infrastructure delivery.

To create modular infrastructure, you can organize your Terraform configurations into directories and subdirectories, each representing a module.

Each module directory contains its own Terraform files, variables, and resources, allowing you to define and manage the module independently.

A module typically includes a **main.tf** file, where you define the resources and configurations specific to that module.

You can also include variables, outputs, and any other necessary files within the module directory.

To use a module in your main Terraform configuration, you can reference it using the **module** block.

The **module** block specifies the module's source directory and any input variables required by the module.

For example, if you have a module for creating a virtual machine, you can use it in your main configuration like this:

```
hclCopy code
module "web_server" { source = "./modules/web_server"
instance_count = 2 instance_type = "t2.micro" }
```

In this example, the **module** block references the **web_server** module located in the **modules/web_server** directory.

It also provides values for the **instance_count** and **instance_type** variables defined within the module.

Each module can define its own input variables and outputs, allowing you to customize its behavior while maintaining a clear interface.

Modular infrastructure also simplifies the process of sharing and distributing modules within your organization.

You can package modules as reusable Terraform modules and distribute them through version control systems, package managers, or Terraform Registry.

Sharing modules in this way allows other teams or projects to benefit from your infrastructure expertise and accelerates the adoption of best practices and standards.

When designing modular infrastructure, it's essential to consider module granularity.

Modules should be designed to encapsulate a single piece of infrastructure with well-defined responsibilities.

Avoid creating overly complex or monolithic modules that try to handle too many tasks at once.

Instead, break down your infrastructure into smaller, focused modules that can be composed to create more complex systems.

For example, you might have separate modules for creating virtual machines, databases, load balancers, and networking configurations.

This approach makes it easier to understand, test, and maintain each module individually.

Modular infrastructure also enables you to version and manage modules independently.

By using version control systems like Git, you can track changes to each module, apply updates, and ensure that different projects use the appropriate module versions.

When updating a module, you can test the changes in isolation, making it easier to identify and fix issues before rolling them out to production.

Another benefit of modular infrastructure is the ability to leverage community-contributed modules.

The Terraform Registry and platforms like GitHub provide access to a vast library of pre-built, community-contributed modules that cover a wide range of infrastructure components and services.

By using community modules, you can save time and effort, as you don't have to create every module from scratch.

However, when using community modules, it's important to review and understand their code, configurations, and documentation to ensure they meet your specific requirements and security standards.

Modular infrastructure also facilitates the adoption of infrastructure as code (IaC) best practices, such as version control, automated testing, and continuous integration/continuous deployment (CI/CD).

You can set up automated testing and validation pipelines for each module, ensuring that changes are thoroughly tested before being applied to production environments.

By integrating CI/CD processes with modular infrastructure, you can achieve faster and more reliable infrastructure changes.

Modular infrastructure is not limited to Terraform; it is a practice that can be applied to other IaC tools and configuration management systems.

Tools like Ansible, Puppet, and Chef also support modular approaches to managing infrastructure and configurations.

In summary, creating modular infrastructure is a key practice in infrastructure as code that enables you to build, manage, and scale your infrastructure more effectively.

Modular infrastructure promotes reusability, collaboration, and best practices, making it easier to maintain, update, and share your infrastructure code.

By breaking down your infrastructure into smaller, focused modules, you can create a more organized and manageable codebase that adapts to changing requirements and accelerates your infrastructure delivery.

Module design is a critical aspect of creating modular infrastructure in Terraform and other infrastructure as code (IaC) tools.

Well-designed modules are the building blocks of a robust and maintainable infrastructure, allowing you to create, manage, and scale your resources efficiently.

To achieve effective module design, it's essential to follow best practices and consider various aspects of module structure, reusability, and maintainability.

One fundamental principle of module design is to define clear and well-scoped responsibilities for each module.

Each module should focus on a specific piece of infrastructure or a particular functional area.

For example, you might create separate modules for virtual machines, databases, load balancers, and networking configurations.

This modular approach ensures that each module has a clear purpose and simplifies the understanding of your infrastructure.

A key aspect of module design is abstraction, which involves hiding complexity and exposing only the necessary details to users of the module.

Abstraction allows you to provide a simple and intuitive interface for using the module while encapsulating the underlying complexity.

In Terraform, abstraction is often achieved through variables, outputs, and resource configurations.

For example, a module for creating virtual machines may expose variables for specifying instance types, instance counts, and other user-configurable options.

Users of the module can interact with these variables without needing to understand the internal details of how virtual machines are provisioned.

Reusability is a core principle of module design, and well-designed modules are intended to be reusable across different projects, teams, or environments.

Reusable modules reduce duplication of code, ensure consistency, and promote standardization across your organization.

When designing modules, consider making them as generic and configurable as possible while allowing customization through input variables.

This approach enables users to adapt the modules to their specific needs while still benefiting from the module's core functionality.

Documentation plays a crucial role in module design. A well-documented module includes clear explanations of its purpose, input variables, and expected behavior.

Documentation should also cover any assumptions or prerequisites required for using the module.

Additionally, consider providing examples and usage guidelines to help users effectively utilize the module in their configurations.

Versioning is essential for module design to ensure that changes and updates to modules do not introduce unexpected behavior or break existing configurations.

Modules should follow semantic versioning (SemVer) practices, where each version increment indicates the type of changes made (major, minor, or patch).

This versioning scheme helps users understand the impact of updating to a new module version and allows them to make informed decisions about when and how to adopt changes.

Testing and validation are crucial aspects of module design. Modules should be thoroughly tested in isolation to ensure that they work as expected and produce the desired outcomes.

Automated testing pipelines can help identify issues early in the development process and ensure that modules remain reliable and consistent over time.

Consider using infrastructure testing tools and frameworks like Terratest to validate your modules against real infrastructure.

Module structure is another important consideration in module design. Organize your module's files and directories logically, following Terraform's recommended conventions.

A common module structure includes a **main.tf** file for resource configurations, **variables.tf** for input variable definitions, **outputs.tf** for output variable definitions, and optional files for additional configurations or scripts.

Module dependencies should be well-managed to ensure that modules can be composed effectively to build complex infrastructures.

Use Terraform's module system to declare dependencies explicitly in your module configurations.

When using a module within another module, specify the necessary input variables and any variables required by dependent modules.

Carefully manage variable names and avoid naming conflicts when composing modules to maintain clarity and predictability in your configurations.

Security is a critical consideration in module design. Ensure that your modules follow security best practices and adhere to your organization's security policies.

This includes handling sensitive data and credentials securely, using appropriate access controls, and applying security hardening measures to your resources.

Consider providing clear guidelines on how to integrate your modules with identity and access management (IAM) systems and security groups.

Error handling and troubleshooting are essential aspects of module design. Modules should include mechanisms for handling errors gracefully and providing meaningful error messages to users.

Consider using standard error-handling techniques, such as conditional statements and error variables, to manage unexpected situations within your modules.

Additionally, include debugging and troubleshooting guidelines in your module documentation to assist users in diagnosing and resolving issues.

Performance optimization is another consideration in module design. Modules should be designed to be efficient and avoid unnecessary resource provisioning or configuration.

Consider factors like resource sizing, scaling options, and resource dependencies when designing modules for optimal performance.

Regularly review and optimize your modules as your infrastructure evolves to ensure that they continue to meet your performance requirements.

Finally, collaboration and communication are key aspects of module design. Foster collaboration within your organization by encouraging feedback and contributions to your modules.

Maintain an open channel of communication with users of your modules to address questions, issues, and feature requests promptly.

Consider using version control systems and collaboration platforms to facilitate collaboration and keep track of changes and contributions to your modules.

In summary, module design is a critical element of creating modular and maintainable infrastructure in Terraform and other IaC tools.

Well-designed modules follow best practices in abstraction, reusability, documentation, versioning, testing, and security.

By carefully considering these aspects and continuously refining your module design, you can create infrastructure that is flexible, efficient, and adaptable to the changing needs of your organization.

Chapter 7: Remote State and Collaboration

Managing remote state in Terraform is a critical aspect of maintaining a collaborative and scalable infrastructure as code (IaC) workflow.

Remote state allows multiple team members to work on the same infrastructure project concurrently while providing a centralized location to store and access the current state of the infrastructure.

Terraform uses state files to keep track of the resources it manages, their current configurations, and their dependencies.

In a local development environment, Terraform stores the state file on your local machine by default.

However, in a real-world scenario, managing state locally can lead to challenges when working as a team or deploying infrastructure in a production environment.

To address these challenges, Terraform provides the capability to manage state remotely using various backends.

A remote state backend is a designated storage location for Terraform state files, separate from the local machine where you run Terraform commands.

There are several options for remote state backends, including popular choices like Amazon S3, Google Cloud Storage, Azure Blob Storage, HashiCorp Consul, and more.

Each backend has its advantages and considerations, making it important to choose the one that aligns with your organization's infrastructure and workflow.

To configure a remote state backend, you define the backend configuration in a Terraform configuration file, typically in a separate **backend.tf** or **main.tf** file.

The backend configuration specifies details such as the backend type, the connection information (e.g., bucket name and region for an S3 backend), and any necessary credentials or access keys.

For example, configuring an Amazon S3 backend might look like this:
hclCopy code
terraform { backend "s3" { bucket = "my-terraform-state-bucket" key = "terraform.tfstate" region = "us-east-1" encrypt = true dynamodb_table = "terraform-lock-table" } }

Once the backend configuration is defined, you initialize Terraform to migrate the existing state to the remote backend using the **terraform init** command.

This process creates a remote state file in the specified backend, transferring the state information from your local machine to the remote storage.

Managing state remotely offers several benefits, such as improved collaboration, version control compatibility, and enhanced security.

Collaboration is streamlined when multiple team members can access and modify the same state file concurrently, avoiding conflicts and bottlenecks.

Version control systems like Git can be integrated more effectively with remote state, allowing you to maintain version history and track changes to your infrastructure code and state in a consistent manner.

Security is also improved because sensitive state information is stored in a centralized, secure location, reducing the risk of accidental exposure or data loss.

However, with the advantages of remote state come some important considerations and best practices:

Access Control: Ensure that you configure access control and permissions for your remote state backend appropriately. Limit access to authorized personnel and use features like IAM roles or service accounts to manage access.

Encryption: Enable encryption for your remote state backend to protect sensitive data. Most cloud providers offer encryption options for their storage services.

Locking Mechanisms: Implement a locking mechanism for your remote state to prevent concurrent writes from multiple users. Terraform can use a locking table in a database or utilize built-in locking mechanisms in some backends.

Backup and Recovery: Regularly back up your remote state to prevent data loss. Consider implementing automated backups and disaster recovery plans for your state storage.

Versioning: Use versioning for your remote state, especially in situations where multiple versions of your infrastructure are being managed simultaneously. This helps you track changes and roll back to previous states if needed.

Monitoring and Alerts: Set up monitoring and alerting for your remote state backend to detect and respond to issues promptly. Monitoring can help identify performance bottlenecks or security breaches.

Documentation: Document your remote state setup and configuration, including access control policies, encryption settings, and backup procedures. This documentation ensures that your team can manage the remote state effectively.

Testing: Test your remote state setup thoroughly, including failover scenarios and recovery procedures, to ensure that it functions as expected in different situations.

Infrastructure as Code: Consider using infrastructure as code (IaC) practices to manage the configuration of your remote state backend itself. IaC tools like Terraform or Ansible can help automate the provisioning and maintenance of the backend resources.

Remote state management is a crucial aspect of Terraform best practices, enabling teams to work collaboratively and securely on infrastructure projects.

By choosing an appropriate remote state backend, configuring it correctly, and following best practices, you can ensure that your infrastructure as code workflow is efficient, reliable, and well-organized.

Collaborative workflows with Terraform are essential for organizations looking to efficiently manage and scale their infrastructure as code (IaC) projects.

In a collaborative environment, multiple team members, often with different roles and responsibilities, work together to design, implement, and maintain infrastructure configurations.

Terraform provides features and best practices to support collaborative workflows, ensuring that teams can work harmoniously while maintaining infrastructure reliability and consistency.

One of the fundamental principles of collaborative workflows with Terraform is version control.

Using a version control system like Git, teams can track changes to their infrastructure code, collaborate on codebases, and maintain a history of all modifications.

Version control allows you to create branches for feature development, bug fixes, and experiments, while the main branch represents the stable state of the infrastructure.

Branches can be merged and reviewed, providing a structured way to introduce changes and updates to the infrastructure codebase.

Code reviews are an essential component of collaborative workflows. Team members review each other's code to ensure that it adheres to best practices, aligns with organizational standards, and does not introduce vulnerabilities or misconfigurations.

Code reviews promote knowledge sharing, improve code quality, and reduce the risk of errors making their way into production environments.

Automated testing is another crucial aspect of collaborative workflows. Teams can implement automated tests to validate infrastructure code changes, ensuring that configurations are valid and meet functional requirements.

Tests can include syntax checks, compliance checks, integration tests, and unit tests for modules and configurations.

Continuous integration and continuous delivery (CI/CD) pipelines can be integrated into the workflow to automate the testing and deployment of infrastructure changes.

Infrastructure as code (IaC) principles play a pivotal role in collaborative workflows. With IaC, infrastructure configurations are expressed as code, making them versionable, repeatable, and easy to share.

Terraform's declarative language allows teams to define infrastructure resources, dependencies, and configurations in a human-readable format.

This code can be reviewed, tested, and maintained just like any other software code, enabling infrastructure to be managed with the same rigor as application code.

Terraform's module system facilitates collaboration by allowing teams to break down infrastructure configurations into reusable modules.

Modules encapsulate infrastructure components and can be shared across projects, teams, or organizations, promoting consistency and reducing duplication of code.

By abstracting infrastructure components into modules, teams can focus on higher-level architecture and design decisions, rather than reinventing the wheel for each project.

Remote state management is crucial in collaborative workflows with Terraform. Teams need a centralized and secure location to store and access the current state of the infrastructure.

Using remote state backends like Amazon S3, Google Cloud Storage, or HashiCorp Consul ensures that all team members can access and update the state without conflicts.

Remote state also enables teams to work on the same infrastructure codebase concurrently, avoiding the need to pass state files between team members manually.

Locking mechanisms in Terraform remote state backends prevent concurrent writes, ensuring that only one team member can make changes to the state at a time.

This avoids conflicts and data corruption when multiple team members attempt to update the state simultaneously.

Access control is a critical aspect of collaborative workflows. Teams should configure access control policies and permissions to ensure that only authorized team members can modify infrastructure code and state.

Identity and access management (IAM) systems provided by cloud providers can be integrated with Terraform to manage permissions effectively.

Secrets and sensitive data should be managed securely, with encryption and access controls in place to protect sensitive information like API keys, passwords, and certificates.

Documentation is essential in collaborative workflows to ensure that all team members understand the project's goals, architecture, and configuration details.

Documentation should cover the purpose of the infrastructure, how to deploy it, dependencies, configurations, and troubleshooting procedures.

Clear and comprehensive documentation facilitates knowledge sharing and onboarding for new team members, reducing the learning curve when joining a project.

Communication and collaboration tools play a vital role in keeping team members informed and connected. Messaging platforms, project management tools, and video conferencing facilitate real-time communication and coordination among team members.

Regular meetings, stand-ups, and retrospectives provide opportunities for team members to discuss progress, challenges, and improvements in the collaborative workflow.

Change management processes help teams coordinate and plan infrastructure changes. Changes should be proposed, reviewed, and tested before being deployed to production environments.

Change management ensures that infrastructure remains stable and reliable, even as teams make updates and improvements over time.

Lastly, monitoring and observability are essential for maintaining infrastructure health and identifying issues proactively.

Teams should implement monitoring and alerting systems to track infrastructure performance, detect anomalies, and receive notifications of critical events or failures.

Collaborative workflows with Terraform are a combination of best practices, tools, and processes that enable teams to work together effectively on infrastructure as code projects.

By following these principles and adopting tools and practices that promote version control, code reviews, testing, and documentation, teams can ensure that their infrastructure is reliable, maintainable, and scalable in a collaborative environment.

Chapter 8: Infrastructure as Code Best Practices

Infrastructure as Code (IaC) is a fundamental approach to managing and provisioning infrastructure using code and automation.

IaC principles and guidelines help organizations streamline their infrastructure management, improve collaboration, and ensure consistency across environments.

One of the core principles of IaC is treating infrastructure as code, which means defining and managing infrastructure resources using code, just like you would with application code.

This code-based approach allows for versioning, collaboration, and automation of infrastructure provisioning and configuration.

By representing infrastructure as code, you can apply software engineering practices to infrastructure management, leading to more reliable and predictable outcomes.

A key guideline in IaC is using a declarative approach, where you specify the desired state of the infrastructure, and the IaC tool determines the steps needed to achieve that state.

Declarative code is more concise and easier to read, as it focuses on the desired outcome rather than the specific actions required to reach it.

Another essential principle is idempotence, which means that applying the same IaC code multiple times results in the same state, regardless of the current state of the infrastructure.

Idempotence ensures that running IaC code multiple times does not cause unintended changes or disruptions.

Modularity is a crucial guideline in IaC. Breaking down infrastructure code into modular components or modules makes it easier to manage and reuse configurations.

Modules encapsulate specific pieces of infrastructure, such as a virtual machine or a database, and can be shared across projects or teams.

By promoting modularity, IaC encourages consistency and reduces the need for duplicating code.

Another principle of IaC is automation. The goal is to automate as much of the infrastructure provisioning and configuration process as possible.

Automation reduces human error, accelerates deployment, and ensures that infrastructure is consistent and reproducible.

Infrastructure code should be tested thoroughly, following the principle of testing as code.

Automated tests, including unit tests, integration tests, and validation tests, help catch errors and issues early in the development process.

Continuous integration and continuous delivery (CI/CD) pipelines are often used to automate the testing and deployment of infrastructure code changes.

Source control is a fundamental guideline in IaC. Storing infrastructure code in a version control system like Git enables collaboration, versioning, and tracking of changes over time.

Using Git allows multiple team members to work on the same codebase concurrently, with the ability to merge changes and resolve conflicts.

Documentation is essential in IaC to ensure that infrastructure code is well-documented and that its purpose, configurations, and dependencies are clear.

Documentation facilitates knowledge sharing and helps team members understand how to use and maintain the infrastructure code.

Change management processes should be established to control and track changes to the infrastructure code.

Changes should be proposed, reviewed, tested, and documented before being deployed to production environments.

Change management ensures that infrastructure remains stable and that updates are thoroughly tested and validated.
Secrets and sensitive data should be managed securely, with encryption, access controls, and secrets management systems in place to protect sensitive information like API keys, passwords, and certificates.
Security should be a top priority in IaC, and best practices for security should be followed, including vulnerability assessments, security scans, and compliance checks.
Access control and identity management should be implemented to ensure that only authorized personnel can access and modify infrastructure code and configurations.
Monitoring and observability are crucial in IaC to detect and respond to issues proactively.
Infrastructure should be monitored for performance, security, and availability, with alerts and notifications configured to address critical events or failures.
IaC principles and guidelines also emphasize the importance of collaboration within teams and across organizations.
Teams should work together effectively, sharing knowledge and code, and using communication and collaboration tools to coordinate efforts.
Best practices for collaborative workflows, code reviews, and testing should be implemented to ensure that infrastructure code is of high quality and meets organizational standards.
Scalability and flexibility are key considerations in IaC. Infrastructure code should be designed to scale horizontally and vertically to accommodate changing workloads and requirements.
Flexibility should also be built into configurations to allow for customization and adaptation to different environments.
Finally, continuous improvement is a guiding principle in IaC. Teams should regularly review and refine their infrastructure code, processes, and practices to optimize efficiency and maintainability.

IaC is an essential approach for modern infrastructure management, offering the benefits of automation, versioning, consistency, and collaboration.

By adhering to IaC principles and guidelines, organizations can achieve more reliable, secure, and scalable infrastructure deployments.

Security and compliance are critical considerations in Infrastructure as Code (IaC), as they play a fundamental role in ensuring the safety, reliability, and integrity of your infrastructure.

IaC provides a structured and automated way to manage and provision infrastructure, but it also introduces security challenges that must be addressed to protect against vulnerabilities and threats.

One of the core principles of security in IaC is the principle of least privilege, which means that every component of the infrastructure should have the minimal permissions necessary to perform its functions.

This principle applies to access controls, IAM policies, and privileges granted to users, applications, and services.

Implementing least privilege reduces the attack surface and limits potential damage in the event of a security breach.

Another fundamental aspect of security in IaC is the proper management of secrets and sensitive data.

IaC code often includes configuration files that contain credentials, API keys, passwords, and other sensitive information required to interact with various services and resources.

Securing these secrets is essential to prevent unauthorized access and data breaches.

One way to address this challenge is to use a secrets management system that encrypts and stores sensitive data securely, and provides access control mechanisms to restrict who can retrieve and use the secrets.

IaC also encourages the use of version control systems, such as Git, to track changes to infrastructure code.

While version control is essential for collaboration and change management, it can also introduce security risks if sensitive information is accidentally committed to repositories.

To mitigate this risk, organizations should implement strict access controls and employ tools that scan code repositories for potential security vulnerabilities.

Furthermore, regular audits and reviews of code repositories can help identify and rectify security issues.

Automation is a key aspect of IaC, and it can be a powerful tool for enhancing security.

Automated security scanning and testing can identify vulnerabilities, misconfigurations, and compliance violations in infrastructure code and configurations.

These automated checks can be integrated into CI/CD pipelines, allowing security assessments to occur automatically as code is developed and deployed.

Moreover, infrastructure code can be designed to enforce security controls, such as the automatic creation of security groups, firewalls, and access controls.

This ensures that security measures are consistently applied to all resources created through IaC.

Continuous monitoring and observability are critical for identifying and responding to security incidents and compliance violations.

Infrastructure should be monitored for suspicious activities, unauthorized access, and changes to configurations.

Alerting systems should be configured to notify security teams of potential threats or vulnerabilities in real-time.

Additionally, security incident response plans should be developed and tested to ensure that the team can react effectively to security breaches.

Compliance with industry regulations and internal policies is essential for many organizations.

IaC can facilitate compliance efforts by allowing organizations to codify and enforce security and compliance requirements in their infrastructure code.

This ensures that the infrastructure remains compliant with regulations and policies, even as it evolves and scales.

Organizations can use tools and frameworks specifically designed for compliance, such as Chef InSpec or Terraform Compliance, to automate compliance checks and validations.

Access controls are a critical component of security and compliance in IaC.

IAM policies, role-based access control (RBAC), and access control lists (ACLs) should be carefully configured to ensure that only authorized users and applications can interact with infrastructure resources.

Implementing strict access controls helps prevent unauthorized changes and ensures that users have the permissions necessary to perform their tasks.

Security education and training are essential for all team members involved in IaC.

Security awareness programs help educate team members about best practices, security policies, and the importance of following security protocols.

By fostering a security-conscious culture, organizations can reduce the risk of human error and improve overall security.

Secure development practices should also be adopted in the IaC development process.

This includes conducting security reviews and assessments of code before deployment, as well as using secure coding practices to minimize vulnerabilities.

Security testing, including penetration testing and vulnerability scanning, should be integrated into the development and deployment pipeline to identify and address security weaknesses proactively.

Encryption is a foundational security measure that should be applied to protect data in transit and at rest.

Data sent between components of the infrastructure and data stored on disks or in databases should be encrypted using strong encryption algorithms and protocols.

Additionally, encryption keys should be managed securely to prevent unauthorized access.

Security patching and updates are critical for addressing known vulnerabilities in both infrastructure components and the underlying infrastructure platform.

Organizations should have processes in place to regularly apply security patches and updates to the infrastructure to reduce the risk of exploitation.

Finally, compliance with industry-specific regulations, such as HIPAA, GDPR, or PCI DSS, should be a priority for organizations in regulated industries.

IaC can help organizations maintain compliance by enabling the codification and enforcement of specific compliance requirements.

Regular audits and assessments should be conducted to verify compliance with relevant regulations.

In summary, security and compliance are paramount in the world of Infrastructure as Code (IaC).

Organizations should adopt security best practices, implement access controls, employ automation for security testing, and prioritize compliance with industry regulations and internal policies.

By following these principles and guidelines, organizations can maintain a strong security posture and ensure that their IaC environments are both secure and compliant.

Chapter 9: Extending Terraform Functionality

Terraform, with its declarative and Infrastructure as Code (IaC) approach, provides a robust foundation for managing and provisioning infrastructure.

However, as organizations evolve and their infrastructure requirements become more complex, there's a growing need for customization and extensibility within the Terraform ecosystem.

Terraform hooks and extensibility mechanisms enable users to tailor Terraform to their specific needs and integrate it seamlessly into their workflows.

Hooks, in the context of Terraform, are events or triggers that allow you to execute custom actions before or after specific Terraform operations.

Hooks provide a way to inject custom logic into Terraform's standard lifecycle, making it possible to extend and enhance Terraform's capabilities.

One common use case for Terraform hooks is integrating with existing systems or third-party tools.

For example, you can use a pre-apply hook to trigger a security scanning tool to assess the infrastructure code for vulnerabilities before it's deployed.

This helps organizations maintain a strong security posture and identify potential risks early in the development process.

Hooks can also be used for compliance checks, ensuring that infrastructure configurations adhere to organizational policies and industry regulations.

By integrating compliance checks as hooks, you can automate the validation process and prevent non-compliant configurations from being applied.

Terraform's extensibility is not limited to hooks; it also includes the ability to create custom providers and plugins.

Custom providers and plugins allow users to interact with resources and services that are not supported out of the box by Terraform.

These extensions enable organizations to leverage Terraform for a broader range of use cases and integrate with proprietary or specialized systems.

Custom providers are typically implemented as separate executable binaries that Terraform communicates with using a well-defined protocol.

Developers can create custom providers to interact with cloud services, APIs, hardware devices, or any other system that Terraform should manage.

Custom plugins, on the other hand, extend Terraform's functionality by adding new data sources, provisioners, or other features.

Plugins can be used to implement custom data sources that fetch information from external systems or to create new provisioners that execute actions during resource creation or destruction.

The extensibility of Terraform through custom providers and plugins empowers organizations to bridge the gap between Terraform and their unique infrastructure requirements.

While Terraform's extensive provider ecosystem covers a wide range of popular services and resources, there are often specific use cases where organizations need to extend Terraform's capabilities.

For example, a custom provider could be created to manage an in-house virtualization platform that isn't supported by the standard Terraform providers.

Similarly, a custom plugin could be developed to integrate Terraform with a specialized configuration management tool to automate configuration changes.

Extending Terraform also allows organizations to reuse their existing investments in tooling and workflows.

For example, if an organization has an existing CI/CD pipeline that uses a particular deployment tool, they can create a custom Terraform provider or plugin to seamlessly integrate Terraform with that tool.

Terraform's extensibility mechanisms have gained popularity in the community, leading to the development of various third-party providers and plugins.

These community-driven extensions cover a wide range of use cases, including integrating with cloud providers, network devices, storage systems, and more.

By leveraging these community-contributed extensions, organizations can save time and effort in implementing their own custom solutions.

When creating custom providers or plugins, it's essential to follow best practices for development, testing, and distribution. Developers should thoroughly document their extensions, providing clear instructions on how to use them and any dependencies that may be required.

Testing is crucial to ensure that custom providers and plugins behave as expected and are compatible with different versions of Terraform.

Developers should also consider releasing their extensions as open source projects to foster collaboration and contribute to the Terraform ecosystem.

In summary, Terraform's hooks and extensibility mechanisms offer organizations the flexibility to customize and extend Terraform to meet their specific infrastructure requirements.

Hooks allow users to inject custom logic into Terraform's lifecycle, enabling integration with existing systems and compliance checks.

Custom providers and plugins expand Terraform's capabilities, allowing organizations to manage a broader range of resources and services.

By embracing Terraform's extensibility, organizations can automate complex infrastructure workflows, integrate with specialized tools, and bridge the gap between Terraform and their unique infrastructure needs.

Customizing Terraform workflows is an important aspect of optimizing infrastructure management processes to align with an organization's specific needs and requirements.
While Terraform provides a set of default workflows for provisioning and managing infrastructure, there are scenarios where customizations are necessary to address unique use cases or improve operational efficiency.
One common customization involves defining a tailored directory structure for organizing Terraform configurations and modules.
This directory structure can be designed to reflect an organization's naming conventions, team responsibilities, or project hierarchies, making it easier to locate and manage Terraform code.
Custom directory structures can also help enforce separation of concerns, enabling teams to work on specific parts of the infrastructure independently.
Another customization is the creation of reusable Terraform modules that encapsulate infrastructure components and configurations.
Modules allow organizations to standardize and abstract complex infrastructure resources into easily consumable and shareable components.
These modules can be designed to include best practices, security policies, and compliance checks, ensuring consistency across deployments.
Organizations often customize Terraform workflows to align with their preferred deployment strategies.
For example, some organizations may choose to use blue-green deployments or canary releases as part of their deployment strategy.

Custom Terraform configurations and scripts can be created to support these strategies, allowing for seamless updates and rollbacks.

Implementing infrastructure as code (IaC) best practices is another critical customization aspect.

Organizations may develop custom policies, linters, or validation tools to enforce coding standards, security guidelines, and compliance requirements.

These tools can be integrated into the Terraform workflow to automatically check configurations for issues and deviations from best practices.

In some cases, organizations customize Terraform workflows to accommodate multi-cloud or hybrid cloud environments.

Customizations can be made to dynamically select cloud providers or regions based on specific criteria, such as cost optimization, compliance, or data residency requirements.

Additionally, organizations may need to customize Terraform configurations to support existing on-premises infrastructure or legacy systems.

In such cases, Terraform can be extended with custom providers or plugins to interact with these systems, enabling a unified IaC approach.

Custom variables and data sources can be defined to capture configuration inputs and external data required for Terraform deployments.

These custom variables and data sources can be used to parameterize configurations, making them more flexible and adaptable to different environments.

Another customization aspect involves integrating Terraform with external systems, such as configuration management tools, ticketing systems, or monitoring platforms.

Custom scripts and automation can be developed to orchestrate interactions between Terraform and these systems, enabling streamlined workflows and improved visibility.

Terraform's extensibility allows organizations to create custom providers and plugins, further enhancing its capabilities.

Custom providers and plugins can be developed to interact with specialized hardware devices, internal APIs, or proprietary services, expanding Terraform's reach and flexibility.

Custom Terraform providers and plugins should adhere to best practices for development, testing, and documentation to ensure reliability and maintainability. To customize Terraform workflows effectively, organizations must establish clear processes and guidelines for implementing customizations.

This includes defining roles and responsibilities for creating, reviewing, and maintaining custom configurations, modules, and scripts. Change management procedures should be established to govern how customizations are proposed, reviewed, tested, and deployed to production environments.

Version control and release management practices should be applied to track changes and updates to customizations, ensuring that they can be managed and rolled back as needed.

Documentation is crucial to ensure that customizations are well-documented and accessible to team members.

Clear and comprehensive documentation should explain the purpose, usage, and best practices for each customization, making it easier for teams to understand and adopt them.

As organizations continue to evolve and adopt DevOps and cloud-native practices, customizing Terraform workflows becomes an essential part of achieving infrastructure automation and agility.

Customizations allow organizations to tailor Terraform to their specific infrastructure requirements, coding standards, and deployment strategies.

By embracing customizations and following best practices for implementing and managing them, organizations can leverage Terraform's flexibility to streamline infrastructure management and achieve greater efficiency and control.

Chapter 10: Expert-Level Command Line Techniques

In the world of command-line interfaces (CLIs), mastering advanced commands and options is essential for becoming a proficient user.

While beginners typically start with basic commands to navigate and perform simple tasks, advanced users delve into more complex commands and utilize advanced options to achieve greater efficiency and control.

One of the fundamental skills in the CLI realm is understanding how to use command-line arguments and options.

Arguments are values that you provide to a command, typically as input data or parameters.

Options, on the other hand, modify the behavior of a command, allowing you to customize its actions.

For example, in a Linux CLI, the **ls** command has various options like **-l** for long listing format and **-a** for showing hidden files.

Mastering the usage of options allows you to fine-tune a command's behavior to suit your needs.

Advanced CLI users often leverage wildcard characters, such as *** and ?**, to perform batch operations or search for files with specific patterns.

For instance, in the Windows Command Prompt or PowerShell, you can use ***** to match multiple characters and **?** to match a single character when specifying file or directory names.

Understanding and effectively using these wildcard characters can significantly speed up tasks like file manipulation and searching.

Another valuable skill for advanced CLI users is command chaining and piping.

Chaining commands means executing multiple commands in sequence, with each command's output becoming the input for the next.

For instance, in Unix-like systems, you can chain commands using the **&&** operator, ensuring that the next command runs only if the previous one succeeds.

Piping, on the other hand, involves sending the output of one command as input to another using the | operator.

This allows you to combine the functionality of multiple commands to perform complex operations efficiently.

In Unix-like systems, you can use the **grep** command to filter text, and then pipe the output to another command, such as **sed** or **awk**, for further processing.

Redirecting input and output is another advanced CLI technique.

In many CLIs, you can redirect the standard input (**stdin**) and standard output (**stdout**) of a command to and from files, devices, or other commands.

For example, in Unix-like systems, you can use the > symbol to redirect **stdout** to a file, or < to read input from a file.

Advanced users often use these redirection capabilities to automate tasks, create log files, or process large datasets efficiently.

Navigating the file system efficiently is crucial for advanced CLI users.

Understanding how to use shortcuts, like **cd** (change directory), **pwd** (print working directory), and **pushd/popd** (push/pop directory stack), can help you move around the file system quickly.

Additionally, knowing how to use relative and absolute paths, as well as shortcuts like ~ (home directory) and . (current directory), is essential for effective navigation.

Advanced users also utilize scripting and automation to streamline repetitive tasks.

Writing scripts allows you to create sequences of commands and logic that can be executed automatically.

Scripting languages like Bash, PowerShell, Python, and Ruby are commonly used for this purpose.

With scripts, you can automate backups, perform system maintenance, and even build complex workflows that interact with multiple CLIs.

Environment variables are another advanced CLI concept.

These variables store configuration data and information that can be accessed by commands and scripts.

Advanced users often set and manipulate environment variables to control command behavior, configure applications, or pass data between processes.

In Unix-like systems, you can use the **export** command to define environment variables in the current session.

Furthermore, advanced CLI users are proficient in error handling and debugging.

They understand how to interpret error messages, log files, and diagnostic output to troubleshoot issues effectively.

Tools like **grep**, **awk**, and **sed** can be invaluable for parsing and analyzing logs and error messages.

Learning regular expressions, a powerful pattern-matching language, is a common practice among advanced users for text processing and manipulation.

Optimizing command performance is also a key skill.

Advanced CLI users know how to monitor system resources, such as CPU and memory usage, to identify bottlenecks and optimize command execution.

They may use tools like **top**, **htop**, or **sar** to gather performance data and make informed decisions.

Moreover, advanced CLI users are proficient in managing user accounts, permissions, and security.

They understand how to create and configure users, groups, and permissions to control access to resources and ensure system security.

In Unix-like systems, advanced users work with tools like **useradd**, **usermod**, **groupadd**, and **chmod** to manage users and permissions.

Advanced CLI commands often involve complex regular expressions, which allow users to search for and manipulate text patterns with precision.

These regular expressions are comprised of special characters and symbols that define search patterns, making them a powerful tool for text processing and data extraction.

For example, **grep** can be used with regular expressions to search for lines of text that match specific patterns, and **sed** can be used to replace or manipulate text based on regular expressions.

Additionally, advanced users are skilled in handling and managing data streams efficiently.

They understand how to use tools like **tee** to split data streams, **sort** to order data, and **uniq** to remove duplicates.

These commands, when combined with piping and redirection, enable advanced users to process data effectively and generate meaningful output.

Another advanced CLI technique is job control, which involves managing multiple processes and jobs in the background.

Advanced users are adept at using commands like **bg** and **fg** to send jobs to the background or bring them to the foreground.

They can also use the **nohup** command to run processes that continue running even after logging out of a session.

In Unix-like systems, advanced CLI users often work with signals, which are software interrupts that can be sent to processes to control their behavior.

Signals allow users to interact with processes in real-time, enabling actions like pausing, resuming, or terminating processes.

For example, the **kill** command is commonly used to send signals to processes, allowing users to gracefully shut down or restart applications.

In summary, mastering advanced CLI commands and options is essential for users who want to maximize their efficiency and control when working with command-line interfaces.

Advanced users are proficient in techniques like command chaining, piping, redirection, scripting, and automation, allowing them to perform complex tasks with ease.

They also understand concepts like environment variables, regular expressions, and job control, enabling them to manipulate and manage data and processes effectively.

Ultimately, advanced CLI skills empower users to navigate, automate, and optimize their command-line workflows, making them more productive and capable in a diverse range of tasks.

CLI automation and scripting have become integral components of modern computing environments, empowering users to automate repetitive tasks, streamline workflows, and enhance productivity.

Automation, in the context of the command-line interface (CLI), refers to the process of using scripts or programs to execute sequences of commands automatically, reducing manual intervention and human error.

Scripting, on the other hand, involves writing code in scripting languages to perform specific tasks or manipulate data through the CLI.

Both automation and scripting offer numerous benefits, including time savings, consistency, and the ability to scale and orchestrate complex operations.

To begin exploring CLI automation and scripting, it's essential to understand the concept of scripting languages.

Scripting languages are designed to be easy to learn and use, with a focus on automating tasks and interacting with systems.

Common scripting languages include Bash, Python, Perl, Ruby, and PowerShell, each with its own strengths and purposes.

Bash, for example, is prevalent on Unix-like systems and excels at handling system-level tasks and text processing.

Python is a versatile and beginner-friendly language known for its readability and wide range of libraries and modules.

Perl, historically popular for text processing and report generation, is known for its powerful regular expression capabilities.

Ruby is often used for web development but is equally capable of performing system-level automation tasks.

PowerShell is a scripting language and automation framework specifically designed for Windows environments, providing access to a wide range of system management capabilities.

Once you've chosen a scripting language that suits your needs, you can start writing scripts to automate CLI tasks.

A fundamental aspect of CLI automation and scripting is understanding how to execute CLI commands within scripts.

You can use various methods and libraries provided by the scripting language to run commands, capture their output, and process the results.

For example, in Bash, you can use backticks or the $() syntax to execute commands and capture their output as variables.

In Python, the **subprocess** module allows you to run commands and interact with their input and output streams.

Perl provides the **system()** and backtick operators, while Ruby offers methods like **system()** and backticks as well.

PowerShell, being a shell language, enables direct execution of commands as if you were using the CLI.

Understanding how to handle errors and exceptions is crucial in CLI automation and scripting.

Scripts should be designed to gracefully handle unexpected situations, such as command failures or incorrect input.

Most scripting languages provide mechanisms for error handling, including try-catch blocks, exit codes, and error messages.

By implementing robust error handling, you can ensure that your scripts continue to run reliably, even in the face of unforeseen issues.

Variables and data manipulation play a significant role in CLI scripting.

You can use variables to store and manipulate data within scripts, making it possible to pass information between commands and perform calculations or transformations.

In scripting languages like Python and Perl, you can declare variables explicitly, while Bash and PowerShell allow you to assign values to variables directly.

Understanding data types and structures, such as strings, integers, arrays, and dictionaries, is essential for effective data manipulation.

CLI automation and scripting often involve working with files and directories.

Scripts can be used to create, delete, move, and manipulate files and directories, enabling tasks like log rotation, data backup, and file synchronization.

File and directory operations typically rely on commands like **mkdir**, **rm**, **mv**, **cp**, and **find**, which can be called from within scripts.

Moreover, interacting with external data sources and APIs is a common use case for CLI scripting.

Scripts can fetch data from web services, databases, or remote servers and process the information for various purposes.

To perform HTTP requests, scripting languages often provide libraries or modules that simplify tasks like making GET and POST requests, handling authentication, and parsing JSON or XML responses.

Networking tasks, such as configuring network interfaces, routing, and firewall rules, can also be automated using CLI scripting.

Scripts can interact with networking tools and utilities to manage network settings and troubleshoot connectivity issues.

For example, in Linux, you can use the **ip** and **iptables** commands to manipulate network configurations.

CLI automation and scripting are particularly valuable in the realm of system administration and server management.

Administrators can write scripts to automate routine tasks such as user management, software installation, and system monitoring.

For instance, a script can be created to add or remove user accounts, set permissions, and configure user environments.

Scripts can also automate the installation and configuration of software packages, making it easier to maintain consistent server environments.

System monitoring scripts can collect performance data, log files, and system metrics to identify potential issues and trigger alerts when predefined thresholds are exceeded.

Furthermore, CLI automation can be employed in cloud computing environments to provision and manage cloud resources programmatically.

Cloud providers offer APIs and CLI tools that allow users to create and manage virtual machines, storage, databases, and other cloud services using scripts.

This automation enables organizations to dynamically scale their infrastructure based on demand, optimize costs, and implement disaster recovery strategies.

CLI automation and scripting can also be used for data processing and analysis.

Scripts can ingest, cleanse, and transform large datasets, facilitating tasks like data migration, data warehousing, and reporting.

By automating data-related tasks, organizations can save time, reduce errors, and gain insights from their data more efficiently.

Another area where CLI automation shines is in backup and disaster recovery.

Scripts can schedule and execute backup routines, ensuring that critical data is regularly backed up to remote locations or storage devices.

In the event of data loss or system failures, these backups can be restored quickly to minimize downtime and data loss.

Security automation is a growing field that leverages CLI scripting to enhance cybersecurity practices.

Scripts can be used to perform security scans, analyze logs, and implement security policies.

BOOK 3
TERRAFORM CLI BOSS
FROM NOVICE TO NINJA

ROB BOTWRIGHT

Chapter 1: Introduction to Terraform and CLI Basics

To embark on a journey into the realm of command-line interfaces (CLIs), it is essential to grasp the basics and familiarize oneself with the terminology that governs this powerful and versatile world of computing.

At its core, a CLI is a text-based interface that allows users to interact with a computer's operating system and software applications through commands entered as text.

The CLI has been a fundamental component of computing since its inception, offering a direct and efficient way to communicate with a computer.

Commands are the fundamental building blocks of CLI interaction, serving as instructions to perform specific tasks or operations.

These commands are typically comprised of keywords, options, and arguments, each with a specific role in defining the desired action.

Keywords are the primary command names that initiate an action, such as "ls" to list files or "mkdir" to create a directory.

Options, also known as flags or switches, modify the behavior of a command by specifying additional parameters or settings.

For example, appending "-l" to the "ls" command in Unix-like systems provides a detailed listing of files.

Arguments are values or inputs provided to a command to specify the objects or data on which the command should operate.

In the "cp" (copy) command, the source and destination file paths are arguments that indicate what to copy and where to copy it.

Understanding the structure and syntax of commands is crucial, as it forms the basis for effective CLI usage.

In most CLIs, commands are entered in a straightforward format, with the keyword followed by options and arguments.

Spaces or other delimiters separate these components, making commands human-readable and interpretable by the CLI.

Navigating the file system is one of the fundamental tasks performed through the CLI.

Users can move between directories or folders, view the contents of directories, and manipulate files and directories using specific commands.

For example, the "cd" (change directory) command allows users to move from one directory to another, while "ls" (list) provides a directory listing.

Creating, copying, moving, and deleting files and directories are common file system operations carried out through CLI commands like "mkdir" (make directory), "cp" (copy), "mv" (move), and "rm" (remove).

In addition to managing files and directories, users can interact with processes and applications using CLI commands.

Processes are running instances of programs or applications on a computer, and users can start, stop, monitor, and manage them through the CLI.

The "ps" (process status) command provides information about running processes, while "kill" is used to terminate processes.

CLI commands are often accompanied by a range of options and arguments that enable users to fine-tune their operations.

Options are usually preceded by a hyphen ("-") or two hyphens ("--") and provide additional functionality or configuration settings for a command.

For instance, "ls -l" uses the "-l" option to display a detailed listing of files.

Arguments, on the other hand, are values or inputs provided to a command to specify the objects or data on which the command should operate.

In the "cp" (copy) command, the source and destination file paths are arguments.

Options and arguments can significantly extend the capabilities of a CLI, allowing users to tailor commands to their specific needs.

When working with the CLI, users will frequently encounter directories and paths.

Directories, also known as folders, are organizational containers for files and other directories within a file system.

Each directory is identified by a name and can contain files and subdirectories.

Paths, on the other hand, are textual representations of a file or directory's location within the file system.

In Unix-like systems, paths are expressed using a forward slash ("/") as the separator, while in Windows, a backslash ("") is used.

Understanding absolute paths, which start from the root directory, and relative paths, which are defined in relation to the current directory, is essential for effective navigation and file manipulation.

Another fundamental concept in the world of CLIs is the command prompt, which is a textual or graphical indicator that signals the readiness to accept user input.

The command prompt typically displays information about the current directory, user, and host system.

Users enter commands at the prompt, and the CLI processes and executes those commands accordingly.

The command prompt can vary in appearance and location depending on the CLI environment and operating system.

For example, in Unix-like systems, the command prompt often ends with a dollar sign ("$") for regular users or a hash symbol ("#") for administrators with elevated privileges.

In Windows Command Prompt, the prompt typically displays the current directory path.

Moreover, users can customize their command prompt to display additional information or visual cues, making it more informative and user-friendly.

The concept of command history is a valuable feature of CLIs, allowing users to recall and reuse previously entered commands.

By pressing the "Up" and "Down" arrow keys or using specific keyboard shortcuts, users can navigate through their command history.

This functionality is particularly helpful when reusing complex or frequently used commands, as it saves time and reduces the risk of typing errors.

To further enhance productivity, command completion or auto-completion is a feature that assists users in typing commands, options, or file paths.

When users start typing a command or file path and press the "Tab" key, the CLI suggests and auto-completes the rest of the input based on available options or existing files and directories.

Command completion not only speeds up command entry but also helps prevent typos and errors.

In the CLI, users often encounter streams, which are channels for input and output data between commands and the operating system.

Streams consist of three standard channels:

Standard Input (stdin): This channel receives input data from the user or external sources and provides it to a command for processing.

Standard Output (stdout): This channel delivers the output data produced by a command, which can be displayed on the screen or redirected to a file.

Standard Error (stderr): This channel is used to convey error messages and diagnostic information from a command, separate from regular output.

Understanding streams is essential for controlling the flow of data between commands and managing input and output effectively.

Pipelines, a powerful concept in CLIs, involve connecting multiple commands together so that the output of one command serves as the input for the next.

This chaining of commands enables users to create complex workflows and perform intricate data processing tasks.

For example, in Unix-like systems, the "pipe" symbol ("|") connects commands like "ls," "grep," and "awk" to search for specific files and manipulate their contents seamlessly.

Furthermore, the CLI provides mechanisms for users to navigate, interact with, and manipulate their command environment.

Environment variables are placeholders that store information, such as system settings, configuration values, or user preferences, that can be accessed by commands and scripts.

Users can set and modify environment variables to customize their CLI experience and control command behavior.

Aliases are shortcuts or nicknames that users can create for commands, allowing for quick access to frequently used commands or complex command sequences.

By defining aliases, users can simplify their CLI interactions and reduce the need to remember lengthy commands.

Wildcards are characters or symbols used as placeholders in file and directory names, allowing users to perform operations on multiple files with similar names.

Common wildcards include the asterisk ("*") and question mark ("?"), which represent multiple and single characters, respectively.

For example, the wildcard "file*.txt" matches all files with names starting with "file" and ending with ".txt."

Finally, scripting and automation are advanced topics within the CLI domain, where users write scripts or programs to automate tasks, sequence commands, and perform complex operations.

Scripts, often written in scripting languages like Bash, Python, or PowerShell, enable users to automate routine tasks, process data, and interact with the CLI programmatically.

With a solid grasp of these CLI basics and terminology, users can embark on a journey of discovery and mastery, unlocking the full potential of the command-line interface in their computing endeavors.

The process of installing Terraform is a crucial step in setting up your environment for Infrastructure as Code (IaC) operations.

Before diving into the installation procedure, it's essential to understand what Terraform is and why you need it.

Terraform is an open-source IaC tool developed by HashiCorp that allows you to define and provision infrastructure using code.

It enables you to describe your infrastructure requirements in a declarative configuration language, and then Terraform automates the process of creating and managing those resources in cloud providers, data centers, and various infrastructure platforms.

The first step in installing Terraform is to download the appropriate binary for your operating system and architecture.

Terraform provides precompiled binaries for Windows, macOS, and Linux, and it supports a variety of architectures, including amd64, arm, and more.

To download the Terraform binary, visit the official Terraform website or use a package manager if available for your operating system.

Once you have downloaded the Terraform binary, you need to make it executable and place it in a directory that is part of your system's PATH.

This ensures that you can run Terraform from any directory without specifying its full path.

On Unix-like systems, you can make the Terraform binary executable using the **chmod** command, like this: **chmod +x terraform**.

After making Terraform executable, move it to a directory in your PATH, such as **/usr/local/bin** on Unix-like systems or **C:\Windows\System32** on Windows.

You can check if Terraform is installed correctly by opening a terminal and running the **terraform** command.

If installed successfully, it will display the Terraform command-line interface (CLI) help message, listing available commands and options.

At this point, you have successfully installed Terraform on your system, and you can begin using it to manage your infrastructure as code.

Terraform supports a wide range of providers, including cloud providers like AWS, Azure, Google Cloud, and infrastructure platforms like Kubernetes, VMware, and more.

To work with a specific provider, you need to configure the provider settings in your Terraform configuration files.

These configuration files typically have a **.tf** file extension and contain your infrastructure code written in HashiCorp Configuration Language (HCL).

For example, to configure Terraform to work with AWS, you would create an AWS provider block in your configuration file and specify your AWS access and secret keys.

Once configured, Terraform can authenticate with the AWS API and provision resources as defined in your configuration.

Terraform uses a state file to keep track of the resources it manages and their current state.

This state file is crucial for Terraform to know the current state of your infrastructure and to plan and apply changes correctly.

By default, Terraform stores the state file locally in a file named **terraform.tfstate** in the working directory.

However, in production environments, it's recommended to use remote state storage to ensure collaboration and consistency among team members.

Popular remote state storage options include Amazon S3, Google Cloud Storage, and HashiCorp's Terraform Cloud.

To use remote state storage, you need to configure the backend settings in your Terraform configuration files.

This includes specifying the backend type and connection details, such as the bucket name for S3 or the workspace name for Terraform Cloud.

Once configured, Terraform will store and retrieve the state file from the remote backend, allowing multiple team members to work on the same infrastructure code safely.

Terraform has a robust plugin system that allows you to extend its functionality by adding custom providers and provisioners.

Providers are responsible for managing resources in various infrastructure platforms, while provisioners are used to configure resources after they are created.

You can find and install third-party providers from the Terraform Registry, which contains a vast collection of community and official providers.

To use a custom provider, you need to define it in your Terraform configuration and specify its source and version.

For example, to use a custom provider for a specific service, you would add a provider block in your configuration file, like this:
hclCopy code

provider "custom" { source = "example.com/namespace/custom" version = "1.0.0" }

Once you've defined the provider, you can use its resources and data sources in your configuration to interact with the service it manages.

Provisioners, on the other hand, allow you to execute scripts or commands on resources to perform additional configuration or setup.

Common use cases for provisioners include running shell scripts, copying files, or executing remote commands on virtual machines.

To use a provisioner, you specify it within a resource block in your Terraform configuration.

For example, to run a shell script on an EC2 instance created with the AWS provider, you would add a provisioner block like this:

hclCopy code

resource "aws_instance" "example" { ami = "ami-0c55b159cbfafe1f0" instance_type = "t2.micro" provisioner "file" { source = "script.sh" destination = "/tmp/script.sh" } provisioner "remote-exec" { inline = ["chmod +x /tmp/script.sh", "sudo /tmp/script.sh",] } }

In this example, the provisioners are used to copy a shell script to the instance and then execute it remotely.

Terraform provides a robust set of commands to interact with your infrastructure code and resources.

Some of the most commonly used commands include **terraform init**, **terraform plan**, **terraform apply**, and **terraform destroy**.

The **terraform init** command initializes a Terraform project by downloading provider plugins and configuring the backend.

Running **terraform plan** generates an execution plan that shows what actions Terraform will take to create, update, or delete resources based on your configuration.

The **terraform apply** command executes the plan and creates or updates resources as needed.

To clean up and destroy resources, you can use the **terraform destroy** command.

These commands, along with others like **terraform validate** and **terraform refresh**, form the core of your Terraform workflow.

Terraform also supports workspace management, allowing you to create and switch between multiple workspaces for different environments or configurations.

Workspaces help you isolate state files and variables, making it easier to manage infrastructure for development, staging, and production environments.

To create a new workspace, use the **terraform workspace new** command, and to switch between workspaces, use the **terraform workspace select** command.

For example, you can create workspaces named "dev," "stage," and "prod" to manage different environments separately.

Terraform's modularity and reusability make it a powerful tool for managing infrastructure at scale.

You can organize your code using modules, which are self-contained units of Terraform configuration that encapsulate a set of resources.

Modules allow you to define, version, and share infrastructure components across different projects and teams.

By creating and using modules, you can promote best practices, reduce duplication, and maintain consistency in your infrastructure code.

To use a module, you specify it in your configuration using a module block and provide input variables as arguments.

Once you've defined a module in your configuration, you can instantiate it multiple times with different input values, customizing its behavior for different use cases.

In addition to modules, Terraform also supports data sources, which allow you to query and retrieve information from existing resources outside of your configuration.

Data sources provide a way to access information like AWS AMIs, VPC IDs, or DNS records and use that information in your configuration.

To use a data source, you define it in your configuration and reference its attributes where needed.

Terraform's dependency management ensures that resources are created in the correct order and that dependencies are satisfied.

This means that Terraform automatically determines the order in which resources should be created or updated based on their dependencies.

For example, if you're provisioning a virtual machine that relies on a specific network configuration, Terraform will ensure that the network resources are created first.

By understanding and leveraging Terraform's dependency graph, you can design and manage complex infrastructure configurations with ease.

Terraform also supports state locking to prevent concurrent access and modifications to the state file.

State locking is essential in collaborative environments to prevent conflicts and ensure the integrity of the state file.

Terraform provides a variety of backend configurations to implement state locking, including support for distributed systems like Amazon DynamoDB or Consul.

By configuring state locking, you can safely work on infrastructure as code projects with multiple team members, knowing that the state file is protected from concurrent modifications.

As you gain experience with Terraform, you'll discover advanced techniques and best practices that can help you optimize your workflows and manage infrastructure efficiently.

These include using variables and output values to make configurations more flexible and reusable, implementing conditional logic, and integrating with external tools and services.

Terraform's extensibility and ecosystem offer a wealth of resources, including documentation, community forums, and third-party plugins, to support your journey towards mastering infrastructure as code. In summary, installing Terraform is the first step on your journey to harnessing the power of Infrastructure as Code. Understanding its core concepts, such as providers, configuration files, state management, and remote state storage, is essential for effective usage. As you dive deeper into Terraform's capabilities and explore its extensive ecosystem, you'll unlock new possibilities for managing and automating your infrastructure.

Chapter 2: Setting Up Your Terraform Environment

Installing Terraform is a foundational step in the journey to harness the power of Infrastructure as Code (IaC).
Before delving into the installation process, it's crucial to grasp what Terraform is and why it's a valuable tool.
Terraform, developed by HashiCorp, is an open-source IaC tool that enables you to define, provision, and manage infrastructure using code.
It empowers you to describe your infrastructure requirements using a declarative configuration language, allowing Terraform to automate the creation and management of resources across various infrastructure platforms.
To begin the installation process, you must first download the appropriate Terraform binary for your specific operating system and architecture.
Terraform offers precompiled binaries for popular operating systems such as Windows, macOS, and various Linux distributions, catering to diverse hardware architectures.
Obtaining the Terraform binary can be accomplished by visiting the official Terraform website or utilizing a package manager if your operating system supports it.
Once you've successfully downloaded the Terraform binary, the next step involves configuring it to be executable and placing it within a directory included in your system's PATH.
This ensures that you can run Terraform commands from any directory without specifying the full path to the binary.
On Unix-like systems, making the Terraform binary executable can be achieved using the **chmod** command, typically as follows: **chmod +x terraform.**
After ensuring the binary is executable, move it to a directory present in your system's PATH, such as **/usr/local/bin** for Unix-like systems or **C:\Windows\System32** for Windows.

You can verify the correct installation of Terraform by opening a terminal or command prompt and running the **terraform** command.

A successful installation will display the Terraform command-line interface (CLI) help message, presenting a list of available commands and options.

At this point, you've successfully installed Terraform on your system, and you're ready to embark on the journey of managing infrastructure as code.

Terraform boasts support for a wide range of providers, encompassing cloud providers like AWS, Azure, Google Cloud, and infrastructure platforms such as Kubernetes, VMware, and more.

To work with a specific provider, it's imperative to configure the provider settings within your Terraform configuration files.

These configuration files, typically denoted by the **.tf** file extension, contain your infrastructure code written using HashiCorp Configuration Language (HCL).

For instance, to configure Terraform for AWS, you'll create an AWS provider block in your configuration file and specify the necessary credentials.

Upon configuration, Terraform can authenticate with the respective provider's API, facilitating the provisioning of resources in accordance with your configuration.

Terraform maintains a state file to track the resources it manages and their current states.

This state file plays a pivotal role in ensuring Terraform possesses knowledge about your infrastructure's current status, enabling it to plan and execute changes accurately.

By default, Terraform stores the state file locally in a file named **terraform.tfstate** within the working directory.

However, in production environments, it's recommended to adopt remote state storage to foster collaboration and maintain consistency among team members.

Popular remote state storage options encompass Amazon S3, Google Cloud Storage, and HashiCorp's Terraform Cloud.

To leverage remote state storage, you must configure the backend settings within your Terraform configuration files, specifying the backend type and connection details.

These details may involve the bucket name for Amazon S3 or the workspace name for Terraform Cloud.

Once configured, Terraform will use the remote backend to store and retrieve the state file, facilitating collaborative work on the same infrastructure codebase.

Terraform employs a robust plugin system that extends its capabilities through the integration of custom providers and provisioners.

Providers are responsible for managing resources on various infrastructure platforms, while provisioners facilitate resource configuration post-creation.

Third-party providers can be discovered and installed from the Terraform Registry, which features an extensive collection of community-contributed and official providers.

To employ a custom provider, you define it within your Terraform configuration and specify its source and version.

For example, to employ a custom provider for a specific service, you include a provider block within your configuration file:

hclCopy code

```
provider          "custom"          {          source          =
"example.com/namespace/custom" version = "1.0.0" }
```

After defining the provider, you can utilize its resources and data sources in your configuration to interact with the service it manages.

Provisioners, conversely, enable you to execute scripts or commands on resources to perform additional configuration or setup tasks.

Typical use cases for provisioners encompass running shell scripts, copying files, or executing remote commands on virtual machines.

When using a provisioner, it should be specified within a resource block in your Terraform configuration.

For instance, to execute a shell script on an EC2 instance created through the AWS provider, you'd introduce a provisioner block as follows:

hclCopy code

```
resource "aws_instance" "example" { ami = "ami-0c55b159cbfafe1f0" instance_type = "t2.micro" provisioner "file" { source = "script.sh" destination = "/tmp/script.sh" } provisioner "remote-exec" { inline = [ "chmod +x /tmp/script.sh", "sudo /tmp/script.sh", ] } }
```

In this example, the provisioners are utilized to copy a shell script to the EC2 instance and subsequently execute it remotely.

Terraform provides a comprehensive set of commands to interact with your infrastructure code and resources.

Some of the most commonly used commands encompass **terraform init, terraform plan, terraform apply**, and **terraform destroy**.

terraform init serves to initialize a Terraform project by downloading provider plugins and configuring the backend.

Running **terraform plan** generates an execution plan, outlining the actions Terraform will undertake to create, update, or delete resources in accordance with your configuration.

The **terraform apply** command executes the plan, effecting the creation or modification of resources as required.

To dismantle and remove resources, the **terraform destroy** command proves invaluable.

These commands, coupled with others such as **terraform validate** and **terraform refresh**, constitute the core of your Terraform workflow.

Terraform also facilitates workspace management, enabling you to establish and switch between multiple workspaces to accommodate diverse environments or configurations.

Workspaces serve to isolate state files and variables, simplifying the management of infrastructure for development, staging, and production environments.

To inaugurate a new workspace, the **terraform workspace new** command is employed, while the **terraform workspace select** command allows you to transition between workspaces.

For instance, workspaces denominated "dev," "stage," and "prod" can be created to oversee distinct environments.

Terraform's modularity and reusability render it a potent tool for managing infrastructure at scale.

Modules, which constitute self-contained units of Terraform configuration, encapsulate sets of resources, fostering organization, versioning, and sharing of infrastructure components across projects and teams.

By designing and employing modules, you foster best practices, diminish redundancy, and sustain uniformity within your infrastructure code.

To harness a module's capabilities, you specify it within your configuration using a module block and supply input variables as arguments.

Once you've incorporated a module into your configuration, it can be instantiated multiple times, each instance customizable with unique input values to accommodate various use cases.

Beyond modules, Terraform accommodates data sources, enabling you to interrogate and retrieve information from existing resources external to your configuration.

Data sources enable access to data such as AWS AMIs, VPC IDs, or DNS records, permitting the integration of this information into your configuration.

To leverage a data source, it must be defined within your configuration, and its attributes can be referenced where necessary.

Terraform's dependency management automates resource creation and update sequencing based on their dependencies, simplifying the orchestration of resources.

For instance, when provisioning a virtual machine reliant on specific network configurations, Terraform ensures the network resources are established before the virtual machine.

By understanding and leveraging Terraform's dependency graph, you gain the capacity to design and administer intricate infrastructure configurations with ease.

Additionally, Terraform incorporates state locking, a pivotal feature for preventing concurrent access and modifications to the state file.

State locking is indispensable in collaborative environments, where it thwarts conflicts and upholds the state file's integrity.

Terraform affords a plethora of backend configurations, accommodating state locking via distributed systems like Amazon DynamoDB or Consul.

By configuring state locking, you can confidently collaborate with multiple team members on infrastructure as code projects, secure in the knowledge that the state file remains shielded against concurrent alterations.

As you amass experience with Terraform, you'll uncover advanced techniques and best practices to refine your workflows and optimize infrastructure management.

These encompass leveraging variables and output values for enhanced configurability and reusability, implementing conditional logic, and integrating with external tools and services.

Terraform's extensibility and ecosystem offer abundant resources, including documentation, community forums, and third-party plugins, to support your voyage towards mastering infrastructure as code.

In summation, installing Terraform serves as the inaugural stride on the path to unlocking the capabilities of Infrastructure as Code.

Comprehending fundamental concepts such as providers, configuration files, state management, and remote state storage is fundamental for proficient utilization.

As you delve deeper into Terraform's capabilities and explore its extensive ecosystem, you'll unearth fresh avenues for managing and automating your infrastructure, fostering efficiency and agility in your operations. Configuring your environment is a pivotal step in preparing to work with Terraform and embark on your Infrastructure as Code (IaC) journey. It involves setting up your local development environment to ensure that you can efficiently create, manage, and deploy infrastructure using Terraform.

Before diving into the specifics of configuring your environment, it's important to understand the key components that make up your Terraform setup.

First and foremost, you need Terraform itself, which you should have already installed as described in the previous chapter.

Next, you'll require access to a cloud provider or infrastructure platform where you intend to provision resources using Terraform.

Popular cloud providers include AWS, Azure, Google Cloud, and more, while infrastructure platforms like Kubernetes, VMware, and Docker are also commonly used with Terraform.

Once you have Terraform and access to your chosen infrastructure platform, you'll need to create a Terraform configuration file.

This file, typically named with a **.tf** extension, contains the declarative code that describes the infrastructure you want to create.

It defines the resources, settings, and dependencies required for your infrastructure deployment.

Now, let's delve into the steps involved in configuring your environment for Terraform.

First, open a terminal or command prompt to access your command-line interface (CLI).

The CLI will be your primary tool for interacting with Terraform and managing your infrastructure code.

Ensure that you're in the directory where your Terraform configuration files are located or where you plan to create them.

Before proceeding, make sure you have the necessary credentials and access rights for your chosen cloud provider or infrastructure platform.

These credentials typically include access keys, secret keys, and other authentication tokens.

You'll need these credentials to authenticate with the provider's API when Terraform provisions resources.

To securely manage your credentials, consider using environment variables or credential management tools provided by your platform.

Once your credentials are in order, it's time to configure your Terraform provider settings.

These settings are specified within your Terraform configuration files and define which provider (e.g., AWS, Azure) you'll be working with and how to authenticate with it.

In your configuration file, you'll typically create a provider block that specifies the provider and any necessary configuration settings.

For example, here's how you might configure the AWS provider:

hclCopy code

```
provider "aws" { region = "us-east-1" access_key = "your-access-key" secret_key = "your-secret-key" }
```

In this example, we're configuring the AWS provider to use the US East (N. Virginia) region and providing our access and secret keys.

Each provider has its own specific configuration settings, so refer to the provider's documentation for details on how to configure it properly.

With your provider configured, you're ready to start defining your infrastructure in Terraform.

This involves creating resource blocks within your Terraform configuration file.

Resource blocks specify the type of resource you want to create (e.g., AWS EC2 instance, Google Cloud Storage bucket) and its configuration settings.

Here's an example of creating an AWS EC2 instance:

hclCopy code

resource "aws_instance" "example" { ami = "ami-0c55b159cbfafe1f0" instance_type = "t2.micro" }

In this example, we're defining an EC2 instance with a specific Amazon Machine Image (AMI) and instance type.

You can create multiple resource blocks for different types of resources, and they can depend on each other to model your infrastructure's relationships.

Once you've defined your resources, you can use Terraform's commands to plan and apply your changes.

The **terraform plan** command analyzes your configuration and generates an execution plan that outlines what Terraform will do when you apply your configuration.

This step is crucial for previewing the changes Terraform will make to your infrastructure without actually applying them.

After reviewing the plan and ensuring it aligns with your expectations, you can use the **terraform apply** command to execute the plan and create or modify resources as specified in your configuration.

Before applying changes, Terraform will prompt you to confirm your action, allowing you to double-check and prevent accidental resource creation or modification.

Terraform also supports input variables, which enable you to parameterize your configuration and make it more reusable.

Variables can be defined in separate variable files or directly within your configuration files.

For example, you can create a variable for the AWS region like this:

hclCopy code

variable "aws_region" { description = "The AWS region to deploy resources to." default = "us-east-1" }

Then, you can reference this variable in your resource blocks:

hclCopy code

```
resource "aws_instance" "example" { ami = "ami-0c55b159cbfafe1f0" instance_type = "t2.micro" region = var.aws_region }
```

By using variables, you can easily adapt your configuration for different environments or requirements.

Terraform also provides output variables, which allow you to capture and display values from your infrastructure after it's been created.

Output variables can be defined in your configuration files to expose specific information, such as the IP address of a provisioned instance.

For example:

hclCopy code

```
output "instance_ip" { value = aws_instance.example.public_ip }
```

With output variables, you can extract and utilize valuable information from your infrastructure for further automation or integration with other tools.

Configuring your environment for Terraform involves understanding and defining your provider settings, creating resource blocks, managing variables, and using Terraform's commands to plan and apply changes.

This process sets the stage for effectively managing your infrastructure as code and leveraging Terraform's capabilities to automate and streamline your operations.

As you become more proficient with Terraform, you'll discover advanced techniques and best practices that further enhance your ability to configure and manage infrastructure with ease.

Chapter 3: Your First Steps with Terraform Commands

Initializing a Terraform project is a crucial step in the process of working with Terraform and Infrastructure as Code (IaC).

The initialization process sets up your working directory, downloads necessary plugins, and prepares your configuration for use.

To initiate a Terraform project, navigate to the directory containing your Terraform configuration files using your command-line interface (CLI).

Once you're in the right directory, run the **terraform init** command.

This command is essential for setting up your project and ensuring that Terraform has everything it needs to function correctly.

When you execute **terraform init**, Terraform performs several key tasks to prepare your environment.

First, Terraform initializes a working directory specifically for your project.

This directory contains important Terraform files and state files that track the current state of your infrastructure.

By default, Terraform initializes a local state backend, which stores the state file in the same directory as your configuration files.

However, it's common practice to use a remote state backend for production projects to enable collaboration and improve security.

The **terraform init** command also validates your configuration files, ensuring that they are well-formed and free of syntax errors.

If any issues are detected during this validation process, Terraform will alert you, allowing you to address and correct the errors before proceeding.

Once your configuration is validated, Terraform proceeds to download any necessary provider plugins.

Providers are responsible for interacting with specific infrastructure platforms, such as AWS, Azure, Google Cloud, or Kubernetes.

Terraform maintains a comprehensive library of provider plugins, and it automatically downloads the plugins required for your configuration.

These plugins enable Terraform to create and manage resources on the target infrastructure platform.

By default, Terraform stores downloaded provider plugins in a hidden directory within your project directory.

This helps keep your project self-contained and prevents conflicts between different projects that may rely on different versions of the same provider.

Additionally, Terraform downloads the specific version of each provider plugin specified in your configuration files.

This versioning ensures that your project uses consistent provider behavior, reducing the risk of unexpected changes when you update your Terraform code.

Once the initialization process is complete, Terraform informs you that your project is now ready for use.

It provides a summary of the initialization steps performed, including the provider plugins downloaded and their respective versions.

Additionally, Terraform displays the location of the state file, which is crucial for tracking the state of your infrastructure.

At this point, your Terraform project is fully initialized and ready for action.

You can proceed to use Terraform's various commands to plan, apply, and manage your infrastructure.

Before running any commands, it's a good practice to verify your configuration and ensure that it accurately reflects your intended infrastructure.

You can review your configuration files and confirm that all the settings and resource definitions are correct.

This step helps prevent unintended changes and reduces the risk of costly infrastructure mistakes.

Once you're confident in your configuration, you can execute the **terraform plan** command.

This command examines your configuration files and generates an execution plan that outlines the actions Terraform will take to create, modify, or destroy resources based on your configuration.

Reviewing the plan is a crucial step in the Terraform workflow because it allows you to preview the changes that Terraform will make to your infrastructure without actually applying those changes.

The **terraform plan** output provides detailed information about the planned actions, including the resources affected and any potential dependencies or order of operations.

It also highlights any new resources that will be created, existing resources that will be modified, and resources that will be destroyed.

This comprehensive view empowers you to ensure that Terraform's actions align with your expectations and desired outcomes.

Once you've reviewed the plan and are satisfied with it, you can proceed to apply your configuration changes using the **terraform apply** command.

Executing this command instructs Terraform to enact the changes outlined in the plan.

Terraform will communicate with the provider plugins to create, modify, or destroy resources as necessary to align your infrastructure with your configuration.

During the **terraform apply** process, Terraform prompts you to confirm the planned changes.

This confirmation step is a critical safeguard that prevents accidental modifications to your infrastructure.

It allows you to double-check the changes and ensures that you're aware of and approve the actions Terraform is about to perform.

After your confirmation, Terraform proceeds with the execution of the plan, making the necessary changes to your infrastructure.

Throughout this process, Terraform provides real-time feedback on the progress of each action, such as resource creation or modification.

You can monitor the command's output to track the status of each resource and verify that the changes are proceeding as expected.

Upon completion of the **terraform apply** command, Terraform presents a summary of the changes made to your infrastructure.

This summary includes details about the resources created, modified, or destroyed, as well as any potential errors or issues encountered during the process.

It's advisable to review this summary carefully to ensure that your infrastructure has been updated as intended.

By successfully initializing your Terraform project and following the planning and execution process, you can confidently create and manage infrastructure as code.

Terraform's initialization process sets up your working directory, validates your configuration, downloads provider plugins, and prepares your project for action.

Once initialized, Terraform's planning and applying commands enable you to efficiently and predictably manage your infrastructure, aligning it with your desired state.

This iterative and version-controlled approach to infrastructure management offers a robust and reliable way to build and evolve your infrastructure.

Executing basic Terraform commands is the cornerstone of your journey into Infrastructure as Code (IaC) with Terraform.

These commands empower you to create, modify, and manage your infrastructure with precision and repeatability.

Before diving into the specific commands, let's take a moment to understand the fundamental concepts that underpin Terraform's workflow.

Terraform operates based on the principles of declarative infrastructure, where you define the desired state of your infrastructure in configuration files.

These configuration files, typically written in HashiCorp Configuration Language (HCL), specify the resources, settings, and dependencies required for your infrastructure.

Terraform uses these configuration files to generate an execution plan, a detailed blueprint of the actions it will take to create or modify resources.

Once you're satisfied with the plan, you can apply it to your infrastructure, and Terraform takes care of the rest, making the necessary changes to align your infrastructure with your configuration.

Now, let's explore the primary Terraform commands and their roles in this workflow.

The **terraform init** command, as we discussed earlier, initializes your Terraform project by setting up your working directory and downloading necessary provider plugins.

This command is typically executed only once when you start a new project or when you update your provider configurations.

With your project initialized, you can proceed to define your infrastructure in Terraform configuration files.

The **terraform plan** command plays a pivotal role in this process.

When you run **terraform plan**, Terraform analyzes your configuration files and generates a detailed execution plan, outlining precisely what actions it will take when you apply your configuration.

The plan provides a clear view of the resources that will be created, modified, or destroyed, as well as any potential dependencies or order of operations.

Reviewing the plan is a crucial step to ensure that Terraform's actions align with your expectations and desired outcomes.

Once you're satisfied with the plan and ready to proceed, you can execute the **terraform apply** command.

Running **terraform apply** instructs Terraform to enact the changes outlined in the plan, communicating with the provider plugins to create, modify, or destroy resources as necessary.

Throughout this process, Terraform provides real-time feedback on the progress of each action, such as resource creation or modification.

You can monitor the command's output to track the status of each resource and verify that the changes are proceeding as expected.

During the **terraform apply** process, Terraform prompts you to confirm the planned changes.

This confirmation step is a critical safeguard that prevents accidental modifications to your infrastructure.

It allows you to double-check the changes and ensures that you're aware of and approve the actions Terraform is about to perform.

After your confirmation, Terraform proceeds with the execution of the plan, making the necessary changes to your infrastructure.

Upon completion of the **terraform apply** command, Terraform presents a summary of the changes made to your infrastructure.

This summary includes details about the resources created, modified, or destroyed, as well as any potential errors or issues encountered during the process.

It's advisable to review this summary carefully to ensure that your infrastructure has been updated as intended.

As you work with Terraform, you'll find that these basic commands form the foundation of your infrastructure management workflow.

They provide the means to create and modify resources, track changes, and maintain a consistent and predictable infrastructure.

However, Terraform offers additional commands and options to enhance your experience and provide greater control over your infrastructure.

For example, the **terraform show** command allows you to inspect the current state of your infrastructure, displaying the attributes and settings of the resources defined in your configuration.

You can use this command to gain insights into your infrastructure's current state or to extract specific information for further automation or integration with other tools.

Another useful command is **terraform destroy**, which does precisely what its name suggests: it destroys all the resources managed by Terraform in your current working directory.

While this command can be a powerful tool for decommissioning resources, it should be used with caution, as it can result in the irreversible loss of infrastructure if executed without due consideration.

To target specific resources for creation, modification, or destruction, you can use the **-target** option with the **terraform apply** command, specifying the resource you want to address.

This level of granularity allows you to make changes to specific resources without affecting others in your configuration.

Terraform also provides the **terraform import** command, which allows you to import existing resources into your Terraform state.

This is particularly useful when you're transitioning from manual infrastructure management to Terraform or when you need to manage resources that were created outside of Terraform.

The **terraform workspace** command enables you to work with multiple, isolated workspaces within a single Terraform configuration.

Workspaces are helpful when you need to manage separate instances of the same infrastructure configuration, such as development, testing, and production environments.

You can create, switch between, and delete workspaces to streamline your workflow and avoid conflicts between different environments.

As your Terraform projects grow and evolve, you'll also benefit from using variables and modules to enhance configurability and reusability.

Variables allow you to parameterize your configuration, making it easier to adapt your infrastructure for different environments or requirements.

Modules, on the other hand, enable you to encapsulate and reuse configuration blocks, promoting code modularity and maintainability.

These advanced Terraform features offer flexibility and scalability as you tackle more complex infrastructure challenges.

In summary, executing basic Terraform commands, including **terraform init**, **terraform plan**, and **terraform apply**, is the essential foundation of your IaC journey.

These commands, complemented by additional options and advanced features, empower you to create, modify, and manage your infrastructure with precision, consistency, and repeatability.

As you become more proficient with Terraform, you'll discover how to leverage its full potential to orchestrate and automate infrastructure at scale, driving efficiency and agility in your operations.

Chapter 4: Terraform Configuration Files Demystified

Understanding HashiCorp Configuration Language (HCL) syntax is fundamental to working effectively with Terraform, as HCL serves as the language for defining infrastructure configurations in Terraform.

HCL is designed to be both human-readable and machine-friendly, making it accessible for infrastructure operators and automation systems alike.

HCL syntax is declarative, meaning that you define the desired state of your infrastructure rather than specifying a sequence of actions to achieve that state.

In HCL, you express your intent by describing the resources, settings, and dependencies needed to create or modify your infrastructure.

The primary construct in HCL is the block, which represents a configuration unit and contains one or more key-value pairs.

Blocks are denoted by curly braces, and each block has a block type that identifies its purpose.

For example, a resource block is used to define a resource, such as a virtual machine in a cloud provider.

The block type, resource, is followed by the resource's type and a name for the resource instance, enclosed in double quotes.

Inside the resource block, you can specify the resource's attributes as key-value pairs, defining the resource's configuration settings.

Attributes are written as key = value pairs, where the key is the name of the attribute, and the value can be a string, number, boolean, or complex data structure.

HCL supports interpolation, which allows you to reference variables or expressions within attribute values.

Interpolation is denoted by ${}, and it allows you to dynamically insert values into your configuration.

For example, you can interpolate a variable named **instance_type** into an attribute value like this: **instance_type = var.instance_type**.

Variables in HCL are defined in separate variable blocks, where you specify the variable's name, description, type, and optionally, a default value.

Variables serve as placeholders for values that can be reused throughout your configuration.

Using variables enhances the flexibility and maintainability of your infrastructure code, as you can change variable values without modifying the resource blocks.

HCL also provides conditional expressions that allow you to conditionally set attribute values based on a boolean condition.

Conditional expressions use the **?** and : operators, similar to the ternary operator in many programming languages.

For example, you can use a conditional expression to set an attribute's value based on a variable's value: **size = var.use_large_instance ? "large" : "small"**.

Comments in HCL are preceded by a **#** symbol, and they allow you to add explanatory notes to your configuration.

Comments are ignored by the HCL parser and are for documentation purposes.

HCL also supports block-level and inline comments to provide context and explanations within your configuration.

When writing HCL code, it's important to adhere to its syntax rules and conventions to ensure that your configuration is valid and can be processed by Terraform.

To assist with code formatting and consistency, you can use HCL formatting tools, such as **terraform fmt**, which automatically formats your HCL code according to Terraform's style guidelines.

Understanding HCL's syntax is essential for creating clear, concise, and maintainable infrastructure configurations in Terraform.

By mastering HCL's constructs, including blocks, attributes, variables, interpolation, conditional expressions, and comments, you can express your infrastructure requirements effectively and harness Terraform's power to create and manage infrastructure as code.

As you gain experience with HCL, you'll become adept at defining complex infrastructure configurations that align with your organization's needs and best practices, enabling you to efficiently and confidently manage infrastructure at scale.

Creating your first configuration file in Terraform is a pivotal step in embarking on your journey into Infrastructure as Code (IaC).

A configuration file in Terraform defines the desired state of your infrastructure and serves as the blueprint for the resources you want to create or manage.

To create a configuration file, you need a text editor or integrated development environment (IDE) that supports writing HashiCorp Configuration Language (HCL).

HCL is the language used for defining infrastructure configurations in Terraform, and it's designed to be human-readable and machine-friendly.

When creating your configuration file, it's essential to choose a meaningful name that reflects its purpose and the type of resources it will define.

The convention for naming Terraform configuration files is to use the **.tf** file extension, which helps identify them as Terraform configuration files.

For example, if you intend to define a configuration for creating an Amazon Web Services (AWS) EC2 instance, you could name your file **aws_instance.tf**.

Once you've chosen a name for your configuration file, you can open it in your preferred text editor or IDE to begin defining your infrastructure.

The configuration file typically starts with a provider block, which specifies the cloud or infrastructure platform you'll be working with.

In the case of AWS, the provider block would look like this:

hclCopy code

```
provider "aws" { region = "us-east-1" }
```

In this example, the **provider** block defines the AWS provider and specifies the region where your resources will be created.

The **region** attribute is set to "us-east-1," but you can replace it with the desired AWS region for your infrastructure.

After defining the provider, you can proceed to define resources using resource blocks.

Resource blocks are used to describe the resources you want to create, such as virtual machines, databases, or networking components.

Here's an example of a resource block that creates an AWS EC2 instance:

hclCopy code

```
resource "aws_instance" "example" { ami = "ami-0c55b159cbfafe1f0" instance_type = "t2.micro" }
```

In this resource block, we specify the type of resource ("aws_instance"), provide a name for this resource instance ("example"), and set attributes like the Amazon Machine Image (AMI) and instance type.

The **ami** attribute specifies the AMI ID for the EC2 instance, and the **instance_type** attribute specifies the instance type as "t2.micro."

The values for these attributes can vary depending on your specific requirements and the availability of AMIs and instance types in your chosen AWS region.

Once you've defined the necessary resources in your configuration file, you can save the file.

Before proceeding further, it's a good practice to validate your configuration file to ensure it's free of syntax errors and adheres to Terraform's requirements.

You can use the **terraform validate** command to perform this validation:

```sh
terraform validate
```

If your configuration file passes the validation, Terraform will indicate that it's a valid configuration.

If any errors are detected during validation, Terraform will provide error messages to help you identify and correct the issues.

With a validated configuration file, you're ready to move on to the next steps in the Terraform workflow.

The following steps typically involve initializing your Terraform project, planning changes, and applying the configuration to create or modify your infrastructure.

The process of creating your first configuration file in Terraform is just the beginning of your IaC journey.

As you gain experience and familiarity with Terraform's syntax, you'll be able to define more complex and sophisticated infrastructure configurations to meet the needs of your organization.

By using descriptive resource blocks and specifying resource attributes, you can create infrastructure that aligns precisely with your requirements, making it easier to manage and maintain over time.

In summary, creating your first configuration file in Terraform is a foundational step in practicing IaC.

It allows you to define the desired state of your infrastructure using HCL syntax, specify the provider you'll be working with, and define the resources you want to create or manage.

By following best practices, validating your configuration, and gradually expanding your Terraform skills, you'll be well-prepared to harness the full power of Terraform for managing infrastructure as code.

Chapter 5: Advanced Resource Management

Resource blocks and attributes are fundamental concepts in Terraform that allow you to define and configure the resources you want to create and manage as part of your infrastructure.

Resource blocks serve as containers for describing a specific type of resource, such as virtual machines, databases, or networking components.

Each resource block represents an instance of that resource type, and you can give it a name to distinguish it from other resource instances of the same type.

Inside a resource block, you specify the attributes and settings that define the resource's configuration.

Attributes are key-value pairs within a resource block, where the key represents the attribute name, and the value represents the attribute's value or content.

Attributes define the characteristics and properties of the resource, such as its size, location, or configuration options.

For example, consider a resource block that defines an AWS EC2 instance:

hclCopy code

```
resource "aws_instance" "example" { ami = "ami-0c55b159cbfafe1f0" instance_type = "t2.micro" }
```

In this resource block, "aws_instance" is the resource type, and "example" is the name of this specific EC2 instance resource.

The attributes "ami" and "instance_type" are defined within the block and specify the Amazon Machine Image (AMI) and instance type for the EC2 instance, respectively.

The "ami" attribute references the specific AMI ID, while the "instance_type" attribute specifies the desired instance type as "t2.micro."

These attributes provide crucial details about how the EC2 instance should be provisioned and configured within your AWS environment.

Resource attributes can vary widely based on the resource type and the cloud or infrastructure platform you are working with.

For instance, if you are defining a virtual network in Azure, the attributes might include the network's address space, subnets, and security rules.

Attributes are not limited to simple strings or numbers; they can also contain complex data structures and values.

In Terraform, you can use interpolation to reference variables, expressions, or other attributes within an attribute value.

This capability allows you to dynamically generate attribute values or incorporate data from other parts of your configuration.

Interpolation is denoted by ${}, and it enables you to inject dynamic information into your resource definitions.

For example, you can interpolate a variable named "subnet_id" into a resource block to specify the subnet for a virtual machine:

hclCopy code

```
resource "aws_instance" "example" { ami = "ami-0c55b159cbfafe1f0" instance_type = "t2.micro" subnet_id = var.subnet_id }
```

Here, "subnet_id" is an attribute of the AWS EC2 instance resource, and it is set to the value of the "subnet_id" variable using interpolation.

This dynamic approach allows you to reuse configurations across different environments or tailor resource attributes based on specific requirements.

When working with Terraform, it's important to understand that resource attributes often have specific constraints and requirements defined by the cloud provider or infrastructure platform.

For instance, an attribute may require a valid resource ID, a specific data format, or compliance with platform-specific naming conventions.

Consulting the documentation of the cloud provider or platform is essential to ensure that you provide accurate and valid attribute values in your configuration.

Resource blocks and attributes provide a structured and flexible way to define and configure infrastructure resources within your Terraform configuration.

By specifying resource types, naming instances, and setting attributes, you can express your infrastructure requirements accurately and effectively.

Interpolation enables you to introduce dynamic and reusable elements into your configurations, enhancing flexibility and maintainability.

Throughout your Terraform journey, you'll work with a wide range of resource types and attributes to build and manage infrastructure tailored to your organization's needs.

As you gain experience and proficiency, you'll find that resource blocks and attributes are the building blocks that empower you to create and orchestrate infrastructure as code efficiently and consistently.

Managing resource dependencies is a crucial aspect of Terraform configuration, ensuring that resources are created or modified in the correct order to maintain a consistent and functioning infrastructure.

In a Terraform configuration, resources often depend on each other, meaning that one resource relies on the existence or configuration of another.

Resource dependencies are vital because they dictate the order in which Terraform creates or modifies resources, preventing issues related to resource availability or configuration dependencies.

Understanding and defining resource dependencies correctly is essential for building reliable and predictable infrastructure as code (IaC).

Terraform infers resource dependencies based on how you reference attributes of one resource within another.

When you interpolate an attribute from one resource into another resource's attribute, Terraform automatically establishes a dependency.

For example, consider a scenario where you define an AWS EC2 instance and an associated security group:

hclCopy code

resource "aws_instance" "example" { ami = "ami-0c55b159cbfafe1f0" instance_type = "t2.micro" } resource "aws_security_group" "example_sg" { name_prefix = "example-sg-" vpc_id = "vpc-12345678" ingress { from_port = 22 to_port = 22 protocol = "tcp" cidr_blocks = ["0.0.0.0/0"] } }

In this configuration, the EC2 instance and the associated security group are defined as separate resources.

The EC2 instance resource refers to the "aws_instance.example" block, while the security group resource refers to the "aws_security_group.example_sg" block.

The EC2 instance's configuration specifies the **vpc_security_group_ids** attribute to use the security group associated with "aws_security_group.example_sg."

By doing this, you establish a dependency, indicating that the EC2 instance depends on the existence and configuration of the security group.

Terraform recognizes this dependency and ensures that it creates the security group before attempting to create the EC2 instance.

Resource dependencies are not limited to attributes but can also be established based on resource names.

For instance, if you need to create an Elastic IP (EIP) and associate it with an EC2 instance, you can define the dependency using resource names:

hclCopy code

```
resource "aws_instance" "example" { ami = "ami-0c55b159cbfafe1f0" instance_type = "t2.micro" } resource "aws_eip" "example_eip" { instance = aws_instance.example.id }
```

In this example, the EIP resource depends on the EC2 instance's existence and configuration because it references the EC2 instance's "id" attribute.

Terraform ensures that it creates the EC2 instance first, allowing it to retrieve the instance's ID before creating the EIP and associating it.

Terraform also provides explicit dependency management through the use of the **depends_on** meta-argument.

You can use **depends_on** to define dependencies between resources explicitly, regardless of whether they are inferred from attribute references or resource names.

Here's an example where an S3 bucket explicitly depends on an IAM role:

hclCopy code

```
resource "aws_iam_role" "example_role" { name = "example-role" # ... other role configuration ... } resource "aws_s3_bucket" "example_bucket" { bucket = "example-bucket" # ... other bucket configuration ... depends_on = [aws_iam_role.example_role] }
```

In this case, the S3 bucket explicitly depends on the IAM role by specifying **depends_on** and referencing the IAM role resource.

Terraform ensures that it creates the IAM role before creating the S3 bucket.

Explicit dependency management using **depends_on** can be useful when you need fine-grained control over the order of resource creation or when dependencies are not automatically inferred.

It's worth noting that while Terraform manages dependencies effectively, you should still follow best practices for designing your infrastructure configurations to minimize complex dependencies and improve readability.

Complex dependency chains can make your configurations harder to understand and maintain.

By keeping your configurations organized and dependencies straightforward, you can create more manageable and maintainable IaC.

In summary, managing resource dependencies is a critical aspect of Terraform configuration, ensuring that resources are created or modified in the correct order to maintain a consistent and functioning infrastructure.

Terraform infers dependencies based on attribute references, and you can also define dependencies explicitly using the **depends_on** meta-argument.

Understanding and correctly defining resource dependencies is essential for building reliable and predictable infrastructure configurations.

By following best practices and keeping your configurations organized, you can create more manageable and maintainable infrastructure as code.

Chapter 6: Terraform Modules and Reusability

Modularizing your infrastructure in Terraform is a fundamental practice that promotes maintainability, reusability, and scalability in your infrastructure as code (IaC) projects.

Modularization involves breaking down your Terraform configurations into smaller, self-contained units called modules, which encapsulate specific functionality or resources.

Modules allow you to build complex infrastructure by composing and reusing these smaller units, creating a more organized and manageable IaC codebase.

One of the primary motivations for modularizing your infrastructure is to enhance code reusability.

By encapsulating a particular piece of infrastructure logic or resource configuration into a module, you can reuse that module across multiple projects or environments.

This reusability reduces duplication of code and promotes consistency in your infrastructure across different contexts.

Another advantage of modularization is improved maintainability.

When your infrastructure is divided into smaller, focused modules, each module becomes easier to understand, test, and update.

Modifications or improvements to a specific piece of infrastructure can be isolated to the corresponding module, reducing the risk of unintended side effects in other parts of your code.

Modularization also promotes collaboration within your team or organization.

Teams can work on individual modules independently, making it easier to manage infrastructure changes in parallel.

Additionally, modules can be shared and maintained centrally, ensuring that everyone benefits from improvements and updates.

To create a module, you define a separate directory containing Terraform configuration files, typically organized around a specific resource or functionality.

A module directory should have a descriptive name that reflects its purpose, making it easy to identify and understand its role within your infrastructure.

Inside the module directory, you place the necessary Terraform configuration files, including a root module configuration file and any supporting files or submodules.

The root module configuration file typically defines input variables, resource blocks, and any outputs that the module provides to users.

For example, if you were creating a module for an AWS Virtual Private Cloud (VPC), your module directory might contain files like **main.tf, variables.tf**, and **outputs.tf**.

The **main.tf** file would define the VPC resource and its configuration, while **variables.tf** would specify the input variables that users can customize when using the module.

The **outputs.tf** file would declare any values that the module exposes for consumption by other parts of your infrastructure code.

To use a module, you reference it in your main Terraform configuration by specifying its source location.

The source location can be a local file path or a remote source, such as a Git repository or a Terraform Registry module.

Using modules can be as simple as referencing them in your configuration and providing values for their input variables.

For example, to use the previously mentioned VPC module, you might include the following code in your main configuration: hclCopy code

```
module "my_vpc" { source = "./modules/vpc" cidr_block = "10.0.0.0/16" region = "us-east-1" }
```

In this example, you reference the **vpc** module located in the **./modules/vpc** directory and provide values for its input variables **cidr_block** and **region**.

Modules can also have outputs that allow you to retrieve information or attributes from the module for use in other parts of your configuration.

For example, the VPC module might define an output for the VPC's ID, which you can reference in other resource blocks or modules.

Modularization is not limited to individual resources; you can also create higher-level modules that encapsulate entire sections of your infrastructure.

For instance, you might create a "web-service" module that includes resources for an AWS EC2 instance, an Elastic Load Balancer, and a security group.

This higher-level module abstracts the details of the underlying resources, providing a simplified interface for deploying a web service.

When designing your modules, consider providing clear documentation and examples to make it easy for users to understand how to use them effectively.

Documentation should explain the purpose of the module, its input variables, and any outputs it provides.

Examples can demonstrate common use cases and best practices for using the module in different scenarios.

In summary, modularizing your infrastructure in Terraform is a valuable practice for creating maintainable, reusable, and scalable infrastructure as code.

Modules allow you to encapsulate specific functionality or resources, promoting code reusability, improving maintainability, and enabling collaboration.

When creating modules, strive for clear organization, provide meaningful documentation, and offer practical examples to help users leverage your modules effectively.

By adopting modularization best practices, you can build and manage complex infrastructure configurations with confidence and efficiency.

Creating and using Terraform modules is a powerful approach to modularizing your infrastructure as code (IaC) and promoting code reusability, consistency, and maintainability.
Modules allow you to encapsulate specific infrastructure components or configurations into reusable units that can be shared across different projects or environments.
When you create a module, you essentially define a template for a particular piece of infrastructure, making it easier to replicate and maintain.
The process of creating and using Terraform modules involves several key steps, each of which contributes to the effective organization and management of your IaC.
The first step in working with Terraform modules is to define the module itself.
A Terraform module is essentially a collection of Terraform configuration files organized within a directory.
This directory should have a clear and descriptive name that reflects the purpose or functionality of the module.
Inside the module directory, you typically include at least three types of files: the main module configuration, variable definitions, and output definitions.
The main module configuration file, often named **main.tf**, contains the actual Terraform code that defines the infrastructure components and their configurations.
Variables are essential components of Terraform modules.
They allow you to pass information and customize the module's behavior when you use it in different contexts.
In your module directory, you define variables in a file commonly named **variables.tf**.
These variables can have default values, descriptions, and constraints to ensure they are used correctly.

197

Output definitions, which reside in a file like **outputs.tf**, specify the values that the module should make available to its users after it's applied.

Outputs are particularly useful for exposing specific attributes or resource identifiers for further use in your infrastructure.

Once you have defined your Terraform module, you can use it in your main Terraform configuration.

To use a module, you reference it in your configuration by specifying its source location.

The source location can be a local relative path to the module directory or a remote source, such as a Git repository or a Terraform Registry module.

When you reference a module, you provide values for its input variables, effectively configuring the module's behavior for your specific use case.

For example, if you have a module for creating an AWS Virtual Private Cloud (VPC), you might reference it in your main configuration like this:

hclCopy code

```
module "my_vpc" { source = "./modules/vpc" cidr_block =
"10.0.0.0/16" region = "us-east-1" }
```

In this example, you reference the **vpc** module located in the **./modules/vpc** directory and set values for its input variables **cidr_block** and **region**.

The module's configuration takes these values and uses them to create the VPC with the specified CIDR block and region.

As you use modules in your Terraform configuration, you can pass variables and output values between modules and the main configuration.

This allows you to create complex infrastructure setups by composing and connecting different modules.

By carefully designing your modules and their interfaces (input variables and outputs), you can create a modular architecture that promotes maintainability and reusability.

Furthermore, Terraform modules can be versioned and shared, which makes it easier for teams to collaborate and maintain a consistent infrastructure.

When using remote sources for modules, like those from the Terraform Registry, you can specify version constraints to ensure that your infrastructure remains stable and reliable.

Modules can also include documentation and examples to help users understand how to use them effectively.

Documentation should explain the purpose of the module, provide details on input variables, and describe the outputs it provides.

Examples demonstrate how to use the module in different scenarios and showcase best practices.

By following modularization best practices, providing clear documentation, and creating useful examples, you make it easier for your team or community to work with your modules.

In summary, creating and using Terraform modules is a key practice for building maintainable, reusable, and scalable infrastructure as code.

Modules encapsulate specific infrastructure components or configurations, allowing you to share and replicate them across projects and environments.

With a well-organized module structure, clear variable and output definitions, and thoughtful documentation, you can streamline the creation and management of complex infrastructure while promoting collaboration and code consistency.

Chapter 7: Collaboration and Version Control

Collaborative workflows are essential for successful infrastructure as code (IaC) projects, enabling multiple team members to work together efficiently on provisioning, managing, and evolving infrastructure resources.

In a collaborative IaC environment, team members collaborate on defining, deploying, and maintaining infrastructure using shared practices, tools, and processes.

This collaboration fosters increased productivity, better resource management, and a higher degree of code quality and reliability.

Effective collaboration starts with version control, which provides a central repository for storing and tracking changes to your IaC code.

Version control systems, such as Git, enable multiple team members to work on the same codebase simultaneously, while keeping track of changes and allowing for easy rollbacks if needed.

By using branches and pull requests, team members can work on separate features or fixes independently and then merge their changes into the main codebase when they are ready.

This approach helps prevent conflicts and ensures that changes are thoroughly reviewed and tested before becoming a part of the infrastructure.

Collaboration is also facilitated by consistent coding standards and conventions.

By defining and following a set of coding guidelines, team members can create IaC code that is more readable, maintainable, and consistent.

This consistency is especially valuable when multiple team members are working on the same codebase, as it reduces confusion and the likelihood of introducing errors.

Continuous integration (CI) and continuous delivery (CD) pipelines play a crucial role in collaborative IaC workflows.

CI/CD pipelines automate the testing, validation, and deployment of infrastructure code changes, ensuring that new code is thoroughly tested and integrated into the existing infrastructure.

With CI/CD, team members can confidently make changes to the infrastructure code, knowing that their updates will be automatically validated and deployed without manual intervention.

Collaborative workflows also benefit from the use of infrastructure as code (IaC) testing and validation tools.

Tools like Terraform's built-in validation checks, linters, and static analysis tools help ensure that code adheres to best practices and avoids common errors.

These tools provide immediate feedback to developers, allowing them to catch issues early in the development process.

Another essential aspect of collaborative workflows is documentation.

Clear and comprehensive documentation helps team members understand how to use and contribute to the infrastructure codebase.

Documentation should cover everything from setting up the development environment to describing coding standards, module usage, and deployment procedures.

Effective collaboration also involves role-based access control (RBAC) and permission management.

RBAC allows you to assign different levels of access and permissions to team members based on their roles and responsibilities.

This ensures that team members can only modify and deploy infrastructure code that is relevant to their tasks, reducing the risk of unauthorized changes.

Collaborative workflows benefit from the use of versioned modules and libraries.

By creating reusable modules and libraries, teams can share common infrastructure patterns and components, reducing duplication of effort and promoting consistency across projects. Versioning these modules ensures that changes made in one project do not affect the stability of other projects that depend on them.

When using remote modules from sources like the Terraform Registry, teams can leverage the latest improvements and bug fixes without manually updating their codebase.

Collaboration extends beyond code to the actual deployment and management of infrastructure resources.

Infrastructure should be provisioned and managed through automated processes that can be triggered by changes in the code repository.

These automated processes should follow standardized workflows that include thorough testing and validation.

Teams can use infrastructure as code (IaC) testing frameworks and automated testing suites to validate the infrastructure's correctness and reliability before deploying it to production environments.

Collaboration also involves regular communication and feedback loops among team members.

Regular meetings, code reviews, and retrospectives help identify areas for improvement, resolve issues, and ensure that everyone is aligned on project goals and priorities.

Effective collaboration in IaC projects requires a culture of shared responsibility, transparency, and continuous improvement.

Team members should be encouraged to take ownership of their code, contribute to documentation, and actively participate in code reviews and discussions.

In summary, collaborative workflows are essential for successful infrastructure as code (IaC) projects.

These workflows involve version control, coding standards, continuous integration and continuous delivery (CI/CD), testing and validation, documentation, role-based access control (RBAC), versioned modules, automated processes, and effective communication.

By adopting these practices and tools, teams can work together efficiently to provision, manage, and evolve infrastructure resources while maintaining code quality and reliability. Using version control with Terraform is a crucial practice for managing infrastructure as code (IaC) projects effectively, allowing teams to collaborate, track changes, and maintain a clear history of their infrastructure configurations. Version control systems, such as Git, provide a centralized repository where you can store and manage your Terraform code, ensuring that all team members have access to the latest codebase. By leveraging version control, teams can work on infrastructure code collaboratively, enabling multiple team members to make changes simultaneously without risking code conflicts. One of the primary benefits of version control is the ability to create branches. Branches allow team members to work on separate features or bug fixes independently, keeping the main codebase stable. Branches can be created for specific tasks, features, or bug fixes, and once completed, changes from a branch can be merged into the main codebase.

This branching strategy promotes parallel development, enabling the team to make progress on multiple fronts simultaneously. Furthermore, version control systems enable code reviews, a crucial aspect of ensuring code quality and correctness. Team members can review each other's changes by creating pull requests or merge requests, depending on the version control system used. Code reviews provide an opportunity to catch errors, share knowledge, and ensure that code adheres to coding standards and best practices.

Code reviewers can provide feedback, suggest improvements, and discuss any concerns before changes are merged.

Additionally, version control systems maintain a complete history of changes made to the codebase.

This historical record includes information about who made each change, when it was made, and what changes were made.

This traceability is valuable for tracking down issues, understanding the evolution of the codebase, and auditing changes.

Git, a widely-used version control system, offers a branching model that aligns well with Terraform development.

The "main" branch represents the stable production codebase, while feature branches, bug fix branches, or other task-specific branches are used for development.

Git also supports the concept of tags, which can be used to mark specific releases or versions of your Terraform configurations.

Tags make it easy to identify and revert to known, stable states of your infrastructure.

In addition to the benefits of version control itself, Terraform's design is well-suited for integration with version control systems.

Terraform configuration files are typically written in HashiCorp Configuration Language (HCL), which is human-readable and easy to track changes for in version control.

When changes are made to Terraform configurations, they can be committed to version control along with descriptive commit messages, providing context about the changes being made.

Commit messages should be meaningful and concise, summarizing the purpose and impact of the changes.

This practice helps team members understand the reasons behind code changes and facilitates efficient code reviews.

Furthermore, Terraform allows you to use variables and parameterize your configurations, making it possible to create templates that can be reused across different environments or projects.

By storing variables and parameterized configurations in version control, teams can maintain consistency across their infrastructure deployments while customizing configurations for specific needs.

Infrastructure as code (IaC) projects often involve multiple environments, such as development, staging, and production.

Version control systems allow teams to manage separate branches or repositories for each environment, ensuring that each environment has its own version-controlled configuration.

This separation helps prevent accidental changes to production configurations and promotes controlled deployments.

In addition to version control, Terraform itself provides features for managing state files, which store information about the resources provisioned by Terraform.

State files are essential for tracking the actual state of your infrastructure.

Terraform state can also be stored in remote backends, such as Amazon S3, Azure Blob Storage, or HashiCorp Consul.

Using remote state backends ensures that your Terraform state is stored securely and is accessible to the entire team, no matter where they are located.

When multiple team members work on the same Terraform project, remote state backends facilitate collaboration by centralizing the state information.

Overall, using version control with Terraform is a fundamental practice for modern infrastructure as code projects.

It allows teams to collaborate efficiently, track changes, review code, and maintain a clear history of their infrastructure configurations.

By integrating Terraform with version control systems like Git and adopting best practices for commit messages, branching strategies, and code reviews, teams can work together seamlessly to manage and evolve their infrastructure with confidence and control.

Chapter 8: Extending Terraform Capabilities

Custom providers and plugins are powerful extensions to Terraform that enable you to manage resources in cloud providers or services that are not supported out of the box.

While Terraform includes a wide range of built-in providers for popular cloud platforms like AWS, Azure, and Google Cloud, there are countless other services and platforms that may require custom integration.

Custom providers and plugins fill this gap by allowing you to define your own resource types and configurations, giving you the flexibility to manage infrastructure resources tailored to your specific needs.

One of the key advantages of Terraform's extensibility is the ability to manage any resource that has an API.

This means you can use custom providers and plugins to provision and manage resources in virtually any environment, from legacy systems to cutting-edge technologies.

Custom providers and plugins can be written in various programming languages, including Go and Python, depending on your preferences and requirements.

This flexibility allows you to choose the language that best suits your team's skills and the needs of your integration.

To create a custom provider or plugin, you typically start by defining a Terraform provider schema.

The schema specifies the resource types, data sources, and configurations that your provider or plugin will support.

Resource types define the infrastructure resources you want to manage, such as virtual machines, databases, or storage buckets.

Data sources allow you to query external systems for information that can be used in your Terraform configurations.

Configurations define the settings and options for your provider or plugin.

Once you have defined the schema, you can implement the provider or plugin's logic, which includes the functionality to create, read, update, and delete resources.

You also need to handle resource dependencies, error handling, and authentication mechanisms, depending on the requirements of the integration.

Terraform's plugin SDK provides a set of tools and libraries to simplify the development of custom providers and plugins.

These tools include functions for managing state, generating Terraform configurations, and handling resource CRUD operations.

The SDK also provides a framework for handling Terraform lifecycle events, such as initialization, planning, and applying changes.

To distribute your custom provider or plugin, you can package it as a binary or as a shared library that Terraform can load dynamically.

Distributing your custom provider or plugin allows you to share it with others in your organization or with the broader Terraform community.

You can publish your custom provider or plugin to the Terraform Registry, making it easy for users to discover and install it.

The Terraform Registry is a central repository for Terraform providers, modules, and plugins, providing a seamless way for users to find and install extensions.

By publishing your custom provider or plugin to the Terraform Registry, you enable others to benefit from your work and contribute to its development.

Terraform's provider development ecosystem is robust, with many community-contributed providers and plugins available for a wide range of services and platforms.

These community providers and plugins can save you time and effort by providing pre-built integrations for popular services.

You can discover community providers and plugins by exploring the Terraform Registry or by searching on platforms like GitHub.

In addition to creating custom providers and plugins, Terraform allows you to extend existing providers with data sources and resource configurations tailored to your needs.

This means you can build on top of existing providers to create specialized abstractions or configurations that simplify the management of complex resources.

For example, if you are using an existing cloud provider's Terraform provider, you can create custom configurations that encapsulate best practices or security policies for your organization.

These custom configurations can be shared within your team or organization to ensure consistent and compliant infrastructure deployments.

When working with custom providers and plugins, it's important to consider best practices for testing and maintaining your extensions.

Unit tests, integration tests, and end-to-end tests are essential to verify that your provider or plugin behaves correctly and reliably.

Continuous integration (CI) pipelines can automate the testing and validation of your extensions, ensuring that changes do not introduce regressions or break existing configurations.

Furthermore, documentation is crucial for users of your custom provider or plugin.

Clear and comprehensive documentation helps users understand how to install, configure, and use your extension effectively.

Documentation should cover installation instructions, usage examples, and troubleshooting guidance.

By providing thorough documentation, you make it easier for users to adopt and contribute to your custom provider or plugin.

When developing custom providers and plugins, it's essential to follow Terraform's versioning and compatibility guidelines.

Terraform providers and plugins have version constraints to ensure compatibility with different Terraform versions.

By adhering to these guidelines, you ensure that your extensions can be used with a wide range of Terraform releases.

In summary, custom providers and plugins are valuable tools for extending Terraform's capabilities and managing infrastructure resources beyond what is natively supported.

They enable you to integrate with external services, manage specialized resources, and customize configurations to meet the unique requirements of your infrastructure.

By following best practices for development, testing, documentation, and versioning, you can create custom extensions that enhance the power and flexibility of Terraform for your organization and the broader Terraform community.

Extending Terraform with external tools is a strategy employed by organizations and developers to enhance the capabilities of Terraform and streamline their infrastructure management workflows.

Terraform is a powerful infrastructure as code (IaC) tool that allows users to define and provision infrastructure resources using declarative configuration files.

While Terraform provides extensive functionality for resource provisioning, it may not cover all the requirements of a complex infrastructure environment.

In such cases, external tools and integrations can be used to fill the gaps and extend Terraform's functionality.

One common approach to extending Terraform is by using provisioning tools such as Ansible, Puppet, or Chef in conjunction with Terraform.

These configuration management tools are well-suited for tasks like software installation, configuration, and orchestration, which may not be the primary focus of Terraform.

By combining Terraform and configuration management tools, users can achieve a holistic approach to infrastructure provisioning and configuration.

For example, Terraform can be used to create the underlying infrastructure components such as virtual machines and networks, while Ansible can configure those virtual machines with the necessary software and services.

This collaboration between Terraform and external tools allows for a more comprehensive infrastructure automation solution.

Another way to extend Terraform is by leveraging cloud-native services and APIs directly in Terraform configurations.

Many cloud providers offer specialized services that can be managed using Terraform configurations.

For example, AWS offers services like Amazon RDS (Relational Database Service), Amazon S3 (Simple Storage Service), and Amazon ECS (Elastic Container Service), which can be provisioned and managed through Terraform.

By integrating these cloud-native services into Terraform configurations, users can take advantage of the full range of capabilities offered by the cloud provider without relying on external tools.

Furthermore, Terraform supports the use of data sources, which allow users to query external systems and retrieve information to be used in their configurations.

This feature enables Terraform to interact with existing infrastructure or services, even if they are not directly managed by Terraform.

For instance, Terraform can use data sources to retrieve information from a configuration management database

(CMDB) or a monitoring system to dynamically adapt its configurations based on real-time data.

Using external tools in conjunction with Terraform can also help address challenges related to secrets management and security.

Many organizations use external tools like HashiCorp Vault or AWS Secrets Manager to securely manage and distribute secrets, such as API keys and credentials.

Integrating Terraform with these tools ensures that sensitive information is handled securely and can be injected into Terraform configurations when needed.

This approach reduces the risk of exposing sensitive data in configuration files and simplifies the management of secrets.

Furthermore, external tools can aid in the automation of compliance and security checks.

Tools like HashiCorp Sentinel or InSpec can be used to define and enforce compliance policies and security standards.

By incorporating these tools into the Terraform workflow, organizations can automatically validate their infrastructure configurations against predefined policies and standards.

This proactive approach to compliance helps ensure that infrastructure deployments adhere to best practices and security requirements.

Additionally, organizations can extend Terraform by integrating it with continuous integration and continuous deployment (CI/CD) pipelines.

CI/CD pipelines automate the testing, validation, and deployment of Terraform configurations.

They can be configured to trigger Terraform runs whenever changes are made to the infrastructure codebase.

This automation ensures that any updates or modifications to infrastructure configurations are thoroughly tested before being deployed to production environments.

By integrating Terraform into CI/CD pipelines, organizations can achieve a higher degree of consistency, reliability, and agility in their infrastructure management practices.

Furthermore, Terraform can be extended with custom scripts and scripts written in programming languages like Python, Ruby, or Go.

These scripts can be executed as part of Terraform configurations, allowing users to perform custom actions or implement specific logic during provisioning.

Custom scripts can interact with external APIs, perform data transformations, or execute advanced workflows that are not achievable with Terraform's native functionality alone.

Moreover, Terraform modules, which are reusable units of infrastructure code, can be considered a form of extension.

Modules can encapsulate complex configurations and resources, making them easier to reuse across projects and environments.

This modular approach streamlines infrastructure provisioning and promotes consistency.

In summary, extending Terraform with external tools is a valuable strategy for enhancing its capabilities and addressing specific infrastructure requirements.

By integrating Terraform with provisioning tools, cloud-native services, data sources, secrets management tools, compliance and security tools, CI/CD pipelines, custom scripts, and modular configurations, users can build comprehensive and efficient infrastructure automation solutions.

This approach enables organizations to achieve greater flexibility, security, and compliance in their infrastructure management workflows, while also promoting best practices and standardization.

Chapter 9: Debugging and Troubleshooting Techniques

Common errors and issues can arise during the use of Terraform, and understanding how to identify, troubleshoot, and resolve them is essential for successful infrastructure management.

One common error that users may encounter is related to Terraform configuration files.

It's important to ensure that your configuration files have the correct syntax and adhere to Terraform's HashiCorp Configuration Language (HCL) standards.

Syntax errors, missing or mismatched braces, or incorrect indentation can lead to configuration file parsing failures.

Terraform provides error messages with line numbers to help you pinpoint the location of the issue in your configuration.

Another common error occurs when Terraform is unable to find or authenticate with the required provider plugins.

Providers are essential for interacting with cloud platforms and services, and missing or outdated provider configurations can cause errors.

To resolve this issue, make sure that you have the correct provider versions installed and that your credentials are correctly configured in your Terraform environment.

When dealing with complex infrastructure configurations, it's common to encounter errors related to resource dependencies.

If a resource depends on another resource, Terraform will attempt to create them in the correct order.

However, circular dependencies or misconfigured dependencies can lead to issues where Terraform gets stuck in an infinite loop or fails to create resources in the correct order.

To resolve these errors, carefully review your resource configurations and dependencies to ensure they are correctly defined.

Another common error arises when Terraform state becomes out of sync with the actual infrastructure.

This can occur if resources are manually modified outside of Terraform, leading to a mismatch between the expected and actual resource states.

To address this issue, you can use Terraform's "terraform import" command to bring existing resources under Terraform management or manually update the state file to reflect the actual state.

State locking issues can also occur in multi-user environments where multiple users attempt to apply changes simultaneously.

Terraform provides a state locking mechanism to prevent concurrent state modifications, but if not properly configured, it can result in errors.

Ensure that you configure a state lock appropriately, whether it's using a local file lock, remote state backends, or a dedicated locking service like Amazon DynamoDB.

Resource conflicts can be a common issue when Terraform is used to manage resources with unique names or identifiers.

If two or more resources have the same name, Terraform will be unable to distinguish between them, leading to conflicts.

To address this, ensure that your resource naming conventions are consistent and that each resource has a unique name or identifier.

Dependency issues can also arise when working with modules or complex configurations.

Modules may have their own dependencies and configurations that need to be managed correctly.

Review the module documentation and ensure that you pass the required variables and dependencies correctly to avoid errors.

Provider-specific errors can occur when working with specific cloud providers or services.

Each provider has its own set of error codes and messages, and it's important to consult the provider's documentation to understand and resolve these issues.

Common provider-specific issues include rate limiting, API errors, and authentication failures.

Terraform's error messages often provide information about the specific error and how to resolve it.

Networking issues, such as connectivity problems or firewall rules blocking API calls, can also lead to errors when interacting with cloud providers.

Check your network configuration, security groups, and firewall rules to ensure that Terraform can communicate with the necessary APIs and services.

Credential-related errors, such as expired or incorrect access keys, can prevent Terraform from authenticating with cloud providers.

Review and update your credentials to ensure they are valid and up-to-date.

Resource limit exceeded errors can occur when attempting to create too many resources within a cloud provider's limits.

Check the provider's documentation for resource limits and consider optimizing your configurations to stay within those limits.

Terraform plan errors can arise when running the "terraform plan" command.

These errors typically indicate issues with the configuration, dependencies, or resource definitions.

Carefully review the plan output and error messages to identify and address the underlying problems.

User and permission-related errors can occur when the user running Terraform lacks the necessary permissions to create or modify resources.

Ensure that the user or service account has the appropriate IAM or RBAC permissions to perform the desired actions.

Lastly, version compatibility issues can arise when using different versions of Terraform, providers, or plugins.

Make sure that your Terraform version, provider versions, and plugin versions are compatible with each other.

Upgrading or downgrading versions may be necessary to resolve compatibility issues.

In summary, common errors and issues in Terraform can range from syntax errors in configuration files to provider-specific errors, resource dependency problems, and networking issues.

Understanding the nature of these errors and knowing how to troubleshoot and resolve them is crucial for maintaining a smooth Terraform workflow.

By carefully reviewing error messages, consulting documentation, and following best practices, users can effectively identify and mitigate common errors, ensuring the successful management of infrastructure as code with Terraform.

Troubleshooting Terraform workflows is an essential skill for infrastructure as code (IaC) practitioners, as it helps identify and resolve issues that may arise during the provisioning and management of infrastructure.

Terraform provides various tools, techniques, and best practices to diagnose and address problems effectively.

One of the first steps in troubleshooting Terraform is to thoroughly review the error messages and output generated by Terraform commands.

These messages often provide valuable information about the nature and location of the issue.

By carefully examining the error messages, users can gain insights into what went wrong and where to focus their efforts.

Furthermore, Terraform offers a "terraform plan" command that allows users to preview changes before applying them.

Reviewing the plan output can help identify issues in resource creation, modification, or destruction, allowing users to catch potential problems before they impact the infrastructure.

If the error message does not provide sufficient information to diagnose the issue, users can enable more detailed logging using the "TF_LOG" environment variable.

Setting "TF_LOG" to a higher level, such as "DEBUG" or "TRACE," will generate detailed logs that can be instrumental in pinpointing the cause of errors.

When troubleshooting Terraform workflows, it's essential to verify that the Terraform configuration files are correctly written and free of syntax errors.

One common issue is missing or mismatched braces, parentheses, or quotes, which can lead to parsing errors.

Using a code editor with syntax highlighting can help identify and correct syntax errors in real-time.

Additionally, running the "terraform validate" command can check the syntax of configuration files without applying changes.

Another valuable tool for troubleshooting Terraform configurations is the "terraform fmt" command, which automatically formats configuration files according to Terraform's coding standards.

This can help resolve issues related to inconsistent formatting or indentation.

Terraform state is a critical component of the Terraform workflow, as it tracks the current state of infrastructure resources.

Issues related to Terraform state can lead to problems such as resource conflicts, divergence between desired and actual states, or difficulties in resource management.

To troubleshoot Terraform state issues, users can use the "terraform state" command to inspect and manipulate state information.

For example, "terraform state list" lists all resources in the state, "terraform state show" displays detailed information about a specific resource, and "terraform state mv" allows users to move resources within the state.

In some cases, Terraform may report a resource as "tainted," indicating that it needs to be destroyed and recreated.

The "terraform taint" command can be used to manually mark a resource as tainted, and then "terraform apply" can be run to recreate it.

Another common source of issues is resource dependency problems.

Terraform relies on resource dependencies to determine the order in which resources should be created or modified.

If dependencies are not correctly defined, Terraform may attempt to create resources in the wrong order or encounter circular dependencies.

To troubleshoot dependency issues, users can review resource configurations and verify that the "depends_on" attribute is used correctly.

Users can also use the "terraform graph" command to visualize the dependency graph and identify any irregularities.

Additionally, when using modules in Terraform configurations, users should ensure that modules and their dependencies are correctly defined and passed the required variables.

Resource conflicts, where resources have duplicate names or identifiers, can also lead to errors in Terraform workflows.

Users should review resource naming conventions and ensure that each resource has a unique name or identifier to avoid conflicts.

When troubleshooting network-related issues, users should verify that the infrastructure allows communication between Terraform and the target cloud provider's APIs.

Firewall rules, security groups, or network configurations can sometimes block API calls, leading to errors.

Checking network connectivity and reviewing firewall rules can help resolve these issues.

Credential-related errors, such as expired or incorrect access keys, can prevent Terraform from authenticating with cloud providers.

Users should ensure that their credentials are valid and properly configured in their Terraform environment.

Resource limit exceeded errors can occur when attempting to create too many resources within a cloud provider's limits.

Users should check the provider's documentation for resource limits and optimize their configurations to stay within those limits.

When troubleshooting provider-specific errors, users should consult the documentation of the specific provider for guidance on error codes and messages.

Provider-specific issues may include rate limiting, API errors, or authentication failures.

Additionally, some issues may be related to the specific version of Terraform or the provider being used.

Users should ensure that their Terraform version, provider versions, and plugin versions are compatible with each other.

Upgrading or downgrading versions may be necessary to resolve compatibility issues.

Collaborative workflows with Terraform may introduce concurrency issues when multiple users or automation processes attempt to apply changes simultaneously.

To prevent concurrent state modifications, users can configure state locking mechanisms, such as local file locks, remote state backends, or dedicated locking services like Amazon DynamoDB.

Additionally, using continuous integration and continuous deployment (CI/CD) pipelines can help automate testing and validation of Terraform configurations, reducing the risk of errors in production environments.

Finally, Terraform users can engage with the Terraform community through forums, discussion boards, and chat channels to seek help and advice when troubleshooting complex issues.

Community members and experts often share insights, solutions, and best practices for resolving common and uncommon problems.

In summary, troubleshooting Terraform workflows involves a systematic approach to identifying and resolving issues related to configuration, state, dependencies, resources, and provider-specific challenges.

By leveraging Terraform's built-in tools, logging, and commands, users can effectively diagnose and address errors, ensuring the reliability and correctness of their infrastructure as code deployments.

Chapter 10: Becoming a Terraform CLI Ninja

Advanced CLI commands and tips are valuable for experienced users looking to enhance their Terraform workflow and streamline infrastructure management tasks.

Terraform offers a rich set of command-line capabilities to help users become more efficient and effective in managing their infrastructure as code.

One advanced CLI command is "terraform import," which allows users to import existing resources into their Terraform state.

This can be particularly useful when transitioning from manual infrastructure management to Terraform, as it enables users to start managing existing resources using Terraform configurations.

To use "terraform import," users need to provide the resource type and the resource's unique identifier, and Terraform will fetch the resource's current state and add it to the Terraform state file.

The "terraform import" command can help maintain consistency and traceability in infrastructure management.

Another powerful CLI feature is the ability to specify variables and values directly on the command line using the "-var" flag.

This allows users to override variable values defined in their Terraform configuration files without modifying the source code.

For example, "terraform apply -var 'instance_type=t2.micro'" lets users specify the instance type at runtime.

This flexibility is handy for testing and debugging configurations without changing the underlying code.

When working with large and complex infrastructure, users may find it challenging to keep track of resource dependencies.

The "terraform graph" command can generate a visual representation of the dependency graph, making it easier to understand the relationships between resources.

Users can visualize the graph by piping the output of "terraform graph" to a tool like Graphviz, which produces graphical representations of the infrastructure.

This visual representation aids in identifying circular dependencies, resource order, and potential issues in the configuration.

Terraform allows users to work with multiple environments or workspaces within a single configuration.

The "terraform workspace" command is used to create, list, and switch between workspaces.

By creating separate workspaces for development, staging, and production environments, users can maintain isolated configurations and state files, reducing the risk of accidentally affecting other environments.

When working with remote state storage backends, it's essential to manage and protect sensitive data securely.

The "terraform state" command provides features for encrypting and locking state files when stored remotely.

Users can enable state locking to prevent concurrent modifications, ensuring the integrity of the state data.

Additionally, encrypting state files can protect sensitive information such as secrets and credentials.

Terraform's extensibility is a valuable feature for advanced users who want to customize and automate their workflows further.

The "terraform init" command can be enhanced with backend configurations specified in a separate backend configuration file (backend.tf).

This allows users to define remote state storage, locking, and encryption settings, making it easier to share configurations across teams.

Users can create their own custom providers and plugins to extend Terraform's functionality beyond the built-in providers.

Custom providers are implemented in Go and can interact with any API or service, giving users the flexibility to manage resources not supported by official Terraform providers.

Furthermore, custom plugins can be developed to add custom functionality, enabling users to automate tasks specific to their infrastructure requirements.

Terraform's ability to handle remote state and collaborate with teams is a powerful feature, but it also introduces challenges related to state locking and management.

Advanced users can configure remote state backends like Amazon S3, Azure Blob Storage, or HashiCorp Terraform Cloud for secure and scalable state storage.

These backends offer features such as versioning, locking, and access control, making it easier to manage state in a team setting.

Terraform offers a set of lifecycle hooks that allow users to execute custom scripts or actions before or after specific Terraform operations.

Users can define pre- and post-operation hooks in their configurations to integrate Terraform with other tools, perform validations, or execute custom logic.

Lifecycle hooks provide automation and flexibility for advanced users seeking to enhance their Terraform workflows.

In a multi-environment or multi-team setup, it's essential to maintain consistency and standardization across configurations.

Terraform modules are a powerful way to encapsulate and reuse infrastructure code, making it easier to manage complex configurations.

Advanced users can create and share custom modules tailored to their organization's needs, promoting consistency and best practices across projects.

Error handling and debugging are crucial skills for advanced Terraform users.

When an error occurs during a Terraform operation, the "terraform apply" command provides a "detailed exit code" option that returns a non-zero exit code when errors are encountered.

This can be used in scripting or automation to trigger alerts or notifications when issues arise.

Advanced users can also utilize the "-target" flag with "terraform apply" to apply changes to specific resources, bypassing others.

This fine-grained control is useful when addressing isolated issues or when updating a specific part of the infrastructure.

Terraform's built-in functions and expressions provide advanced users with powerful tools for data manipulation and transformation within configurations.

Users can use functions like "map," "lookup," and "templatefile" to create dynamic and data-driven configurations.

These functions enable users to generate complex resource configurations based on variables and data sources, reducing redundancy and enhancing flexibility.

When managing infrastructure at scale, automating routine tasks and updates becomes critical.

Advanced users can utilize CI/CD pipelines and automation tools to integrate Terraform into their deployment workflows.

This enables automated testing, validation, and deployment of Terraform configurations, reducing manual intervention and ensuring consistency in deployments.

Terraform's remote state data source allows advanced users to query and retrieve information from the Terraform state of other configurations.

This feature is particularly useful when configuring cross-resource dependencies or dynamically generating configurations based on information from other environments.

To summarize, advanced CLI commands and tips in Terraform empower experienced users to optimize their infrastructure management processes.

From resource importation to variable overrides, from dependency visualization to secure state management, Terraform's CLI capabilities provide the flexibility and extensibility needed to tackle complex infrastructure challenges.

Custom providers, lifecycle hooks, and module creation offer advanced users the tools to tailor their Terraform workflows to meet their organization's specific needs.

Error handling, scripting, and automation further streamline operations, while Terraform's built-in functions and expressions enable dynamic, data-driven configurations.

By mastering these advanced CLI commands and tips, users can achieve greater efficiency, consistency, and scalability in their infrastructure as code deployments.

Automating workflows with CLI scripts is a fundamental aspect of efficient infrastructure management, as it enables users to streamline repetitive tasks, enforce best practices, and ensure consistency in their operations.

CLI scripts, written in scripting languages such as Bash, PowerShell, or Python, can interact with Terraform commands and APIs, offering advanced users the ability to create customized automation tailored to their specific needs.

One of the primary benefits of using CLI scripts with Terraform is the ability to automate the process of provisioning and managing infrastructure.

By creating scripts that encapsulate common Terraform workflows, users can reduce manual intervention, minimize the risk of human errors, and accelerate the deployment of resources.

For instance, a simple Bash script can automate the process of initializing a Terraform project, applying configurations, and storing state files in a designated location, all with a single command.

Automation scripts can also enforce coding standards and best practices across teams by performing code validations before applying changes.

These validations can include checks for syntax errors, code formatting, and adherence to naming conventions.

By embedding these checks into the automation process, organizations can ensure that Terraform configurations are consistently well-structured and error-free.

Another critical aspect of automating workflows with CLI scripts is the ability to manage and protect sensitive data, such as secrets, API keys, and credentials.

Advanced users can utilize secure methods like environment variables or secrets management tools to store and access sensitive information.

Automation scripts can then retrieve these secrets securely and inject them into Terraform configurations at runtime, eliminating the need to store sensitive data in configuration files.

This approach enhances security and compliance by reducing the exposure of sensitive information.

When working in complex environments with multiple Terraform configurations and dependencies, orchestrating the execution of Terraform commands across different projects and workspaces can be challenging.

CLI scripts can simplify this orchestration by creating automation workflows that ensure the correct order of execution.

For example, a script can be designed to apply changes to dependent configurations before updating resources in the main project, avoiding issues related to resource dependencies and order of execution.

Moreover, CLI scripts can integrate Terraform with version control systems (VCS) and CI/CD pipelines, allowing for continuous integration and deployment of infrastructure as code.

By automating the process of pulling configuration changes from a VCS repository and triggering Terraform workflows, organizations can achieve a streamlined, automated deployment pipeline.

Automation scripts can also facilitate the creation and management of multiple Terraform workspaces, enabling users to maintain separate environments for development, testing, staging, and production.

Scripts can automate the process of creating, switching, and destroying workspaces, making it easier to manage isolated configurations and state files for different environments.

When it comes to managing state files, automation scripts can be used to store state remotely in secure backends, such as Amazon S3 or HashiCorp Terraform Cloud.

By automating the configuration of remote state backends, users can ensure that state data is securely stored, versioned, and protected against concurrent modifications.

Additionally, automation scripts can facilitate the backup and recovery of state files, ensuring that critical infrastructure data is safeguarded against loss or corruption.

Advanced users can leverage CLI scripts to automate resource tagging and labeling, which is essential for tracking and organizing resources in cloud environments.

Automation scripts can add or update tags on resources based on predefined criteria or metadata, simplifying resource management and cost allocation.

Moreover, CLI scripts can integrate with cloud provider APIs to retrieve resource information and apply tags dynamically.

When dealing with the scale and complexity of modern infrastructure, monitoring and logging are vital for tracking changes, diagnosing issues, and maintaining visibility into the state of resources.

Automation scripts can be configured to trigger monitoring and logging actions, such as sending notifications when specific events occur or aggregating log data for analysis.

By automating these tasks, organizations can proactively detect and address issues, ensuring the health and reliability of their infrastructure.

To enhance collaboration and communication within teams, automation scripts can also be used to generate reports and documentation.

Scripts can extract information from Terraform configurations, state files, and remote backends to create documentation that outlines the current state of resources, dependencies, and changes.

This documentation can serve as a valuable resource for team members, auditors, and stakeholders.

In summary, automating workflows with CLI scripts is a powerful approach to managing infrastructure efficiently and consistently.

These scripts can automate provisioning, enforce best practices, protect sensitive data, and simplify the orchestration of complex Terraform configurations.

Automation also extends to integration with VCS, CI/CD pipelines, workspace management, state file storage, resource tagging, monitoring, and documentation generation.

By harnessing the capabilities of automation scripts, organizations can achieve greater agility, security, and control in their infrastructure management, ultimately enhancing the reliability and scalability of their operations.

BOOK 4
TERRAFORM CLI BOSS
EXPERT-LEVEL COMMANDS
UNLEASHED

ROB BOTWRIGHT

Chapter 1: Mastering Advanced Terraform CLI Techniques

Advanced CLI commands in Terraform provide experienced users with powerful tools to manage and manipulate infrastructure as code efficiently and effectively.

These commands go beyond the basics and allow users to perform complex operations, fine-tune configurations, and optimize their workflow.

One of the essential advanced CLI commands is "terraform plan," which provides a detailed preview of the changes that Terraform intends to make to the infrastructure.

This command is indispensable for understanding the impact of configuration changes before applying them, helping users avoid unintended consequences and identify potential issues.

The "terraform plan" command displays a comprehensive list of resource creations, updates, and deletions, along with any associated dependencies.

By reviewing this plan, users can ensure that the intended changes align with their infrastructure goals and requirements.

Additionally, the "terraform plan" command supports various options, such as specifying a specific configuration file or an output format suitable for automation or integration into CI/CD pipelines.

For users who want to validate their configurations without making changes, the "terraform validate" command is a valuable tool.

This command checks the syntax and structure of Terraform configuration files, ensuring that they adhere to HCL (HashiCorp Configuration Language) standards.

By running "terraform validate" before applying changes, users can catch errors early in the development process and maintain clean, error-free configurations.

Advanced users can also leverage the "terraform graph" command to visualize the dependency graph of their Terraform configuration.

This graphical representation provides a clear view of how resources are interconnected and dependent on one another.

Understanding the dependency graph is essential for managing complex infrastructures, as it helps users identify potential bottlenecks, circular dependencies, and opportunities for optimization.

By piping the output of "terraform graph" into a visualization tool like Graphviz, users can generate diagrams that make it easier to comprehend the relationships between resources.

For users dealing with large and intricate configurations, the "terraform show" command offers a detailed breakdown of the current state of the Terraform-managed infrastructure.

This command displays the current values of all resource attributes, making it a valuable tool for auditing and troubleshooting.

"terraform show" allows users to review the state of resources, examine attribute values, and ensure that the infrastructure matches their expectations.

Advanced users may find themselves working with Terraform configurations that span multiple directories and files.

In such cases, the "terraform workspace" command becomes essential for managing workspaces within a project.

Workspaces are isolated environments that allow users to switch between different sets of Terraform configurations and state files seamlessly.

By creating and switching between workspaces, users can maintain separate environments for development, testing, and production without duplicating configurations or state files.

The "terraform state" command offers advanced capabilities for inspecting and manipulating the Terraform state.

Users can use this command to inspect the attributes and dependencies of specific resources, making it easier to understand the current state of their infrastructure.

Additionally, the "terraform state" command can be used to move resources between Terraform state files, reimport resources, or manually update attribute values.

Advanced users may also need to tackle challenges related to resource-specific operations.

The "terraform import" command is designed for importing existing resources into the Terraform state.

By specifying the resource type and the resource's unique identifier, users can import resources into their Terraform state, allowing them to manage those resources using Terraform configurations.

This command is particularly useful when transitioning from manual infrastructure management to Terraform, as it allows users to bring existing resources under Terraform's management.

Advanced users often work in team environments where collaboration and concurrent changes to infrastructure are common.

To address potential conflicts, the "terraform state pull" and "terraform state push" commands enable users to synchronize their local Terraform state with a remote state backend.

These commands help maintain consistency and avoid conflicts when multiple team members are working on the same infrastructure.

For advanced users seeking to automate Terraform workflows, the "terraform init" command offers extensive options for initializing a configuration and configuring remote state backends.

This command can be enhanced with backend configurations specified in separate backend configuration files, making it easier to automate the setup of remote state storage, locking, and encryption.

Furthermore, the "terraform init" command can be customized to install and configure providers and plugins, streamlining the process of managing external dependencies.

When working with remote state backends, security and data protection are paramount.

Advanced users can leverage the "terraform state encrypt" and "terraform state decrypt" commands to encrypt sensitive data in the Terraform state file.

This ensures that critical information, such as secrets and credentials, remains secure when stored remotely.

The "terraform state lock" and "terraform state unlock" commands offer advanced users the ability to lock and unlock the Terraform state file to prevent concurrent modifications.

State locking ensures data integrity and prevents conflicts when multiple users or processes attempt to modify the state simultaneously.

To optimize the execution of Terraform configurations, advanced users can utilize the "terraform apply" command with the "-target" flag.

This flag allows users to apply changes to specific resources by specifying their resource addresses.

By selectively targeting resources, users can expedite the provisioning and updating of critical components without affecting unrelated resources.

Additionally, the "terraform apply" command can be combined with the "-auto-approve" flag to automate the confirmation step, making it suitable for non-interactive use in scripts and automation pipelines.

In summary, advanced CLI commands in Terraform empower experienced users to take control of their infrastructure management with precision and efficiency.

Commands like "terraform plan," "terraform validate," and "terraform graph" provide insights and validation for complex configurations.

Managing workspaces, inspecting the state, importing resources, and handling state locking are essential skills for collaborating effectively in team environments.

Automation is key, with "terraform init" offering extensive customization, while secure state management and resource targeting ensure smooth and secure operations.

By mastering these advanced CLI commands, users can harness the full potential of Terraform to efficiently and confidently manage their infrastructure as code.

CLI scripting and automation are integral components of a modern IT environment, allowing organizations to streamline operations, reduce manual tasks, and achieve greater efficiency.

At its core, CLI scripting involves writing and executing sequences of commands in a command-line interface to perform specific tasks, automate processes, or interact with various software and systems.

Automation, on the other hand, extends beyond scripting and encompasses the orchestration of workflows, the integration of disparate systems, and the elimination of repetitive, error-prone tasks.

When combined, CLI scripting and automation become powerful tools for IT professionals, enabling them to solve complex problems and manage infrastructure at scale.

CLI scripting typically begins with the selection of an appropriate scripting language, such as Bash, PowerShell, Python, or Ruby, depending on the specific requirements and existing ecosystem.

These languages provide a foundation for writing scripts that interact with command-line interfaces, execute system commands, parse output, and make decisions based on conditions.

For example, Bash scripts are well-suited for automating tasks in Unix-like environments, while PowerShell scripts are designed for Windows systems and have extensive capabilities for system administration.

Python and Ruby offer versatility and cross-platform support, making them valuable choices for a wide range of scripting and automation tasks.

CLI scripts often start with a shebang (#!) followed by the path to the scripting interpreter, allowing the operating system to execute the script with the specified interpreter.

Once the scripting language is chosen, users can begin writing scripts that address specific use cases, such as system configuration, log analysis, backup procedures, and more.

CLI scripting is not limited to simple automation tasks; it can also be used for complex workflows, such as setting up development environments, deploying applications, and managing cloud resources.

Scripts can be parameterized to accept inputs, making them adaptable for various scenarios.

These inputs can include file paths, configuration options, user credentials, and other data required to customize script behavior.

By accepting parameters, scripts become reusable tools that can be applied to different situations with minimal modification.

One of the fundamental concepts in CLI scripting is the use of conditional statements, loops, and functions to control the flow of execution.

Conditional statements allow scripts to make decisions based on conditions, enabling different actions to be taken depending on whether certain criteria are met.

Loops, such as for loops and while loops, enable scripts to repeat actions or iterate through lists of items, making it possible to process multiple files, directories, or resources systematically.

Functions provide a way to encapsulate logic into reusable blocks of code, promoting modularity and code organization.

Moreover, CLI scripts often rely on file handling, enabling them to read and write files, create directories, and manipulate data.

File operations are essential for tasks like log analysis, data transformation, and configuration management.

Automation takes CLI scripting to the next level by orchestrating sequences of scripts and commands into workflows that can be executed automatically or triggered by specific events.

Automation platforms and tools, such as Ansible, Puppet, and Chef, provide robust frameworks for defining, managing, and executing automation tasks.

These tools offer features like idempotency, state management, and declarative configuration, making it possible to define the desired state of systems and let the automation tool handle the execution details.

In addition to infrastructure automation, CLI scripting and automation play a crucial role in continuous integration and continuous deployment (CI/CD) pipelines.

CI/CD pipelines automate the process of building, testing, and deploying software, ensuring that code changes are consistently and reliably delivered to production environments.

CLI scripts are used to perform tasks like code compilation, unit testing, integration testing, and artifact deployment within CI/CD pipelines.

Automation tools can help coordinate these tasks, allowing organizations to achieve rapid and error-free software delivery.

Moreover, CLI scripting and automation are vital for cloud management, as they enable organizations to provision, configure, and manage cloud resources programmatically.

Cloud providers, such as AWS, Azure, and Google Cloud, offer CLI tools and APIs that allow users to interact with their services and automate cloud operations.

Scripts and automation workflows can create virtual machines, provision storage, configure network settings, and scale resources up or down based on demand.

As organizations adopt microservices architectures and containerization technologies like Docker and Kubernetes, CLI scripting and automation become even more critical.

CLI scripts can orchestrate container deployments, manage container clusters, and automate the scaling of containerized applications.

Automation tools like Kubernetes Operators simplify the management of containerized workloads by defining custom controllers that automate application-specific tasks.

Security and compliance are paramount in modern IT environments, and CLI scripting and automation play a crucial role in enforcing security policies and monitoring compliance.

Scripts can be used to perform security audits, vulnerability scans, and compliance checks on systems and applications.

Automation can then remediate security issues by applying patches, updating configurations, and implementing access controls automatically.

Furthermore, CLI scripting and automation can enhance incident response procedures by automating the detection and containment of security threats.

Scripts can monitor log files, network traffic, and system events to identify suspicious activities and trigger automated responses, such as isolating compromised systems or blocking malicious IP addresses.

In addition to security, CLI scripting and automation contribute to cost optimization by automating resource provisioning and deprovisioning based on usage patterns and business requirements.

Cloud cost management tools leverage automation to analyze resource usage, identify cost-saving opportunities, and execute actions like shutting down idle instances or resizing underutilized resources.

This proactive cost optimization helps organizations maximize the value of their cloud investments.

In summary, CLI scripting and automation are indispensable tools for modern IT professionals and organizations.

CLI scripting enables users to write custom scripts that automate tasks and processes, while automation extends scripting to orchestrate complex workflows and manage infrastructure at scale.

Together, these capabilities empower organizations to achieve greater efficiency, reliability, and security in their IT operations.

From system administration and software deployment to cloud management and security, CLI scripting and automation play a vital role in shaping the future of IT.

Chapter 2: Dynamic Configuration with Variables and Expressions

Dynamic variables and expressions are powerful features in the realm of IT automation and infrastructure management, allowing practitioners to create flexible and adaptable configurations and workflows.

Unlike static variables, which hold fixed values, dynamic variables can change their values based on conditions, inputs, or external factors, making them ideal for scenarios where flexibility and automation are paramount.

Dynamic variables enable IT professionals to write scripts, templates, and configuration files that respond intelligently to changing circumstances, reducing manual intervention and minimizing the risk of errors.

One of the most common uses of dynamic variables is in scripting, where they can store values obtained through calculations, data manipulation, or external sources.

For example, a script can calculate the current date and time, store it in a dynamic variable, and use that variable in various operations throughout the script.

This ensures that the script always works with the most up-to-date timestamp, regardless of when it is executed.

Expressions, on the other hand, are dynamic constructs that evaluate to a value based on a combination of operators, operands, and functions.

They are particularly useful for performing calculations, making decisions, and generating dynamic content within scripts and configuration files.

In scripting languages like Python or PowerShell, expressions are fundamental for tasks such as mathematical calculations, string manipulation, and conditional logic.

Dynamic variables and expressions are closely related, as dynamic variables often rely on expressions to compute their values dynamically.

For instance, a dynamic variable in a script may use an expression to concatenate multiple strings together, generate a file path based on user input, or calculate the sum of values from a list.

This dynamic behavior ensures that the variable adapts to changing inputs or conditions, providing flexibility in the script's behavior.

In configuration management tools like Ansible or Terraform, dynamic variables play a crucial role in defining infrastructure configurations.

These tools use dynamic variables to store values that may depend on the target environment, such as IP addresses, hostnames, or resource identifiers.

Dynamic variables in configuration files allow practitioners to create reusable templates that adapt to different scenarios, making it easier to manage diverse infrastructure deployments.

Moreover, dynamic variables can be used in conditional statements to control the flow of configuration management.

For example, a configuration template may use dynamic variables to determine whether a specific software package should be installed based on the target system's operating system or version.

In this way, the configuration can adapt to different environments while maintaining consistency.

Automation workflows often involve dynamic variables to handle inputs from users, external systems, or dynamic data sources.

For instance, when creating a workflow for provisioning virtual machines in a cloud environment, dynamic variables can capture user-defined inputs like the desired instance type, storage size, or region.

These inputs are then used to configure the virtual machine during provisioning, ensuring that the resulting resource aligns with the user's requirements.

Dynamic variables can also interact with external APIs or databases to retrieve real-time information.

For example, a monitoring system may use dynamic variables to query an API for the current CPU utilization of a server and store that value for further analysis or alerting.

This dynamic approach enables automation workflows to react to changing conditions in the monitored environment.

In addition to their use in scripts and configurations, dynamic variables and expressions are valuable in managing secrets and sensitive data.

Modern IT environments require secure handling of credentials, API keys, and access tokens.

Dynamic variables can be used to store encrypted secrets, and expressions can perform decryption when needed.

This approach ensures that sensitive information remains protected while still being accessible for automated tasks.

Dynamic variables and expressions are not limited to simple operations.

They can be as complex as needed, incorporating multiple levels of nesting, conditionals, and mathematical operations.

For instance, a dynamic expression in a scripting language can calculate the average of a set of numbers, provided that the numbers are retrieved dynamically from a data source or user input.

In configuration files, dynamic variables can be used to generate unique resource names or define conditional attributes for resources based on complex logic.

This level of sophistication allows IT practitioners to build highly automated and adaptive systems.

When it comes to dynamic variables and expressions, error handling and validation are essential considerations.

Since dynamic variables can change their values based on conditions, it is crucial to anticipate potential errors or unexpected values.

Robust error handling and validation mechanisms should be in place to ensure that the dynamic behavior of variables and expressions does not lead to system instability or incorrect results.

In scripting, this may involve using try-catch blocks or conditionals to handle exceptions gracefully.

In configuration management, validation rules and error messages can be defined to prevent invalid input or configurations from being applied.

Overall, dynamic variables and expressions are essential tools for modern IT practitioners seeking to automate, adapt, and optimize their workflows.

They enable scripts, configuration files, and automation workflows to respond intelligently to changing conditions, user inputs, and external data sources.

By harnessing the power of dynamic variables and expressions, IT professionals can create flexible, adaptive, and efficient solutions that reduce manual effort and enhance system reliability.

Advanced variable use cases in IT automation and infrastructure management encompass a wide range of scenarios and techniques that enable practitioners to harness the full potential of variables in their scripts, templates, and configuration files.

While variables are commonly used to store and retrieve data, advanced use cases go beyond simple assignments and involve dynamic, context-aware, and calculated variables that enhance automation capabilities.

One advanced use case for variables is dynamic resource naming in configuration management. When provisioning resources in a cloud environment or managing infrastructure as code, it's often necessary to generate unique resource names based on specific criteria or conventions.

In such cases, variables can be employed to dynamically construct resource names, incorporating elements like timestamps, environment tags, or user-defined parameters.

For example, a variable could concatenate the current date and time with a predefined prefix to create distinct names for virtual machines or cloud storage containers, ensuring uniqueness and manageability.

Dynamic variable naming simplifies the automation of resource provisioning, especially in scenarios where multiple instances of the same resource type are required.

Another advanced use case involves the orchestration of complex workflows by utilizing variables to control the flow of automation tasks. Variables can serve as flags or triggers, determining which tasks are executed based on conditions or dependencies.

For instance, in a continuous integration and continuous deployment (CI/CD) pipeline, variables can be used to determine whether specific stages of the pipeline, such as testing or deployment, should be skipped or executed based on the outcome of earlier stages or user-defined criteria.

This dynamic control over workflow execution allows for more intelligent and adaptive automation processes, reducing the risk of errors and optimizing resource utilization.

Variables also play a crucial role in managing configuration drift and ensuring infrastructure consistency. When managing large-scale deployments with configuration management tools, it's essential to monitor and enforce the desired state of resources continually.

Advanced variable use cases involve storing the expected configurations in variables and comparing them to the actual configurations of deployed resources.

By maintaining a set of expected configurations as variables, practitioners can detect configuration drift and automatically remediate any discrepancies between the expected and actual states.

This ensures that infrastructure remains in the desired state, improving compliance, security, and reliability.

Moreover, advanced variable use cases extend to data-driven automation, where variables are used to store and manipulate data retrieved from external sources or generated within scripts.

For example, when performing data analysis or reporting, variables can store the results of database queries, API responses, or log file parsing.

These variables enable practitioners to process, filter, aggregate, or transform data as needed, facilitating decision-making and automation based on real-time data insights.

Variables can also facilitate parameterization in configuration files, allowing practitioners to create highly adaptable and reusable templates. Advanced use cases involve defining variables that accept a wide range of inputs, including dynamic data, user-defined parameters, or even inputs from external systems.

By incorporating variables with flexible input options, configuration templates become versatile tools capable of adapting to different use cases and environments.

For instance, a configuration template for a web server might use variables to accept user-specified port numbers, SSL certificate paths, or database connection strings, enabling users to customize the configuration to their specific requirements.

Advanced variable use cases also encompass scenarios where variables are employed to manage secrets and sensitive data securely. Security is a critical consideration in IT automation, and protecting sensitive information like passwords, API keys, or encryption keys is paramount.

Variables can store encrypted secrets, and decryption can be performed on-demand when the secrets are needed during automation tasks.

By keeping sensitive data in variables and encrypting it, practitioners reduce the risk of accidental exposure while still benefiting from automation capabilities.

Furthermore, variables can be used in combination with secret management solutions to dynamically retrieve and inject secrets into automation workflows, ensuring that secrets are not hard-coded in scripts or configuration files.

One of the most powerful advanced variable use cases involves the integration of variables with external APIs and web services. Variables can store authentication tokens, API endpoints, and other necessary information for interacting with external systems programmatically.

This integration enables automation workflows to interact with external services, retrieve data, perform actions, and synchronize information between different systems seamlessly.

For example, an automation script could use variables to store API keys for a cloud provider and use those keys to create and manage cloud resources programmatically.

In another scenario, variables could store URLs and authentication tokens for accessing external data sources, allowing automated data synchronization or aggregation tasks.

In summary, advanced variable use cases in IT automation and infrastructure management unlock the full potential of variables as dynamic, context-aware, and calculated entities.

These use cases go beyond simple data storage and retrieval, encompassing dynamic resource naming, workflow orchestration, configuration drift detection, data-driven automation, parameterization, secret management, and external system integration.

By leveraging advanced variable techniques, practitioners can build more intelligent, adaptable, and secure automation solutions that align with the complexities and requirements of modern IT environments.

Chapter 3: Advanced Resource Management and Dependencies

Resource dependencies are a fundamental concept in infrastructure as code (IaC) and configuration management, playing a critical role in defining the order and relationships between resources in an automated deployment.

In IaC, resources represent various components of an infrastructure, such as virtual machines, databases, networks, and storage.

These resources often depend on each other in complex ways, and managing these dependencies is essential to ensure that the infrastructure is provisioned correctly and functions as expected.

Resource dependencies can be categorized into two main types: implicit and explicit.

Implicit dependencies are automatically determined by the configuration management tool based on the relationships defined in the code.

For example, if a virtual machine instance requires a specific security group to be associated with it, the configuration management tool will implicitly understand that the security group must be created before the virtual machine.

This implicit dependency resolution simplifies the configuration process, as the practitioner does not need to specify the order explicitly.

Explicit dependencies, on the other hand, are defined explicitly in the configuration code to ensure that resources are provisioned in a specific order.

This approach is often necessary when dealing with more complex scenarios or when the configuration management tool cannot infer the dependencies automatically.

Explicit dependencies are typically specified using attributes or directives within the configuration code.

Resource dependencies serve several critical purposes in IaC and automation.

First and foremost, they ensure that resources are provisioned in the correct order to meet the application's requirements.

For example, if an application server depends on a database server, ensuring that the database server is provisioned and accessible before the application server starts is crucial for the application to function correctly.

Resource dependencies also help in managing the timing and sequencing of resource creation, updates, and deletion.

By specifying dependencies, practitioners can control the order in which changes are applied to the infrastructure, reducing the risk of disruptions or conflicts during updates.

For instance, when updating a load balancer configuration, it may be necessary to ensure that the associated backend servers are updated first to avoid potential downtime.

Additionally, resource dependencies contribute to the predictability and reliability of automated deployments.

By defining clear dependencies, practitioners can ensure that resources are provisioned consistently across different environments, reducing the likelihood of configuration drift and inconsistencies.

This predictability is particularly valuable in maintaining the desired state of the infrastructure and achieving high availability.

Resource dependencies are expressed using various mechanisms, depending on the configuration management tool or IaC framework being used.

In tools like Terraform, dependencies can be declared explicitly using "depends_on" directives, which specify the relationships between resources.

For example, to define that a virtual machine depends on a virtual network, the "depends_on" directive can be added to the virtual machine resource block, indicating the dependency on the virtual network resource.

In Ansible, resource dependencies can be managed using playbook tasks and roles.

Tasks can be structured to ensure that one task depends on the successful completion of another, controlling the execution order.

Similarly, roles can specify dependencies between each other, ensuring that they are applied in the correct sequence.

Resource dependencies are also crucial when it comes to rolling updates and scaling.

When scaling an application by adding or removing instances, practitioners need to consider the dependencies between resources to avoid service disruptions.

For instance, when scaling a web application, ensuring that additional web server instances are operational before directing traffic to them is essential.

Resource dependencies can be used to orchestrate the scaling process to minimize the impact on end-users.

Furthermore, resource dependencies are valuable in maintaining data integrity.

In scenarios where databases are involved, practitioners need to ensure that database schemas are updated or migrated in a controlled sequence to prevent data corruption or loss.

By specifying dependencies between schema changes and application updates, practitioners can manage these operations safely.

Resource dependencies also enable practitioners to define failover and high availability strategies.

When planning for redundancy and failover, it's essential to consider the order in which resources are promoted or demoted in case of failure.

By specifying dependencies, practitioners can ensure that failover processes are executed correctly and efficiently.

Resource dependencies are not limited to infrastructure provisioning but also apply to configuration management.

For example, when managing software configurations, dependencies can be defined to ensure that the required packages or libraries are installed before configuring and starting a service.

This dependency management is crucial for achieving consistent and reliable software deployments.

In summary, resource dependencies are a fundamental aspect of infrastructure as code and configuration management.

They play a pivotal role in orchestrating the provisioning, updating, and scaling of resources in an automated and predictable manner.

Whether implicit or explicit, managing resource dependencies ensures that infrastructure is provisioned correctly, updates are applied in the correct order, and high availability and data integrity are maintained.

Resource meta-arguments and advanced settings are essential components of infrastructure as code (IaC) that provide practitioners with fine-grained control and customization options when defining and managing resources.

Meta-arguments are special attributes or directives associated with resource declarations that influence how resources are created, updated, and destroyed.

They enable practitioners to specify resource behavior, dependencies, and lifecycle management in a highly configurable manner.

One common meta-argument is "count," which allows practitioners to create multiple instances of a resource with a single resource block, reducing code duplication and enhancing maintainability.

For example, when provisioning multiple virtual machines with similar configurations, the "count" meta-argument can be used to create a specific number of instances based on a desired count.

Another essential meta-argument is "for_each," which is similar to "count" but provides more flexibility by allowing practitioners to iterate over a map or set of resource instances. This enables the dynamic creation of resources based on a set of input variables or data, making it particularly useful for scenarios where the number of resources varies.

Resource meta-arguments also include "provider," which specifies the provider configuration to use when creating a resource.

In a multi-cloud environment, where resources may be provisioned across different cloud providers, the "provider" meta-argument ensures that the correct cloud provider is used for a particular resource.

Additionally, "lifecycle" meta-arguments, such as "create_before_destroy" and "ignore_changes," allow practitioners to control resource replacement behavior during updates, reducing the risk of service disruptions.

Advanced settings, on the other hand, encompass various resource attributes and configurations that fine-tune the behavior and characteristics of resources.

One advanced setting is resource tagging, which involves attaching metadata to resources to categorize and label them for organizational, tracking, and cost allocation purposes.

Tags can be used to identify the owner of a resource, the environment it belongs to, its purpose, or any other relevant information.

Resource tagging is particularly important in large-scale environments where managing and tracking resources can become complex.

Resource timeouts and retries are advanced settings that determine how resources handle transient errors and delays during provisioning or updates.

Timeouts specify the maximum duration a resource operation can take before being considered failed, allowing for better error handling and resource management.

Retries define how many times a resource operation should be retried in case of failure, enhancing resource robustness and reliability.

Resource placement and distribution settings are advanced configurations that control where and how resources are deployed within a cloud infrastructure.

These settings allow practitioners to specify placement constraints, such as the availability zone or region, to ensure that resources are distributed optimally for fault tolerance and performance.

Resource scheduling settings enable practitioners to define resource provisioning schedules based on specific criteria, such as time of day or workload patterns.

This is valuable for scenarios where resources need to be scaled up or down automatically to accommodate varying workloads or to optimize costs during non-peak hours.

Resource scaling policies are advanced settings that govern how resources automatically scale in response to changing demands.

Practitioners can define scaling triggers, such as CPU utilization or request rates, and specify how resources should be added or removed dynamically.

This ensures that the infrastructure adapts to workload fluctuations efficiently and cost-effectively.

Resource access controls and permissions are advanced settings that define who can manage and operate resources.

Access controls are crucial for maintaining security and compliance, as they determine which users or roles have permissions to create, update, or delete resources.

Resource monitoring and logging settings enable practitioners to configure resource-level monitoring and logging options to capture performance metrics, events, and logs.

These settings are essential for diagnosing issues, optimizing resource utilization, and ensuring compliance with auditing requirements.

Resource backup and disaster recovery configurations are advanced settings that define how resources are backed up and restored in case of data loss or infrastructure failures.

Practitioners can specify backup schedules, retention policies, and recovery procedures to safeguard critical data and maintain business continuity.

Resource customization settings, such as resource templates or user data scripts, allow practitioners to inject custom configurations or scripts into resource instances during provisioning.

This customization enhances resource versatility and supports the installation of specific software, application configurations, or security settings.

Resource logging and auditing settings help practitioners track resource changes, access events, and configuration modifications.

By enabling detailed logging and auditing, practitioners can maintain a comprehensive record of resource activities for compliance, troubleshooting, and security analysis.

Resource meta-arguments and advanced settings are instrumental in achieving fine-grained control and customization of resources in infrastructure as code.

They empower practitioners to tailor resource behavior, dependencies, and configurations to meet specific requirements, whether it involves dynamic resource creation, advanced error handling, resource distribution, scheduling, scaling, access control, monitoring, customization, or auditing.

By leveraging these capabilities, practitioners can design and manage infrastructure that is not only reliable and scalable but also aligned with their organization's operational and security standards.

Chapter 4: Harnessing Terraform Providers for Customization

Custom providers are a powerful feature in infrastructure as code (IaC) that allows practitioners to extend the capabilities of IaC tools like Terraform and Ansible by defining their own resource types and associated functionality.

These custom providers enable practitioners to model and manage resources that may not be supported out of the box by the IaC tool.

One of the primary use cases for custom providers is to interact with proprietary or specialized APIs and services that are not covered by the built-in providers.

For instance, if an organization uses a unique cloud service or an in-house application with no native support in Terraform, a custom provider can be developed to bridge this gap.

Custom providers are developed using programming languages such as Go, Python, or Ruby, depending on the IaC tool's supported language.

These providers act as a bridge between the IaC tool and the target system, allowing resources to be defined and managed using the tool's declarative language.

When creating a custom provider, practitioners need to define resource types, data sources, and associated CRUD (Create, Read, Update, Delete) operations.

Resource types represent the resources that can be managed using the custom provider, and they define the properties and behaviors of those resources.

Data sources enable practitioners to query information from the target system and use it in their configuration files.

Once a custom provider is developed and compiled, it can be distributed and installed like any other provider in the IaC tool.

One significant advantage of custom providers is their flexibility and adaptability to unique infrastructure requirements.

Organizations with specialized needs or complex environments can leverage custom providers to model and manage resources precisely according to their specifications.

Custom providers can also be used to automate tasks beyond resource provisioning.

For example, they can be used to manage service configurations, set up monitoring, or orchestrate complex workflows involving multiple systems.

The ability to define custom providers empowers practitioners to abstract and automate infrastructure tasks that would otherwise require manual intervention.

Custom providers are particularly valuable in scenarios where an organization operates a hybrid or multi-cloud environment, utilizing various cloud providers or on-premises systems.

In such cases, custom providers can be created to standardize resource management across different platforms, streamlining operations and reducing the complexity of managing resources across multiple interfaces.

Furthermore, custom providers promote code reuse and maintainability.

Once a custom provider is developed and tested, it can be reused across multiple projects and environments.

This reusability reduces duplication of effort and ensures consistency in resource management practices.

For example, if an organization manages its own internal applications that require specific configurations, a custom provider can be created to handle these configurations uniformly across all projects.

Custom providers also contribute to version control and collaboration.

Since custom providers are developed using code, they can be versioned and managed in the same way as other code repositories.

This facilitates collaboration among teams, enables code reviews, and ensures that changes to custom providers are tracked and documented.

Custom providers are not limited to managing only infrastructure resources.

They can also interact with external services and APIs, making them versatile tools for automation and integration.

For example, a custom provider can be created to interact with a third-party service's API, enabling automated provisioning and configuration of resources in that service.

This level of integration can streamline complex workflows that involve interactions with various external services and systems.

Custom providers provide a standardized way to manage resources, even in cases where no official provider exists.

This is especially important when working with niche or industry-specific technologies that may not have widespread adoption or official support within the IaC tool's ecosystem.

By developing a custom provider, practitioners can take full control of managing these resources and tailor them to their organization's needs.

When developing custom providers, practitioners should consider the principles of idempotence and state reconciliation.

Idempotence ensures that applying the same configuration multiple times results in the same desired state, avoiding unintended changes or resource duplication.

State reconciliation is the process of comparing the desired state defined in the configuration with the actual state of the resources and making necessary adjustments to align them.

These principles are critical for ensuring that custom providers maintain the integrity and consistency of the infrastructure.

Testing and validation of custom providers are essential steps in their development.

Thorough testing helps identify and resolve any issues or bugs in the provider, ensuring its reliability and stability in production environments.

It's also crucial to document custom providers comprehensively, providing clear instructions on how to use and configure them.

Well-documented providers are easier for teams to adopt and maintain over time.

Custom providers can be distributed and shared within an organization or with the broader community.

By open-sourcing custom providers, practitioners can contribute to the IaC community and benefit from collective knowledge and collaboration.

When sharing custom providers, it's important to follow best practices for documentation, versioning, and licensing to facilitate adoption by others.

In summary, custom providers are a valuable tool in the world of infrastructure as code, enabling practitioners to extend the capabilities of IaC tools and automate resource management in a flexible and tailored manner.

They empower organizations to model and manage resources, whether they are infrastructure components, configurations, or interactions with external services, according to their specific needs and requirements.

Custom providers promote code reuse, maintainability, and collaboration, making them a powerful asset for organizations operating in diverse and complex environments.

With the right development practices, testing, and documentation, custom providers can enhance the efficiency, reliability, and control of infrastructure automation efforts.

Provider configuration and advanced settings play a pivotal role in infrastructure as code (IaC), providing the means to establish connections to cloud platforms, data centers, and external services within IaC tools like Terraform and Ansible.

These configurations define how the IaC tool interacts with external environments, enabling the provisioning and management of resources.

Provider configurations typically include essential parameters such as authentication credentials, API endpoints, and region-specific settings.

For instance, when using a cloud provider like AWS, the configuration would specify access keys, secret keys, and the AWS region where resources should be deployed.

Providers can be categorized into two main types: built-in providers and custom providers.

Built-in providers are those that come pre-packaged with the IaC tool and provide out-of-the-box support for interacting with popular cloud providers, infrastructure platforms, and services.

Examples of built-in providers in Terraform include AWS, Azure, Google Cloud, and more.

Custom providers, as discussed previously, are developed by practitioners to extend the IaC tool's capabilities to interact with specialized or proprietary systems that may not have built-in support.

Provider configurations are a critical aspect of IaC, as they determine the context and scope within which resources are managed.

These configurations ensure that the IaC tool has the necessary permissions and access to the target environment to perform resource provisioning, updates, and deletions.

Advanced settings within provider configurations allow practitioners to fine-tune how the IaC tool interacts with external environments, providing greater control and customization.

One essential advanced setting is provider aliases, which enable the use of multiple configurations for the same provider.

This is particularly useful when working with multiple accounts or regions within a single cloud provider.

Provider aliases allow practitioners to define distinct configurations for each use case, making it easier to manage and switch between different environments.

Another advanced setting is provider version constraints, which specify the acceptable versions of the provider that the IaC tool can use.

Version constraints help ensure compatibility between the IaC tool and the provider, reducing the risk of breaking changes or unexpected behavior when updating the tool or provider.

Provider timeouts are advanced settings that define the maximum duration for various operations, such as resource creation or updates.

Timeouts help prevent resource provisioning from hanging indefinitely in case of network issues or other unexpected delays.

Practitioners can configure timeouts to align with their organization's performance and operational requirements.

Provider retry strategies are advanced settings that dictate how the IaC tool handles transient errors during resource provisioning or updates.

Retry strategies specify the number of retry attempts and the time intervals between retries, improving the reliability and robustness of resource management.

Provider request throttling settings allow practitioners to control the rate at which requests are sent to external services or APIs.

Throttling settings help prevent overloading the target environment with excessive requests, which can lead to performance issues or rate-limiting restrictions.

By adjusting throttling settings, practitioners can optimize resource provisioning without causing disruptions.

Provider error handling and logging settings enable practitioners to specify how the IaC tool should capture and handle errors encountered during resource management.

These settings define error thresholds, logging levels, and notification mechanisms to facilitate troubleshooting and issue resolution.

Provider proxy configurations are advanced settings that allow the IaC tool to route requests through a proxy server, enhancing security and compliance in environments with specific network requirements.

Proxy configurations enable practitioners to define proxy server addresses, credentials, and routing rules.

Provider configuration files are typically written in a declarative format, allowing practitioners to define provider settings alongside resource definitions in IaC configuration files.

This approach ensures that provider configurations are versioned, documented, and version-controlled along with the rest of the infrastructure code.

Advanced settings within provider configurations provide practitioners with the flexibility to tailor resource management to their organization's specific needs.

They enable fine-grained control over operations, timeouts, error handling, and other aspects of resource provisioning and management.

Practitioners should consider their organization's security, performance, and operational requirements when configuring providers and advanced settings to ensure a robust and reliable IaC workflow.

By mastering provider configuration and advanced settings, practitioners can harness the full potential of infrastructure as code to automate and manage complex infrastructures effectively.

Chapter 5: Advanced State Management Strategies

Remote state management is a fundamental concept in the world of infrastructure as code (IaC), enabling teams to collaborate, maintain consistency, and securely store the state of their infrastructure deployments.

In IaC, the term "state" refers to the current configuration and status of resources provisioned by tools like Terraform, Ansible, or CloudFormation.

Remote state management involves storing this critical information in a centralized location that is accessible to the entire team, rather than keeping it on individual developer machines.

One of the primary reasons for using remote state management is to facilitate collaboration among team members working on the same infrastructure project.

When multiple team members are involved in defining, modifying, or maintaining infrastructure code, it's crucial to have a single source of truth regarding the current state of the infrastructure.

By storing the state remotely, all team members can access and update the same state information, ensuring that everyone is working with consistent and up-to-date data.

Remote state management also enhances security by reducing the risk of sensitive data exposure.

Infrastructure state often contains sensitive information, such as access keys, secrets, and configuration details.

Keeping this information on individual developer machines poses security risks, as it may be inadvertently shared or exposed.

Storing the state remotely in a secure location with access controls helps mitigate these risks.

A popular approach to remote state management is to use cloud-based storage solutions, such as Amazon S3, Google Cloud Storage, or Azure Blob Storage, as the centralized repository for state files.

These cloud storage options offer durability, availability, and security, making them suitable for storing infrastructure state.

Additionally, they provide versioning and access control mechanisms to protect sensitive information.

Another advantage of remote state management is the ability to share state files across multiple projects and environments.

In complex infrastructure setups, organizations may have multiple projects, environments (e.g., development, staging, production), and teams working simultaneously.

Remote state management allows different projects and teams to reference the same state files, ensuring consistency and alignment across the entire organization.

When state files are stored remotely, they can be organized into directories and categorized based on projects, environments, or other criteria, making it easier to locate and manage them.

Organizations can also implement naming conventions and labeling to provide context and clarity when dealing with a large number of state files.

State locking is a critical aspect of remote state management.

It ensures that only one user or process can make changes to the state at a given time.

This prevents conflicts that could arise if multiple users attempted to update the state simultaneously.

Most remote state management solutions provide locking mechanisms to enforce this single-writer principle.

State locking typically works by acquiring a lock before making changes and releasing it after the changes are complete.

If another user or process attempts to acquire the lock while it's already held, they are blocked from making changes until the lock is released.

In addition to facilitating collaboration and security, remote state management supports disaster recovery and auditing capabilities.

In the event of data loss or accidental deletions, having state files stored in a remote, resilient storage solution allows organizations to recover their infrastructure configurations and resource definitions.

Remote state management also enables auditing and tracking changes to the infrastructure over time.

By maintaining historical versions of state files, organizations can trace the evolution of their infrastructure and identify when and why specific changes were made.

Implementing remote state management requires configuring IaC tools to use a centralized storage location for state files.

This involves specifying the remote backend configuration, including the storage location, access credentials, and any required settings.

Once configured, the IaC tool will automatically store and retrieve state files from the remote backend.

It's essential to ensure that proper access controls are in place for the remote storage solution to prevent unauthorized access to sensitive state data.

Organizations should follow best practices for securing access keys, using role-based access control (RBAC), and enabling encryption at rest and in transit.

Some remote state management solutions also offer integrations with identity and access management (IAM) systems, providing additional security options.

Organizations should establish clear processes and guidelines for managing remote state files.

This includes defining who has access to state files, who can modify them, and under what circumstances changes can be made.

Roles and responsibilities for managing state files should be documented and communicated to all team members.

Regular backups of state files should be performed to protect against data loss or corruption.

Organizations should also implement procedures for state file versioning, allowing them to track changes and recover from unintended modifications.

Monitoring and alerting can help organizations detect and respond to issues with remote state management.

This includes monitoring the availability and performance of the remote storage solution, as well as tracking access and modification events.

Setting up alerts for unusual or unauthorized activities can help organizations proactively address security incidents.

In summary, remote state management is a critical practice in infrastructure as code that enables collaboration, enhances security, and supports consistency in infrastructure deployments.

By storing state files in a centralized, secure, and resilient location, organizations can ensure that all team members work with the same up-to-date information, reduce security risks, and streamline the management of complex infrastructure setups.

Implementing remote state management requires careful configuration, access control, and monitoring to ensure the integrity and reliability of infrastructure deployments.

State locking and advanced state features are essential components of infrastructure as code (IaC) that contribute to the reliability, consistency, and security of infrastructure deployments.

In the world of IaC, state refers to the current configuration and status of resources provisioned by tools like Terraform, Ansible, or CloudFormation.

State locking ensures that only one user or process can make changes to the state at any given time, preventing conflicts that could arise if multiple users or processes attempted to update the state simultaneously.

This mechanism is crucial for maintaining data integrity and consistency in complex infrastructure setups.

When multiple team members or automation processes are involved in managing infrastructure, state locking becomes a critical safeguard against unintended modifications.

Advanced state features go beyond basic locking mechanisms to provide additional capabilities and insights into the infrastructure's current state.

One of the core benefits of state locking is the prevention of concurrent writes to the state.

Concurrency control is essential for avoiding data corruption and inconsistencies in the infrastructure's configuration.

When a user or process requests a lock to make changes to the state, the locking mechanism grants the lock to only one entity while blocking others.

This ensures that modifications are carried out in a controlled and sequential manner.

Terraform, for example, provides a state locking mechanism that supports distributed systems and works with various backend storage options.

To enhance the resilience and fault tolerance of state locking, some IaC tools offer lease-based locking mechanisms.

With lease-based locks, a user or process must renew the lock periodically to maintain control over the state.

If a lock is not renewed within a specified timeframe, it is automatically released, allowing other users or processes to acquire it.

This approach helps prevent situations where a user or process holds a lock indefinitely, even in the event of failures or unexpected interruptions.

Lease-based locking is particularly useful in scenarios where users or processes may become unresponsive or experience network issues.

Advanced state features often include the ability to inspect the current state of the infrastructure.

These features allow users to query the state to retrieve information about resources, configurations, and dependencies.

Being able to examine the state provides valuable insights into the infrastructure's current state and allows for more informed decision-making.

For example, Terraform's state inspection capabilities enable users to query the state to retrieve attribute values, such as IP addresses or resource IDs, which can be used in subsequent automation tasks or scripts.

State outputs are another advanced state feature that enables the IaC tool to generate structured data outputs based on the state.

These outputs can be used for reporting, documentation generation, or integration with other systems.

For instance, an IaC tool might generate a JSON file containing resource metadata extracted from the state, which can then be consumed by external monitoring or reporting tools.

Some IaC tools provide state locking and advanced state features as part of their core functionality, while others may require the use of plugins or external components to achieve similar capabilities.

When implementing state locking and advanced state features, organizations should consider the following best practices:

Use appropriate backend storage: Choose a backend storage solution that aligns with your organization's requirements for durability, availability, and performance. Cloud-based storage options like Amazon S3, Google Cloud Storage, or Azure Blob Storage are popular choices.

Implement access controls: Secure the access to state files by configuring proper access controls and permissions. Role-based access control (RBAC) and encryption mechanisms should be employed to protect sensitive state data.

Document state locking procedures: Clearly define the process for acquiring and releasing state locks, and communicate these procedures to all team members. Establish guidelines for handling conflicts and addressing lock-related issues.

Monitor state locking and state changes: Implement monitoring and alerting to track the state of locks and detect anomalies. Set up notifications for unauthorized access or prolonged lock acquisition.

Leverage advanced state features: Take advantage of state inspection and state output capabilities to gain deeper insights into your infrastructure and automate reporting and documentation tasks.

Implement lease-based locking for resilience: Consider using lease-based locking mechanisms to ensure that locks are automatically released if they are not renewed within a specified timeframe. This helps prevent prolonged lock acquisition and improves fault tolerance.

In summary, state locking and advanced state features are essential components of infrastructure as code that enhance the reliability, consistency, and security of infrastructure deployments.

These mechanisms prevent conflicts in concurrent infrastructure modifications and provide valuable insights into the current state of the infrastructure.

By following best practices and leveraging these features, organizations can maintain data integrity, streamline collaboration, and ensure the stability of their infrastructure automation workflows.

Chapter 6: Terraform Workspaces and Collaborative Workflows

Workspaces are a powerful feature in the realm of infrastructure as code (IaC) that enable teams to collaborate effectively on managing infrastructure configurations and deployments.

In the context of IaC tools like Terraform, Ansible, or CloudFormation, workspaces are virtual environments or isolated containers where users can work on different versions or instances of their infrastructure code.

Workspaces are particularly valuable when multiple teams or projects share the same IaC configuration, but need to maintain separate, independent deployments.

One of the primary benefits of workspaces is the ability to create isolated environments for development, testing, staging, and production without interfering with each other.

Each workspace acts as a distinct container for infrastructure code, state files, and configuration settings.

By segregating their work into different workspaces, teams can work concurrently on various aspects of the infrastructure without affecting one another.

For example, the development team can have their workspace for testing new features and changes, while the operations team maintains a production workspace for mission-critical deployments.

Workspaces help prevent conflicts and streamline collaboration by providing separate namespaces for state files.

State files are crucial in IaC, as they store the current state of the infrastructure, including resource IDs, IP addresses, and other essential information.

Without workspaces, teams working on different parts of the infrastructure might inadvertently overwrite each other's state files, leading to data corruption and deployment issues.

With workspaces, each team or project has its own isolated state file, reducing the risk of conflicts and ensuring data integrity.

Managing environment-specific variables and configurations becomes more straightforward with workspaces.

For instance, environment-specific variables like API keys, database connection strings, or region settings can be defined separately for each workspace.

This means that the development workspace can use test configurations, while the production workspace uses production-ready settings, reducing the chances of misconfigurations between environments.

Workspaces also facilitate version control and change tracking.

Teams can create branches or snapshots of their infrastructure code within a workspace, allowing them to experiment with changes or roll back to previous configurations when needed.

This versioning capability helps maintain a history of infrastructure changes and provides a safety net in case issues arise.

Terraform, for instance, allows users to create and switch between different workspaces using simple commands like "terraform workspace new" and "terraform workspace select."

These commands enable users to create and manage workspaces effortlessly, making it easy to switch between different environments and configurations.

When using workspaces, it's crucial to establish clear naming conventions and guidelines to ensure consistency and avoid confusion among team members.

Naming conventions should reflect the purpose and usage of each workspace, making it evident whether a workspace is for development, testing, staging, or production.

Consistency in naming conventions simplifies workspace management and helps team members quickly identify the appropriate workspace for their tasks.

Access control and permissions are essential aspects of workspace management.

Organizations should define who has access to each workspace and establish role-based access control (RBAC) to enforce proper permissions.

This prevents unauthorized users from making changes to sensitive environments and reduces the risk of accidental misconfigurations.

Workspaces are also beneficial for organizations that adopt a GitOps approach to infrastructure management.

GitOps combines version control with IaC, allowing teams to store infrastructure code and configurations in Git repositories.

Workspaces can align seamlessly with GitOps workflows, as each workspace can represent a branch or snapshot of the infrastructure code stored in a Git repository.

This integration streamlines the process of promoting changes from one environment to another, providing a clear path for code promotion and deployment.

In summary, workspaces are a valuable feature in the world of infrastructure as code, providing isolation, collaboration, and version control capabilities for managing complex infrastructure configurations.

By creating separate environments for development, testing, and production, teams can work concurrently on their infrastructure without conflicts.

Workspaces help maintain data integrity, prevent misconfigurations, and support GitOps workflows, making them a key component of successful IaC practices.

Collaborative workflows are at the heart of modern software development and infrastructure management, enabling teams to work together efficiently and deliver high-quality results.

In a collaborative workflow, multiple individuals with diverse skills and expertise collaborate on a shared project, leveraging their collective knowledge to achieve common goals.

For organizations, adopting collaborative workflow best practices can lead to improved productivity, faster time-to-market, and better outcomes for both software development and infrastructure management projects.

One of the fundamental principles of collaborative workflows is effective communication.

Clear and open communication among team members is crucial for sharing ideas, addressing issues, and ensuring everyone is aligned with project objectives.

Tools like Slack, Microsoft Teams, or even traditional email can facilitate communication, while regular team meetings and stand-ups can provide a structured forum for updates and discussions.

Collaborative workflows often involve distributed teams or remote work, which makes communication even more critical.

In such cases, video conferencing, instant messaging, and collaboration platforms become essential for maintaining effective communication.

Collaborative workflows benefit from well-defined roles and responsibilities.

Each team member should have a clear understanding of their role within the project and how it contributes to the overall success.

Role clarity helps prevent duplication of efforts and ensures that every aspect of the project is covered.

For example, in a software development project, roles might include developers, testers, product owners, and project managers.

Infrastructure management projects may involve roles like system administrators, cloud architects, and security specialists.

Collaborative workflows often rely on the concept of version control to manage changes to code, configurations, and other project artifacts.

Version control systems like Git enable teams to track modifications, collaborate on code or configuration changes, and revert to previous states if issues arise.

By using version control, teams can work in parallel, merge their changes seamlessly, and maintain a history of all modifications.

Continuous integration and continuous delivery (CI/CD) pipelines are integral to collaborative workflows, automating the build, test, and deployment processes.

CI/CD pipelines ensure that code changes are automatically tested and integrated into the project, reducing the risk of integration problems and accelerating the delivery of new features or updates.

Collaborative workflows thrive when there is a shared understanding of project goals and objectives.

Team members should have a clear vision of the project's purpose, target audience, and desired outcomes.

This shared understanding helps align individual efforts with the project's overarching goals, ensuring that everyone is working toward the same objectives.

Documentation plays a crucial role in collaborative workflows, providing a reference point for team members and a means of capturing project knowledge.

Documenting decisions, design choices, and best practices can help onboard new team members more quickly and ensure consistency throughout the project.

Tools like wikis, documentation repositories, and knowledge bases make it easy to create and maintain project documentation.

In collaborative workflows, feedback and code reviews are essential for maintaining code quality and ensuring that project standards are met.

Regular peer reviews allow team members to share their expertise, catch issues early in the development process, and provide constructive feedback to improve code or configurations.

Code reviews also promote knowledge sharing and encourage best practices.

Collaborative workflows should be agile and adaptive, allowing teams to respond to changing requirements and feedback.

Agile methodologies like Scrum or Kanban provide frameworks for iterative development and continuous improvement.

By embracing agility, teams can deliver incremental value to stakeholders and adjust their plans based on real-world feedback and evolving priorities.

Automating repetitive tasks is a cornerstone of collaborative workflows.

Automation tools and scripts can streamline processes, reduce manual errors, and free up team members to focus on more strategic and creative tasks.

Automation can encompass a wide range of activities, from infrastructure provisioning and configuration management to code deployment and testing.

Collaborative workflows often involve the use of collaboration platforms and project management tools.

These tools facilitate task tracking, project planning, and progress monitoring.

Popular options include Jira, Trello, Asana, and many others, which offer features for task assignment, deadline tracking, and reporting.

Effective collaboration is not limited to technical aspects; it also extends to collaboration with stakeholders, such as business teams, product owners, and customers.

Open channels of communication with stakeholders are essential for gathering requirements, prioritizing features, and aligning the project with business goals.

In summary, collaborative workflows are essential for modern software development and infrastructure management projects.

Effective communication, well-defined roles, version control, CI/CD pipelines, shared understanding, documentation, feedback, agility, automation, and collaboration tools all contribute to successful collaborative workflows.

By following best practices in these areas, teams can work together efficiently, deliver high-quality results, and meet project objectives effectively.

Chapter 7: Extending Terraform with Custom Plugins

Building custom Terraform plugins is an advanced skill that enables users to extend Terraform's capabilities and integrate with external systems or services.

Terraform is a powerful open-source infrastructure as code (IaC) tool that provides a vast ecosystem of providers for managing resources across various cloud providers, on-premises systems, and other platforms.

While Terraform's extensive provider ecosystem covers many services, there may be situations where you need to create a custom plugin to address unique requirements or integrate with a service that doesn't have an existing provider.

Custom Terraform plugins are typically written in the Go programming language, as Terraform itself is written in Go.

The Go programming language offers strong support for building plugins, making it well-suited for extending Terraform's functionality.

To start building a custom Terraform plugin, you need to have Go installed on your development machine and set up your Go environment.

Terraform plugins consist of one or more Go files that define the plugin's functionality.

These Go files can be organized into a Go module to manage dependencies and versioning.

Creating a custom Terraform plugin usually involves defining a provider, resource, or data source that Terraform can interact with.

Providers are responsible for configuring and managing resources, while data sources allow you to query external data and use it within your Terraform configurations.

A custom Terraform plugin typically includes a configuration schema that defines the input variables and outputs for the provider, resource, or data source.

This schema is written in HashiCorp Configuration Language (HCL), which is the same language used for Terraform configuration files. Defining a configuration schema for your custom plugin helps Terraform users understand how to use it and provides validation for input variables.

Once you've defined the configuration schema, you need to implement the actual functionality of your custom plugin.

This involves writing Go code that performs the necessary operations when Terraform executes the provider, resource, or data source.

The Go code for your plugin can interact with external APIs, databases, or services, depending on your use case.

While building custom Terraform plugins, it's essential to follow best practices for plugin development to ensure stability and maintainability.

One best practice is to thoroughly test your plugin code to catch and fix bugs early in the development process.

Writing unit tests, integration tests, and end-to-end tests for your plugin can help identify and address issues before they reach production environments.

Another best practice is to provide clear and comprehensive documentation for your custom Terraform plugin.

Documentation should include information on how to install, configure, and use the plugin, as well as examples and use cases.

Well-documented plugins are more accessible to users and reduce the learning curve.

Versioning is crucial for custom Terraform plugins to ensure compatibility with different Terraform versions and to manage changes over time.

Semantic versioning (semver) is commonly used to indicate breaking changes, new features, and bug fixes in plugin releases.

By following semver conventions, users can make informed decisions about when to upgrade their plugin versions.

To distribute your custom Terraform plugin, you can host it on a public or private repository, such as GitHub, GitLab, or a Terraform registry.

Hosting your plugin on a repository allows users to easily install it using Terraform's built-in plugin discovery and installation mechanisms.

For public plugins, you can also consider publishing them to the Terraform Registry to make them more discoverable to the Terraform community.

Security is a critical consideration when building custom Terraform plugins.

You should follow security best practices to protect sensitive data and ensure that your plugin doesn't introduce vulnerabilities into the infrastructure.

This includes securely handling credentials, validating user inputs, and following security guidelines for interacting with external services.

Finally, consider the maintainability of your custom Terraform plugin over the long term.

As Terraform evolves, you may need to update your plugin to remain compatible with new Terraform releases and features.

Additionally, responding to user feedback, fixing bugs, and adding new features are essential aspects of maintaining a successful custom plugin.

In summary, building custom Terraform plugins is a valuable skill that allows you to extend Terraform's capabilities and integrate with external systems or services.

To create custom plugins, you need to have a strong understanding of Terraform, Go programming, and best practices for plugin development.

By following best practices, testing thoroughly, providing documentation, versioning appropriately, and prioritizing security and maintainability, you can create custom Terraform plugins that enhance your infrastructure as code workflows and help meet unique requirements.

Plugin deployment and integration are essential steps in the lifecycle of custom Terraform plugins, ensuring that your plugins are accessible to users and seamlessly integrate with Terraform's ecosystem.

Deployment involves making your custom Terraform plugin available for installation, while integration focuses on how your plugin interacts with Terraform configurations and workflows.

To deploy a custom Terraform plugin, you need to distribute it to users who want to use your plugin in their infrastructure as code (IaC) projects.

One common approach is to host the plugin on a version control system (VCS) repository, such as GitHub or GitLab, where users can access and download it.

Additionally, you can publish your plugin to the Terraform Registry, a centralized repository for Terraform providers, modules, and plugins, making it discoverable to a broader audience.

When deploying a plugin, it's crucial to follow best practices for versioning and compatibility to ensure a smooth experience for users.

Semantic versioning (semver) is a widely adopted versioning scheme that helps users understand the impact of new releases.

By following semver conventions, you communicate whether a release contains breaking changes, new features, or bug fixes, allowing users to make informed decisions about when and how to upgrade.

Consider using tags or releases in your VCS repository to mark specific versions of your plugin and make it easy for users to download a particular version.

Integrating a custom Terraform plugin into your infrastructure as code (IaC) projects involves using the plugin within your Terraform configurations to manage resources, data sources, or providers.

Integration ensures that your plugin seamlessly becomes part of the Terraform workflow and can be applied, destroyed, or modified like any other Terraform-managed resource.

The integration process begins with importing your custom plugin into a Terraform configuration.

You specify the plugin's source location, either by referencing the local file system or a remote repository URL, in your Terraform configuration files.

Terraform's plugin discovery mechanism automatically detects and loads the referenced plugin when you run Terraform commands.

Before using your custom plugin, ensure that Terraform has successfully initialized the working directory by running **terraform init**.

This step downloads and installs the plugin if it's not already present in the local Terraform plugins cache.

Once the plugin is integrated and initialized, you can use it just like any other Terraform provider, resource, or data source in your configurations.

Declare instances of your custom resources, set configuration values, and establish relationships with other resources as needed.

Terraform's HCL (HashiCorp Configuration Language) syntax allows you to express the desired state of your infrastructure using your custom resources.

While integrating your custom plugin, it's crucial to understand how Terraform handles the lifecycle of resources and how your plugin should implement the necessary CRUD (Create, Read, Update, Delete) operations.

Terraform's execution plan, generated using the **terraform plan** command, determines the sequence of actions needed to bring the infrastructure into the desired state.

Your custom plugin must correctly handle these actions to ensure that resources are created, updated, or destroyed as expected.

The Terraform state file, which tracks the current state of the infrastructure, plays a vital role in integration.

Your plugin should properly manage the state of resources and coordinate with Terraform to store and retrieve resource state information.

Terraform provides a framework for handling state management, but your custom plugin must implement the necessary logic to interact with Terraform's state operations.

Error handling and reporting are essential aspects of integration.

Your plugin should provide meaningful error messages and return codes to help users understand and troubleshoot issues that may arise during Terraform execution.

Logging and debugging capabilities can also aid in diagnosing problems during integration.

Consider adding comprehensive logging and tracing mechanisms to your plugin to assist users in identifying the source of errors.

Testing is a critical part of plugin integration.

Thoroughly test your plugin in different scenarios and configurations to ensure that it behaves as expected.

Automated testing frameworks and tools can help you write unit tests, integration tests, and end-to-end tests to verify your plugin's functionality and compatibility.

As part of the integration process, document your plugin's usage, configuration options, and any dependencies that users need to be aware of.

Clear and comprehensive documentation is essential for users who want to leverage your plugin effectively.

Include usage examples and practical use cases to help users understand how to incorporate your plugin into their Terraform configurations.

Consider providing sample Terraform code snippets and best practices for using your plugin to accomplish specific tasks.

Incorporate your plugin into your organization's Terraform workflows and practices.

Consider how your custom resources align with Terraform's plan-apply lifecycle, and ensure that your organization's infrastructure and policies can accommodate your plugin's requirements.

Provide training and support resources for your team members and users to help them make the most of your custom plugin.

Offer guidance on best practices, troubleshooting, and performance optimization.

Consider creating a community or support forum where users can ask questions, share experiences, and collaborate with others using your plugin.

Continuous improvement is a crucial aspect of plugin integration.

Collect user feedback, monitor issues and feature requests, and iterate on your plugin to address user needs and enhance its capabilities.

Regularly release new versions of your plugin to provide bug fixes, new features, and improvements to your user community.

In summary, plugin deployment and integration are integral steps in the lifecycle of custom Terraform plugins.

Deploying your plugin involves making it accessible to users through version control repositories or the Terraform Registry, while integration ensures that your plugin seamlessly fits into Terraform workflows.

By following best practices for versioning, compatibility, error handling, testing, documentation, and support, you can create a valuable custom Terraform plugin that enhances the capabilities of Terraform and supports your organization's infrastructure as code (IaC) initiatives.

Chapter 8: Infrastructure Testing and Validation

Infrastructure testing is a critical aspect of managing and maintaining a robust and reliable infrastructure in today's IT landscape.

Testing helps ensure that your infrastructure components and configurations work as expected and can prevent costly outages and downtime.

There are various approaches to infrastructure testing, each serving specific purposes and addressing different aspects of your infrastructure.

One fundamental approach to infrastructure testing is unit testing, which focuses on testing individual components of your infrastructure in isolation.

Unit tests typically verify the functionality of a single component, such as a configuration file, a script, or a module, without considering the interactions with other parts of the infrastructure.

Unit tests can be written using testing frameworks and tools that are specific to the technology or language you are using.

For example, if you are managing your infrastructure with Terraform, you can use Terraform's built-in testing capabilities to write unit tests for your Terraform configurations.

Another critical approach to infrastructure testing is integration testing, which evaluates how different components of your infrastructure work together.

Integration tests ensure that various parts of your infrastructure can communicate and collaborate effectively.

These tests examine the interactions between different services, applications, or modules to detect potential issues that may arise when they are integrated into the broader infrastructure.

Integration testing often requires setting up a test environment that closely resembles your production environment to simulate real-world scenarios.

In addition to unit and integration testing, infrastructure as code (IaC) validation is a crucial testing approach for ensuring the correctness and consistency of your infrastructure configurations.

IaC validation tools, such as Terraform's **terraform validate** command, check your infrastructure code for syntactical correctness and adherence to best practices.

These tools help identify issues early in the development process, reducing the chances of deploying faulty configurations.

Compliance testing is another essential aspect of infrastructure testing, especially for organizations that must adhere to specific regulatory or security standards.

Compliance tests evaluate whether your infrastructure configurations meet the requirements and guidelines set by regulatory bodies or internal policies.

These tests can include checks for security configurations, access controls, and data protection measures.

Automated compliance testing tools can help streamline the process of verifying compliance with various standards.

Performance testing assesses the performance and scalability of your infrastructure under different load and usage conditions.

This type of testing helps identify bottlenecks, resource limitations, and potential performance degradation before they impact your users or applications.

Performance testing tools can simulate various scenarios to measure the response times, throughput, and resource utilization of your infrastructure components.

Security testing is a critical consideration for infrastructure, as security vulnerabilities can lead to data breaches and system compromises.

Security testing involves scanning your infrastructure for vulnerabilities, misconfigurations, and potential weaknesses.

Tools like vulnerability scanners, penetration testing, and code analysis tools can help identify security issues and provide recommendations for remediation.

Disaster recovery testing is essential for ensuring that your infrastructure can recover from unforeseen disasters or incidents.

This testing approach involves simulating catastrophic events, such as hardware failures, data center outages, or cyberattacks, to validate your disaster recovery plans and procedures.

Testing your infrastructure's ability to failover to backup systems, restore data, and maintain service availability is crucial for business continuity.

High availability testing focuses on verifying that your infrastructure can deliver services with minimal downtime and interruptions. This testing approach assesses the redundancy, failover mechanisms, and load balancing capabilities of your infrastructure components. By conducting high availability testing, you can identify potential single points of failure and implement strategies to enhance the availability of your services.

Configuration drift testing helps detect and prevent configuration inconsistencies that can occur over time due to manual changes or unauthorized modifications. Automated configuration drift detection tools compare the desired infrastructure state defined in your IaC code with the actual state of deployed resources and highlight discrepancies.

By regularly testing for configuration drift, you can maintain the desired infrastructure state and reduce the risk of operational issues. Chaos engineering is an advanced infrastructure testing approach that deliberately introduces failures and disruptions into your infrastructure to assess its resiliency.

Chaos engineering tests aim to uncover weaknesses, uncover hidden dependencies, and improve the overall robustness of your infrastructure. Tools like Chaos Monkey, developed by Netflix, have popularized the practice of chaos engineering.

Load testing is a subset of performance testing that focuses on evaluating how your infrastructure handles a specific level of traffic or workload. Load tests simulate user interactions, requests, or transactions to measure the infrastructure's response under load.

This type of testing helps identify performance bottlenecks and scalability issues and ensures that your infrastructure can handle expected traffic spikes.

Scalability testing assesses your infrastructure's ability to accommodate increasing workloads and adapt to changing demands.

This testing approach involves gradually increasing the load on your infrastructure to determine its limits and scalability factors.

Scalability testing can help you plan for resource provisioning and scaling strategies.

Regression testing is an ongoing testing practice that verifies whether changes to your infrastructure, such as updates, patches, or configuration modifications, introduce new issues or regressions.

By running automated regression tests, you can quickly identify and address any unintended side effects of changes.

In summary, infrastructure testing encompasses various approaches and practices to validate the correctness, performance, security, and resilience of your infrastructure.

Unit testing, integration testing, IaC validation, compliance testing, performance testing, security testing, disaster recovery testing, high availability testing, configuration drift testing, chaos engineering, load testing, scalability testing, and regression testing all play crucial roles in ensuring the reliability and effectiveness of your infrastructure.

Selecting the appropriate testing approaches and tools for your infrastructure and regularly conducting tests can help you proactively identify and mitigate potential issues, ultimately leading to a more stable and robust infrastructure.

Validation and compliance checks are fundamental aspects of infrastructure management that ensure your systems adhere to industry standards, regulatory requirements, and internal policies.

These checks play a crucial role in maintaining the integrity, security, and reliability of your infrastructure.

Validation and compliance checks involve assessing your infrastructure configurations, settings, and controls to confirm that they align with predefined criteria.

One of the primary purposes of validation and compliance checks is to ensure that your infrastructure meets specific security standards and practices.

For example, organizations in the healthcare sector must comply with the Health Insurance Portability and Accountability Act (HIPAA), which mandates stringent data protection and privacy measures. Validation and compliance checks help organizations confirm that their infrastructure safeguards sensitive healthcare data in accordance with HIPAA requirements. Similarly, companies operating in the financial industry must adhere to the Payment Card Industry Data Security Standard (PCI DSS) to protect credit card data. Validation and compliance checks assist these organizations in verifying that their infrastructure meets the PCI DSS guidelines and safeguards cardholder information.

Another essential aspect of validation and compliance checks is ensuring that your infrastructure adheres to best practices and follows recommended configurations.

These checks help identify configuration drift, which occurs when infrastructure settings deviate from the intended state defined in your infrastructure as code (IaC) templates.

Regularly performing validation and compliance checks can detect configuration drift early, allowing you to remediate issues promptly and maintain consistency across your infrastructure.

Validation and compliance checks are not limited to security and configuration standards; they also encompass performance-related criteria.

For instance, organizations often establish service level agreements (SLAs) or key performance indicators (KPIs) to guarantee optimal service delivery.

Validation and compliance checks enable organizations to monitor and assess whether their infrastructure consistently meets these performance benchmarks.

To conduct validation and compliance checks effectively, organizations commonly employ automated tools and solutions.

These tools can scan infrastructure configurations, assess security settings, and generate reports that highlight compliance violations, security vulnerabilities, and performance bottlenecks.

Automated validation and compliance checks reduce the manual effort required for audits and streamline the process of ensuring adherence to standards and policies.

In addition to external standards and regulations, organizations may have internal policies and guidelines that must be enforced through validation and compliance checks.

These internal policies may cover areas such as naming conventions, resource tagging, access controls, and resource lifecycle management.

Validation and compliance checks can validate whether resources in your infrastructure adhere to these internal policies, helping maintain consistency and governance.

For cloud-based infrastructures, cloud service providers offer various tools and services that facilitate validation and compliance checks.

For example, AWS Config allows you to assess resource configurations against predefined rules and provides a historical record of configuration changes.

Azure Policy in Microsoft Azure lets you enforce compliance with company standards and regulatory requirements across your resources.

Google Cloud's Config Validator enables you to validate resource configurations against predefined constraints.

These cloud-native tools streamline the validation and compliance process for organizations using cloud services.

When conducting validation and compliance checks, it's crucial to establish a well-defined process and schedule for assessments.

Regular assessments, whether daily, weekly, or monthly, help organizations maintain a continuous monitoring and improvement cycle.

They ensure that any deviations from standards are identified and addressed promptly, reducing the risk of security breaches and compliance violations.

Furthermore, organizations must prioritize and categorize validation and compliance checks based on their criticality and impact.

High-priority checks should focus on security and compliance with external regulations, while lower-priority checks can address internal guidelines and best practices.

Automation also extends to the remediation of issues identified during validation and compliance checks.

Automated remediation processes can help organizations promptly rectify configuration drift, security vulnerabilities, or non-compliance with standards.

These automated responses can include rolling back changes, applying updates, modifying settings, or notifying relevant stakeholders.

A crucial aspect of validation and compliance checks is documentation.

Organizations should maintain records of assessments, findings, remediation actions, and any changes made to infrastructure configurations.

Documentation serves as evidence of compliance and provides an audit trail for regulatory authorities, internal auditors, and stakeholders.

Furthermore, documentation helps organizations track progress, maintain accountability, and demonstrate their commitment to security and compliance.

In summary, validation and compliance checks are essential components of infrastructure management, ensuring that infrastructure configurations align with industry standards, regulatory requirements, and internal policies.

These checks cover a wide range of areas, including security, configuration, performance, and governance.

Automated tools and solutions simplify the validation and compliance process, helping organizations detect and address issues efficiently.

Regular assessments, prioritization, and documentation are key elements in maintaining a secure, compliant, and well-managed infrastructure.

Chapter 9: Advanced Debugging and Troubleshooting

Advanced troubleshooting techniques are invaluable for IT professionals seeking to resolve complex issues in their infrastructure and applications.

These techniques go beyond basic problem-solving methods and involve in-depth analysis, critical thinking, and a deep understanding of the systems in question.

One of the fundamental principles of advanced troubleshooting is to gather as much information as possible about the issue at hand.

This includes collecting logs, error messages, system configurations, and any relevant historical data.

Having a comprehensive set of information is crucial because it allows you to narrow down the root cause of the problem more effectively.

Once you have gathered sufficient data, the next step is to analyze it systematically.

This involves looking for patterns, trends, and anomalies that may provide clues about what went wrong.

For example, if you're troubleshooting a performance issue in a web application, you might analyze server logs to identify patterns in resource utilization or requests.

Advanced troubleshooting often requires a deep understanding of the technology stack involved.

Whether it's a complex software application or a distributed system, knowing how the different components interact and affect each other is essential.

This knowledge enables you to pinpoint potential bottlenecks, dependencies, and areas of weakness in the system.

Root cause analysis (RCA) is a crucial technique in advanced troubleshooting.

RCA involves identifying the underlying cause of a problem rather than just addressing its symptoms.

By tracing the issue back to its source, you can implement more effective and lasting solutions.

To conduct RCA, you may use techniques such as the "5 Whys" or "Fishbone Diagram" to systematically explore the causes of the problem.

Advanced troubleshooters often leverage diagnostic tools and utilities specific to the technology they are working with.

For example, network administrators might use packet capture tools like Wireshark to analyze network traffic and identify communication issues.

Similarly, software developers may use profiling tools to identify performance bottlenecks in their code.

When dealing with intermittent or hard-to-reproduce issues, advanced troubleshooting may involve setting up monitoring and logging systems that capture relevant data over an extended period.

This continuous data collection helps in capturing critical information when the issue occurs, even if it's sporadic.

When investigating issues in a production environment, it's essential to use non-intrusive techniques that don't disrupt the system's operation.

Advanced troubleshooters often work in environments where downtime is not an option, and they must find solutions without causing further disruption.

For instance, when debugging a live system, they may use debugging tools and techniques that allow them to inspect the system's state without stopping it.

In cases where advanced troubleshooting requires code changes, professionals follow best practices like version control and staging environments to test and implement fixes safely.

Collaboration is a key aspect of advanced troubleshooting, especially when dealing with complex systems involving multiple teams or departments.

Effective communication and knowledge sharing help ensure that everyone involved in resolving the issue is on the same page.

This collaboration can include sharing logs, findings, and insights with relevant team members, coordinating efforts, and seeking input from subject matter experts.

Another advanced troubleshooting technique is the use of "what-if" scenarios.

This involves hypothesizing different scenarios and their potential impact on the system to gain a better understanding of the problem.

By exploring various possibilities, you can narrow down the potential causes and focus your efforts more effectively.

Advanced troubleshooters often rely on a structured approach to problem-solving.

One such approach is the "Troubleshooting Methodology" which involves steps like problem identification, data collection, hypothesis generation, testing, and validation.

This structured approach helps ensure that no critical steps are missed during the troubleshooting process.

Advanced troubleshooting techniques also involve the use of advanced debugging tools and profilers.

These tools provide insights into the inner workings of software applications and can help identify performance bottlenecks, memory leaks, and other issues.

Profiling tools, for instance, can pinpoint which parts of a program are consuming the most resources and causing performance problems.

In some cases, advanced troubleshooters may need to simulate or recreate the issue in a controlled environment.

This allows them to experiment with potential solutions without risking the production system.

Creating a test environment that closely mimics the production environment is crucial for accurate testing and validation.

Advanced troubleshooters are often skilled at scripting and automation.

They create custom scripts and automation workflows to streamline repetitive tasks, gather data, and perform tests systematically.

This automation not only saves time but also reduces the risk of human error during the troubleshooting process.

When dealing with complex issues, documentation becomes even more critical.

Advanced troubleshooters maintain detailed records of their troubleshooting process, including the steps taken, the data collected, the hypotheses tested, and the outcomes.

This documentation serves as a valuable resource for future reference and helps other team members understand the problem and its resolution.

One of the key principles of advanced troubleshooting is persistence.

Complex issues can be challenging to resolve, and it may require multiple iterations of data collection, analysis, and testing to identify and address the root cause.

The ability to persevere and maintain a methodical approach is essential for success.

In summary, advanced troubleshooting techniques involve a combination of skills, tools, and methodologies to tackle complex issues effectively.

These techniques include data collection, analysis, root cause analysis, diagnostic tools, structured problem-solving approaches, collaboration, "what-if" scenarios, simulations, scripting, automation, documentation, and persistence.

By mastering these techniques, IT professionals can become proficient at resolving intricate problems in their infrastructure and applications.

Debugging complex Terraform issues can be a challenging but essential skill for infrastructure as code (IaC) practitioners.

These issues often involve intricate interactions between resources, complex configurations, and dependencies that can be difficult to untangle.

Successful debugging requires a systematic and thorough approach, beginning with the identification of the problem.

The first step in debugging is recognizing that an issue exists, which may be indicated by error messages, unexpected behavior, or failed deployments.

Once the issue is identified, the next step is to gather relevant information to understand its scope and impact.

This information includes error messages, logs, Terraform configuration files, and the state of the infrastructure.

Careful examination of error messages is crucial, as they often provide clues about the nature of the problem and where to focus your debugging efforts.

Logs from Terraform executions, cloud providers, or other services can also be valuable sources of information.

Reviewing Terraform configuration files is essential to ensure that resources are defined correctly and that dependencies are accurately represented.

Understanding the current state of the infrastructure, as stored in the Terraform state file, can help pinpoint the divergence between the desired and actual states.

Once you've gathered sufficient information, you can begin the process of hypothesis generation.

This involves formulating educated guesses about what might be causing the issue based on the available data.

Hypotheses help guide your debugging efforts and provide a starting point for testing and validation.

It's essential to consider various potential causes, as complex issues may have multiple contributing factors.

Testing hypotheses is a critical phase in debugging complex Terraform issues.

This involves conducting experiments, making changes, and observing the results to determine whether a hypothesis is correct.

Testing may require modifying Terraform configuration files, adjusting resource attributes, or altering dependencies to isolate and validate the issue.

While testing, it's essential to make incremental changes and document each step to keep track of your progress.

In some cases, you may need to create a controlled environment or a Terraform module that isolates the problematic components for testing.

Validation is an integral part of debugging, as it confirms whether your tests have successfully identified and resolved the issue.

Validation may involve inspecting the Terraform plan, running Terraform commands, and analyzing the state file to ensure that the desired state is reached.

In complex scenarios, it's common to iterate through the hypothesis generation, testing, and validation phases multiple times.

Debugging complex issues often requires a process of elimination, ruling out potential causes one by one until the root cause is identified.

Collaboration is invaluable when tackling complex Terraform issues.

Engaging with team members, peers, or online communities can provide fresh perspectives, alternative solutions, and additional expertise.

Sharing your findings, hypotheses, and test results with others can lead to breakthroughs in resolving the problem.

Debugging complex Terraform issues may also involve examining external factors that can impact the infrastructure.

These factors may include network issues, cloud provider outages, third-party service dependencies, or changes in the underlying infrastructure.

Being aware of these external influences and considering them in your debugging process is essential.

As you progress in debugging, consider using Terraform-specific tools and commands to aid your efforts.

Terraform provides features like the "terraform graph" command, which generates a visual representation of resource dependencies, helping you understand the relationships between resources.

The "terraform state" command allows you to inspect and manipulate the Terraform state file, which can be useful for verifying the state of resources.

Terraform's "terraform plan" command can help you preview changes and understand the intended modifications before applying them.

Using these tools effectively can streamline the debugging process.

In complex environments, it's important to adopt best practices for Terraform code organization and modularity.

Well-structured code can make debugging easier by isolating issues to specific modules or resource definitions.

Additionally, adopting version control and continuous integration/continuous deployment (CI/CD) practices can help catch issues earlier in the development and deployment lifecycle.

Documentation is a critical aspect of debugging complex Terraform issues.

Recording your findings, steps taken, successful solutions, and lessons learned can be invaluable for future reference and knowledge sharing with your team.

Debugging is not always a linear process, and you may encounter dead ends or setbacks along the way.

Maintaining a patient and persistent approach is crucial, as complex issues may take time to unravel.

While debugging complex Terraform issues can be challenging, it is a skill that improves with practice and experience.

By following a systematic approach, leveraging Terraform-specific tools, collaborating with others, and documenting your findings, you can effectively tackle even the most intricate issues in your infrastructure as code projects.

Chapter 10: Achieving Infrastructure as Code Excellence

Infrastructure as Code (IaC) best practices are essential guidelines for organizations and teams seeking to harness the full potential of IaC for managing their infrastructure.

These practices aim to streamline operations, improve reliability, and enhance collaboration among development and operations teams.

One fundamental IaC best practice is to treat infrastructure as code, meaning that infrastructure configurations are expressed in code and stored in version-controlled repositories.

By doing so, you enable infrastructure to be managed, versioned, and reviewed just like any other software component.

This approach brings consistency, repeatability, and traceability to infrastructure changes.

Version control is a cornerstone of IaC best practices, as it allows teams to track changes, collaborate effectively, and roll back to previous configurations when issues arise.

Using version control systems like Git ensures that every change to the infrastructure code is documented and reversible.

IaC code should be modular and reusable, with well-defined components that can be composed to create more complex infrastructures.

This modularity enhances maintainability and accelerates the deployment of new environments by reusing existing code components.

To ensure consistency and avoid configuration drift, IaC code should be tested thoroughly before deployment.

Automated testing, including unit tests, integration tests, and validation tests, helps catch errors early in the development process and ensures that configurations work as intended.

Continuous integration (CI) and continuous deployment (CD) pipelines are essential for automating the testing and deployment of IaC code.

These pipelines enable teams to automate the building, testing, and deployment of infrastructure, reducing the risk of manual errors and ensuring that code is always deployable.

IaC code should be reviewed by peers or subject matter experts to identify issues, improve quality, and ensure compliance with organizational standards.

Code reviews provide an opportunity for knowledge sharing and collaboration, leading to better code quality and more reliable infrastructure.

Documentation is a critical IaC best practice, as it provides valuable insights into how the infrastructure is configured and how to maintain it.

Clear and up-to-date documentation helps new team members understand the infrastructure, troubleshoot issues, and make informed changes.

Secrets and sensitive information, such as API keys and passwords, should be stored securely and managed separately from the IaC code.

Using secrets management tools and practices ensures that sensitive data is protected and can be rotated easily when necessary.

When deploying infrastructure, it's essential to consider security from the beginning.

Security best practices, such as network segmentation, firewall rules, and regular vulnerability assessments, should be part of the IaC code and deployment process.

Immutable infrastructure is an IaC best practice that involves replacing instances instead of modifying them.

This approach minimizes configuration drift and ensures that the infrastructure is always in a known and consistent state.

Monitoring and logging are crucial for maintaining the health and performance of infrastructure deployed with IaC.

Teams should incorporate monitoring tools and practices to track resource utilization, detect anomalies, and troubleshoot issues proactively.

Regular backups and disaster recovery plans should be part of the IaC strategy to ensure business continuity in case of data loss or infrastructure failures.

Backup procedures should be automated and tested regularly to guarantee data integrity.

Scaling infrastructure horizontally and vertically should be a straightforward process enabled by IaC.

IaC code should allow teams to adjust resource capacities easily to handle changes in demand.

Infrastructure code should be treated as a first-class citizen and undergo the same code review, testing, and validation processes as application code.

This ensures that infrastructure configurations are as reliable and robust as the applications they support.

Using infrastructure as code templates and patterns, teams can define reusable infrastructure configurations for common use cases.

These templates accelerate the deployment of new environments while maintaining consistency and best practices.

Teams should establish well-defined roles and responsibilities for managing infrastructure as code.

Roles may include code authors, reviewers, deployers, and administrators, each with specific responsibilities in the IaC workflow.

Infrastructure changes should go through a defined change management process, including approvals, risk assessments, and documentation.

This process ensures that changes are planned, communicated, and executed in a controlled manner.

As organizations adopt IaC, they should provide training and resources to their teams to ensure that everyone is proficient in using IaC tools and practices effectively.

Knowledge sharing and ongoing education are essential for successful IaC implementation.

IaC code should be regularly audited for compliance with organizational policies, industry regulations, and security standards.

Automated tools and practices can help identify and remediate compliance violations efficiently.

Monitoring and alerting should be configured to detect and notify teams of any changes to the infrastructure that deviate from the desired state defined in the IaC code.

Automated alerting helps teams respond quickly to potential issues and maintain the integrity of the infrastructure.

Immutable infrastructure patterns, where infrastructure instances are replaced rather than modified, should be applied whenever possible to minimize configuration drift and ensure consistency.

Infrastructure changes should be tested in staging or development environments before being applied to production, reducing the risk of introducing errors.

To minimize downtime and ensure smooth deployments, teams should consider blue-green or canary deployment strategies when making infrastructure changes.

These strategies allow new infrastructure to be gradually rolled out while monitoring for issues and performance improvements.

Finally, organizations should regularly evaluate their IaC practices and make adjustments as needed to keep up with evolving technology, industry standards, and organizational requirements.

Continuous improvement is essential to ensure that IaC remains effective and efficient over time.

IaC governance plays a vital role in ensuring the effective and secure management of infrastructure as code within an organization.

Governance encompasses a set of policies, procedures, and practices that guide how IaC is used, deployed, and maintained.

One of the key aspects of IaC governance is defining clear roles and responsibilities for team members involved in the creation and management of infrastructure code.

By establishing these roles, organizations can ensure that individuals understand their responsibilities and accountabilities in the IaC workflow.

IaC governance also involves defining and enforcing coding standards and best practices for infrastructure code.

These standards ensure that code is written consistently, making it easier to review, maintain, and troubleshoot.

Compliance checks can be integrated into the development pipeline to automatically enforce these coding standards.

Security is a paramount concern in IaC governance, and organizations must implement security policies and practices to protect infrastructure code and the resources it manages.

This includes measures such as access controls, encryption, and the regular review of security configurations.

Continuous improvement is an essential element of IaC governance, as it ensures that IaC processes and code are continually refined to meet changing needs and evolving best practices.

Organizations should regularly assess their IaC workflows, tools, and codebase to identify areas for improvement.

To facilitate continuous improvement, organizations should foster a culture of collaboration and knowledge sharing among teams responsible for IaC.

Regular communication and feedback loops can help teams identify challenges and opportunities for enhancement.

Governance also extends to the version control of infrastructure code.

Organizations should establish policies for branching and merging code changes to maintain a clean and coherent version history.

Additionally, version control enables organizations to track changes and roll back to previous configurations when necessary.

Documentation is a critical component of IaC governance, as it provides a comprehensive record of infrastructure configurations and changes.

Documentation should be up to date, clear, and readily accessible to team members, enabling them to understand the infrastructure codebase.

Another important aspect of IaC governance is the establishment of change management processes.

These processes define how changes to infrastructure code are proposed, reviewed, tested, and deployed.

Change management helps maintain a structured and controlled approach to infrastructure modifications.

IaC governance should also address disaster recovery and business continuity.

Organizations should have plans and procedures in place to recover infrastructure quickly in the event of unexpected outages or data loss.

These plans should be tested regularly to ensure their effectiveness.

Testing and validation are key components of IaC governance.

Automated testing should be integrated into the development pipeline to catch errors and ensure that infrastructure code behaves as expected.

Governance policies should define how testing is conducted and what constitutes a successful test.

Scalability is an essential consideration in IaC governance, as infrastructure code should be designed to accommodate growth and changing demands.

Organizations should have guidelines for scaling resources horizontally or vertically as needed.

IaC governance policies should also address the use of third-party modules or code from external sources.

Organizations should have criteria for evaluating and approving the use of external code to ensure security and compatibility.

Resource tagging and naming conventions are crucial aspects of IaC governance, as they help organize and identify resources in cloud environments.

Governance policies should specify naming conventions and tagging requirements for resources.

Cost management is another concern for IaC governance, and organizations should have policies for monitoring and controlling infrastructure costs.

This may include budgeting, resource optimization, and regular cost analysis.

Performance monitoring and optimization should also be addressed in IaC governance.

Organizations should have policies for monitoring the performance of infrastructure resources and optimizing them to meet performance requirements.

IaC governance should encompass compliance with industry standards and regulations relevant to an organization's operations.

Organizations should have processes in place to audit and assess infrastructure code for compliance.

Disaster recovery and incident response plans should be part of IaC governance to ensure a rapid and coordinated response to unexpected events.

These plans should be regularly reviewed and tested to maintain readiness.

Governance should also address the retirement or decommissioning of infrastructure resources.

Organizations should have procedures for retiring resources when they are no longer needed or have reached the end of their lifecycle.

Finally, IaC governance should promote transparency and accountability.

Teams should be accountable for their actions, and policies should be in place to track and report on infrastructure changes.

By implementing robust IaC governance, organizations can maximize the benefits of infrastructure as code while maintaining security, reliability, and compliance.

Conclusion

In this comprehensive bundle, "Terraform CLI Boss: Novice to Command Line Guru," we embarked on an exciting journey through the world of Terraform and its command-line interface. Across four meticulously crafted books, we covered everything from mastering the basics to unleashing expert-level commands, providing you with the knowledge and skills needed to excel in the world of infrastructure as code.

In "Book 1 - Terraform CLI Boss: Mastering the Basics," we laid the foundation for your Terraform journey by introducing you to the fundamental concepts and commands. You learned how to set up your environment, execute your first Terraform commands, and manage state effectively. With this solid base, you were well-prepared to delve deeper into the Terraform ecosystem.

"Book 2 - Terraform CLI Boss: Command Line Wizardry" took you to the next level by exploring advanced configuration management techniques. You became a wizard in harnessing the power of HashiCorp Configuration Language (HCL), dynamically managing workflows with variables, and customizing Terraform with providers and plugins. Your command-line skills evolved, setting you on the path to becoming a true Terraform expert.

In "Book 3 - Terraform CLI Boss: From Novice to Ninja," we continued our journey by guiding you through the intricacies of Terraform modules, workspaces, and collaborative workflows. You transformed into a Terraform ninja, capable of building reusable modules and collaborating seamlessly with your team. As you honed your skills, you gained a deeper understanding of best practices that would serve as your compass in the world of infrastructure as code.

Our final destination in "Book 4 - Terraform CLI Boss: Expert-Level Commands Unleashed" was the realm of true expertise. Here, you unlocked the full potential of Terraform CLI by exploring advanced command-line techniques, infrastructure testing, and validation. You became a master of debugging and troubleshooting, ensuring the reliability and resilience of your Terraform projects. With expert-level commands at your fingertips, you were ready to conquer even the most complex infrastructure challenges.

As you conclude this journey, remember that the Terraform CLI is a powerful tool, and your mastery of it opens doors to endless possibilities in the realm of infrastructure automation. Whether you are a novice starting your journey or a seasoned pro seeking to refine your skills, the "Terraform CLI Boss" bundle has equipped you with the knowledge and tools to thrive in the world of infrastructure as code.

Your command-line journey doesn't end here; it's an ongoing adventure filled with innovation and discovery. Stay curious, keep exploring, and continue honing your skills, for the world of Terraform awaits your command. Thank you for choosing "Terraform CLI Boss: Novice to Command Line Guru" as your trusted guide on this remarkable journey.

www.ingramcontent.com/pod-product-compliance
Lightning Source LLC
Chambersburg PA
CBHW071236050326
40690CB00011B/2145